AFRICAN AMERICANS

VOICES OF TRIUMPH™

PERSEVERANCE

VOICES OF TRIUMPH KENTE CLOTH

Textiles, perhaps more than any other art form, reflect the cultures from which they come. They are at once personal, societal, religious, and political—invaluable vehicles for the spread of ideas from one culture to another. In Africa, woven cloths have served these functions for more than 2,000 years, conveying the vibrant essence of an African aesthetic.

Kente, the type of cloth seen on the cover, is the primary woven fabric produced by the people of the old Ashanti Kingdom of Ghana. This particular cloth was specially designed and woven in Ghana to convey the theme "African Americans: Voices of Triumph."

Although the Ashanti tend to favor strips of uniform color, the varying colors in this kente cloth express the many paths taken by all our people—and especially the multiple destinations of black slaves who were removed from the shores of Africa.

The traditional red, gold, and green repeated in the middle of the design is one of the several variations of the "liberation colors" recognized by all children of African descent all over the world: red for the blood (shed by millions in captivity), gold for the mineral wealth (prosperity), and green for the vegetation of the land of Africa (home).

The weavers of Ghana and other countries throughout West Africa have long adapted foreign elements to suit their own needs, creating unique motifs to express cultural values. Among the motifs incorporated in the design for this cloth is *abusua foa* (the council of elders)—represented by the boxes arranged in an X ("all ideas coming together at one point")— to symbolize leadership, consensus, and the voice of the people.

The stepped border motif, which seems to connect all the strips, symbolizes unity, interdependence, and cooperation as prerequisites for the advancement of the people.

The "shield" motif symbolizes defense against the countless assaults and obstacles encountered in the course of our lifetime.

Finally, the diamond, rarest, hardest, and most precious of all the minerals of Africa, represents the many-faceted soul of the children of Africa in America and reflects their power to endure and their growing triumph in the struggle for freedom and equality.

PERSEVERANCE

BY THE EDITORS OF TIME-LIFE BOOKS
ALEXANDRIA, VIRGINIA

WITH A FOREWORD BY DR. HENRY LOUIS GATES, JR.

TIME-LIFE CUSTOM PUBLISHING
VICE PRESIDENT AND PUBLISHER:
Susan J. Maruyama
Director, Multicultural Markets:
Rosalyn McPherson Andrews
Associate Director, Multicultural Markets:
Russell J. Haskins
Production Manager: Prudence G. Harris
Operations Manager: Phyllis Gardner
Promotions Managers: Rebecca C. Wheeler,
Gary Stoiber
Retail Manager: Lorna Milkovich
Financial Manager: Dana Coleman
Special Contributors: Patricia Loushine,
Becky Merson, Theresa Mixon,
Tracey Warner

Time-Life Books is a division of
Time Life Inc.

PRESIDENT AND CEO, TIME LIFE INC.:
John M. Fahey, Jr.

TIME-LIFE BOOKS
PRESIDENT: John D. Hall
EDITOR-IN-CHIEF: John L. Papanek
Executive Editor: Roberta Conlan
Director of Editorial Resources:
Elise Ritter-Clough
Executive Art Director: Ellen Robling
Director of Photography and Research:
John Conrad Weiser
Assistant Director of Editorial Resources:
Norma E. Shaw

**The Voices of Triumph Development
Team gives special thanks to Quincy
Jones, who joined hands with us early
in the project, supported our vision,
and believed in our goal.**

**AFRICAN AMERICANS:
VOICES OF TRIUMPH**™
Series Directors: Roxie France-Nuriddin,
Myrna Traylor-Herndon
Series Design Director: Cynthia Richardson

Editorial Staff for **PERSEVERANCE**
Senior Editor: Janet P. Cave
Administrative Editor: Loretta Y. Britten
Picture Editor: Sally Collins
Text Editors: Esther Ferington, Paul
Mathless
Senior Art Director: Robert K. Herndon
Art Director: Alan Pitts
Associate Editors/Research: Ruth Goldberg,
Sharon Virginia Kurtz
Writer: Darcie Conner Johnston
Assistant Editors/Research: Michael E.
Howard, Dionne Scott, Terrell Smith,
T. Nieta Wigginton
Assistant Art Director: Kathleen D. Mallow
Senior Copyeditors: Anne Farr (principal),
Colette Stockum
Picture Coordinator: Jennifer Iker

Editorial Operations
Production: Celia Beattie
Library: Louise D. Forstall
Computer Composition: Deborah G. Tait
(*Manager*), Monika D. Thayer, Janet
Barnes Syring, Lillian Daniels

Special Contributors: Karen Grigsby
Bates, George E. Curry, George D.
Daniels, Marfé Ferguson Delano, Betty
De Ramus, Marge duMond, Rosalyn M.
Hamlett, Harvey Loomis, Keith Moore,
Diane Patrick, Sandra Salmans, Jarelle S.
Stein, Karen D. Taylor, Hollie I. West,
Juan Williams (text); Nina D. Barrengos,
Ellen C. Gross, Catherine B. Hackett,
Maurice Hall, Greg S. Johnson, Kather-
ine N. Old, Patricia A. Paterno, Sonia
Reece, Elizabeth Thompson, Amy
Turim, Donna Wells (research); Mel J.
Ingber (index)

Educational Consultants: Constance Jackson,
Shirley Tinsley, Detroit, Michigan, Public
Schools

Correspondents: Elisabeth Kraemer-
Singh (Bonn), Christine Hinze (London),
Christina Lieberman (New York), Maria
Vincenza Aloisi (Paris), Ann Natanson
(Rome). Valuable assistance was also
provided by Marguerite Michaels
(Nairobi); Elizabeth Brown, Katheryn
White (New York); Ann Wise (Rome);
Xavier F. Harispe (Senegal); Traudl
Lessing (Vienna).

First printing. Printed in U.S.A.

TIME-LIFE is a registered trademark of
Time Warner Inc. U.S.A.
VOICES OF TRIUMPH and
AFRICAN AMERICANS:
VOICES OF TRIUMPH
are trademarks of Time Life Inc.

**Library of Congress
Cataloging in Publication Data**
Perseverance / by the editors of
Time-Life Books.
    p.   cm. — (African Americans)
    Includes bibliographical references
    and index.
    ISBN 0-7835-2250-9 (trade)
    ISBN 0-7835-2251-7 (lib.)
    1. Afro-Americans—History. 2. Slavery
—United States. 3. Afro-American pio-
neers—West (U.S.). 4. Afro-Americans—
Civil rights. 5. Civil rights movements—
United States—History.   I. Time-Life
Books.   II. Series.
E185.P425 1993
973'.0496073—dc20   93-19566
                                        CIP

AFRICAN AMERICANS: VOICES OF TRIUMPH™
consists of three volumes: *Perseverance, Leadership,* and *Creative Fire.*
For more information about the VOICES OF TRIUMPH™ volumes and
accompanying educational materials call or write 1-800-892-0316,
Time-Life Customer Service, P.O. Box C-32068, Richmond, Va. 23261-2068,
or ask for VOICES OF TRIUMPH™ wherever books are sold.

African Americans have long been driven to collect, order, and interpret the details of their historical past in Africa and in the New World—in part because of a powerful historical impulse that can be traced to the traditional role of the oral historians, or griots, and in part as a reaction to having been stripped of their culture and their past by slavery.

Indeed, history was the first discipline in which black scholars made their mark, beginning with individuals such as R. B. Lewis and the abolitionist William Wells Brown, who published histories of African Americans as early as the middle of the 19th century. In 1896, when W. E. B. Du Bois received a PhD in history at Harvard, he became the first of a long line of Harvard-educated black historians, including Carter G. Woodson, Rayford Logan, Charles Wesley, and John Hope Franklin, who would narrate the lost saga of the African American past. As Arthur A. Schomburg put the matter three decades later:

"Though it is orthodox to think of America as the one country where it is unnecessary to have a past, what is a luxury for the nation as a whole becomes a prime social necessity for the Negro. For him, a group tradition must supply compensation for persecution, and pride of race the antidote for prejudice. History must restore what slavery took away, for it is the social damage of slavery that the present generation must repair and offset."

African Americans: Voices of Triumph is part of, and extends, this great tradition of recollecting the black past. These books, of which *Perseverance* is the first, are a fulfillment of Schomburg's mandate, bringing to the broadest possible readership—white and black, Asian and Hispanic, male and female, young and old—the compelling drama of the fundamental role that African Americans have played in the making of the American republic.

In reading these pages—which begin with an account of the Songhai Empire and then conduct us through the horrors of the Middle Passage and human bondage, through the Civil War and the long subsequent struggle for human dignity and civil rights—every American will realize how inextricably intertwined is "white" American culture and history with black American culture and history. What is clear is that there would be no nation known as America had no blacks been forcibly imported to these shores.

Voices of Triumph, then, are books written for all Americans, aimed at restoring the lost history of a people to our common storehouse of knowledge. These volumes are part of our attempt to create a living vision of multiculturalism as an antidote to the dangerous temptations of ethnocentrism and cultural chauvinism. Traditionally in America, this task, and the task of shaping and improving our democratic polity, have been entrusted to the schools. Fortunately, our schools are increasingly teaching the story of America not as a people descended from Pilgrims and Puritans but as a plural nation, made up of people who came from different lands and who have been subject to different experiences.

Teaching our children about the various American cultures and their histories can only help to make us all the more sensitive to, and familiar with, that which we bear in common, the shared experiences that unite us, as citizens of this country. For it is only through the sharing of knowledge that we can begin to repair the racial, ethnic, gender, class, and religious divisions that continue to plague our society. Voices of Triumph is a major contribution to this effort. It should be a central part of every household and school library in America. Voices of Triumph is itself a triumph.

Henry Louis Gates, Jr.
W. E. B. Du Bois Professor of the Humanities
Harvard University

EDITORIAL ADVISORY BOARD

BOARD OF CONSULTANTS

DR. BENJAMIN S. CARSON
is Director of Pediatric Neurosurgery at Johns Hopkins Hospital in Baltimore. He is a motivational speaker for young people across the United States.

WILLIAM H. GRAY III
is president and chief executive officer of the United Negro College Fund and a former U.S. Congressman from Philadelphia. He has long been an advocate for education.

GORDON PARKS
came to national attention as an award-winning photographer for *Life*. He is a composer, best-selling author, and film director, and has been widely recognized for his contributions to the fine arts.

REVEREND DR. DEFOREST B. SOARIES, JR.
is pastor of First Baptist Church of Lincoln Gardens in Somerset, New Jersey. He is known for economic empowerment programs and for his work with youth.

FOR PERSEVERANCE:

Dr. Russell L. Adams is chairman of the Department of Afro-American Studies at Howard University. A political sociologist, he has written extensively in the fields of human relations and history. He also has been a curriculum materials consultant to a variety of governmental agencies in the United States and abroad.

Jerald H. Anderson has written extensively on the subject of blacks in the military for the Department of Defense and has developed a college-level course on the same subject. He also has assisted the DOD 50th Anniversary of World War II Commemoration Committee to develop materials that chronicle the wartime contributions of African Americans.

William Loren Katz began researching African Americans in the American West three decades ago and has written several highly acclaimed studies of the subject. His slide lectures based on this research have been presented to audiences in Europe, Africa, and throughout the United States.

Darrell Millner is the chairman of the Department of Black Studies at Portland State University in Portland, Oregon. His research and writing interests include the buffalo soldiers, black cavalry in the Indian wars, blacks and the Oregon Trail, and the history of Afro-Caribbean contributions to the American West.

Dr. Sulayman S. Nyang is the chairman of the Department of African Studies at Howard University. He has served as a member of the board of the African Studies Association and is currently on the editorial board of several international journals. He has written extensively on African, Islamic, and Middle Eastern issues.

Dr. Ronald Walters, chairman of the Department of Political Science at Howard University, has served on the Council of the American Political Science Association and is the founder of the National Congress of Black Faculty. He has held key positions in both of Jesse Jackson's presidential campaigns, and is a frequent guest political analyst on national and local radio and television news programs.

PERSEVERANCE

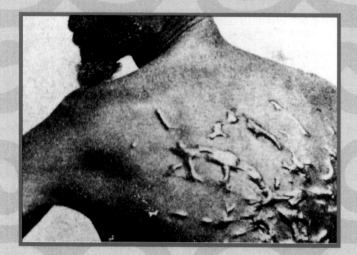

THREE
SOLDIERS IN THE SHADOWS...126

FOUR
ADVOCATES FOR CHANGE...180

A MIGHTY NATION ON THE NIGER

In the days when no European had yet managed to penetrate the interior of West Africa and the horrors of the Atlantic slave trade had not even been imagined, a great civilization arose along the Niger River where it brushes against the southwestern Sahara (*map, opposite*). Established by the Songhai, a nation of black-skinned scholars, warriors, merchants, farmers, and artisans, the empire that bore their name became well known throughout North Africa, Southwest Asia, and Europe for its power and wealth.

The Songhai was the third and greatest of three black kingdoms that waxed and waned in this region between the 8th and 16th centuries. Its predecessors left their names, and their reflected glory, to the modern African nations of Ghana and Mali. Like them, the Songhai Empire echoes down through history, half a millennium after its days of glory, in tales of its most fabled city, Timbuktu—a mysterious and alluring place that still stands at the edge of the Sahara Desert, in the region called the Sahel.

Sometime around AD 800, caravans of traders from the lands north of the desert brought south a new religion, Islam, which played a role in shaping the states of this region. The Islamic, or Muslim, faith was already firmly established in most of the cities of the Sahel by the middle of the 15th century, when the Songhai people began to extend their domain from their capital city of Gao, located about 200 miles down the Niger from Timbuktu.

The empire's founding ruler was Sunni Ali Ber—Ali the Great, of the Sunni dynasty. Sunni Ali began his campaign of conquest in 1468 by taking Timbuktu, which was then ruled by the Tuaregs, a nomadic Berber people. The city, strategically located where the camel caravans made contact with boatmen plying the Niger River with goods from the south, had grown wealthy from trade. Timbuktu succumbed after only a feeble show of resistance, thanks to the treachery of its chief, who hoped to strike a deal with the invaders.

Contemptuous of what seemed to be an effete, submissive population, the Songhai slaughtered hundreds and pillaged the place. Sunni Ali's next target, the city of Djenné, did not surrender till 1473, after a siege that lasted, according to oral histories, for seven years, seven months, and seven days. Admiring the courageous stand of the city's defenders, Sunni Ali annexed Djenné but left its king on his throne and its population unharmed.

As Sunni Ali consolidated his new realm, he strove to reconcile the feelings of the majority of his people, who were rural folk and believed in their traditional deities, with those of the Muslim city dwellers, whose wealth and learning were essential to the empire's government and commerce. He successfully maintained a balance between the two factions for the duration of his 27-year reign.

Sunni Ali's son and successor, Sunni Baru, however, paid little obeisance to the prevailing Islam of the cities. By openly worshiping the old gods, he shattered the fragile unity that his father had worked so long to preserve, and Muslim insurgents, acting in defense of their faith, deposed him in 1493, just six months after he inherited the throne. The leader of the rebels, Muhammad ibn Abubakr Touré, became the new emperor. Going by the name Askia (generally translated as "king") Muhammad, he ruled the Songhai Empire, expanding its domains, for 35 prosperous years.

The death of Askia Muhammad triggered cycles of dynastic infighting. So destructive were these struggles that the final decline of the Songhai Empire had an air of inevitability. Weakened by internal dissension, the empire proved easy pickings for a small Moroccan army that ventured across the Sahara in 1591. The once-invincible Songhai troops found their traditional weapons no match for the Moroccans' new firearms, imported from England. Within months, there was nothing left of the great Songhai Empire except the songs and stories that have kept its memory alive.

THE SONGHAI SEAT OF POWER

After toppling Sunni Baru, Askia Muhammad faced a daunting challenge—how to rebind the pieces of the empire with the glue of good government. In 1495, two years after gaining power, he made hajj, or a pilgrimage, to Mecca, where he met and befriended Muslim scholars. Upon gaining an understanding of Islamic government, he decided to construct his administration according to its principles, although the Songhai monarchy itself rested on a traditional African concept of divine kingship.

To ensure the defense of his realm, Askia Muhammad first established a full-time professional army. Then he turned to the empire's internal organization, creating a layered form of government. Askia Muhammad ruled from a tusk-flanked throne (*left*) in Gao, where he held audiences with emissaries from distant states, meditated on the wisdom of the Koran as verses were recited by Islamic scholars, and received petitions from the peoples of his empire. Below the throne itself were ranked the governors of the four regions into which he divided the empire; each region was in turn divided into provinces run by provincial chiefs.

But the empire's true strength lay in a social structure that spelled out everyone's duties. And with a standing army guarding its borders, the empire's farmers, merchants, fishermen, livestock breeders, and artisans could concentrate on being productive in their vocations.

Even the griots—members of a hereditary caste of storytellers who preserved the people's history by passing it orally from generation to generation—had a responsibility in imperial society beyond their traditional role. The griots were expected to weave glorious tales about the empire's past military exploits to boost the morale of the Songhai soldiers before battle and in the heat of combat.

Slaves occupied the lowest rung of society, but their servitude took an African form in which race was irrelevant and bondsmen were no less human than other workers. Slaves were not simply units of property but could rise on the basis of their service and had the security of knowing that their children could not be sold away from them.

TIMBUKTU: SCHOOL OF THE EMPIRE

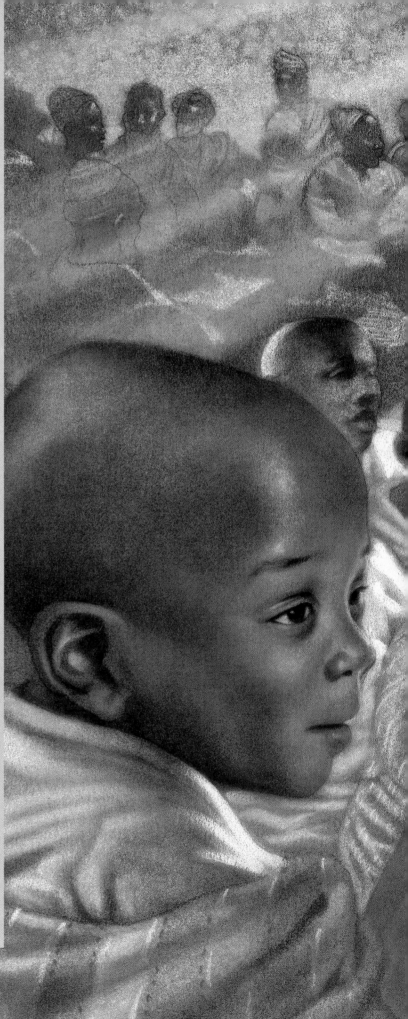

Although it was a prosperous market city of almost 50,000 people, Timbuktu owed its greatest fame to its reputation as a center of intellect, a place where poets and priests could live like princes, where books mattered more than costly raiment or herds of camels. About 4,000 boys were students, and the cultural life of the city was dominated by scholars. According to the 16th-century historian Leo Africanus, serious scholars were "bountifully maintained at the king's cost and charges."

Timbuktu had 150 Koranic schools, where lessons were taught in Arabic, the language of the Prophet Muhammad. In a house of prayer, or mosque (*right*), Songhai boys would practice Arabic speech as their teacher wrote Koranic verses on a slate, while nearby an imam—a prayer leader— might discuss the scripture with a group of men. Advanced study frequently took place in the homes of established scholars who owned large libraries of books that had been laboriously copied by hand. The scholar al-Hajj Ahmad ibn Umar, for example, could choose from among 700 volumes in his own personal library.

For students, the goal of education was to gain sufficient understanding of the principles of Islam to apply them to everyday life. Students strove to sharpen their powers of analysis by studying grammar, literary style, rhetoric, and, occasionally, astronomy, history, mathematics, and medicine. As many as 300 of the city's most advanced scholars also served as community leaders who played a part in regulating public affairs and made sure that the concerns of ordinary people reached the ears of their rulers.

But not all educated people became master scholars or community leaders. Some were scribes, making a living by copying books. Others found work as teachers, mosque functionaries, even tailors. Indeed, the making and embroidering of robes played a unique role in Timbuktu, giving poorer students a trade that would support them in their quest for further learning. During its heyday in the 16th century, Timbuktu had more than 26 tailoring houses and 1,000 learned tailors.

BUILDING A NATION ON SALT AND GOLD

When Askia Muhammad made hajj, he brought along not only 500 cavalrymen and 1,000 foot soldiers but also a treasure of 300,000 pieces of gold, which he dispensed generously along the route and in Mecca. His pilgrimage spread the fame of the Songhai Empire and promoted trade with North African merchants. The merchants craved Songhai gold and offered in return something the Songhai craved even more—salt, for the empire had almost no natural sources of this essential mineral.

The traffic in salt and gold helped finance the development of a strong, well-organized state, in which Timbuktu and other market centers flourished. As early as the 14th century, about two-thirds of the gold used to mint coins in Europe and the Arab world came from this region.

Slabs of salt carved from mines around the Saharan town of Taghaza were carried by camel across the desert to the Niger. The arduous trip typically took at least three months, and five such trips were considered enough for a lifetime. Yet the merchants were highly motivated to brave the desert's hazards, as the books, writing paper, horses, swords, and knives they brought commanded good prices in the bustling city marketplaces (*left*), and their salt was literally worth its weight in gold to the Songhai.

Fortunately, the southern reaches of the Songhai Empire were studded with rich deposits of gold. The exact locations of the gold mines were—and are still today—a great mystery, and to keep them hidden the miners used a strange and secretive way of trading. Caravans would arrive at a spot designated by a go-between; there the traders would unload and spread out their wares, and would then withdraw a good many miles. The miners would appear, inspect the merchandise, leave amounts of gold for what they wanted, and withdraw in turn. If the merchants were satisfied with the price, they would collect the gold and depart. If not, they would leave everything in place to show the miners that they expected to be paid more. Once both sides were happy, each would collect its gold or goods and the business would be concluded—without either side's ever having seen or spoken to the other.

BASTIONS OF RURAL TRADITIONS

People living outside the cities of the Songhai Empire didn't discard their age-old ways when their rulers flirted with or embraced Islam. They continued worshiping their traditional deity, who created the world; they prayed to their deified ancestors; and they believed in the same spirits that in antiquity had guided the lives of their forebears. They may have paid taxes to distant rulers, but their traditional ways sustained them at home.

To rural people, human beings were both biological and spiritual. The spiritual was the most important aspect of a person's existence and survived his or her death. Thus, a beloved grandparent who died would continue to be a part of the community in noncorporeal form.

The rhythms of rural life had a reassuring regularity, as exemplified at right in this picture of a village of the Bambara people, one of the constituent tribes of the Songhai Empire. A woman pounds grain to make flour. The village blacksmith heats iron preparatory to fashioning a household tool or a farming implement. Another woman braids a child's hair. Under a baobab tree, a group of men convene in a village council to hash out a dispute.

Country people lived under a social organization far older and more complex than the stratified society developed by Askia Muhammad. They grouped themselves according to clan, village, ancestry, even craft or vocation. A person born into one of these groupings tended to remain in it for life and to choose a mate from within it.

The seasons set the pace for the ebb and flow of rural life. In the dry months, when agricultural work slowed almost to a stop, life was unhurried, and most activities took place in the village. People visited friends, rebuilt or repaired their grass-thatched houses, and made pottery, mats, baskets, and textiles for domestic use and for commerce. During the rainy season—from May to early September—many villagers moved temporarily to outlying farming hamlets, where they stayed while they cultivated more-distant fields. When the soil closer to home was exhausted, villagers resorted to plots that might lie as much as 20 miles away.

CEREMONY FOR A RICH HARVEST

Farming wasn't something the rural people of the Songhai Empire did simply to produce food. In their scheme of things it was the most exalted occupation, the one activity that brought people into direct involvement with the elements and reaffirmed their place in the universe. And to ensure that their work in the fields would be crowned with a good crop at harvesttime, specially trained dancers—members of a covert males-only society—would perform the Tyi Wara ceremony, dancing in a bent-over position like farmers hoeing the soil (*right*). In this fashion they would appeal for the blessings of Tyi Wara, the god of agriculture.

Tyi Wara was a supernatural being who was believed to have taught humans how to transform weeds into nourishing foodstuffs. Later, when the bounteous crops provided by Tyi Wara made mortals lazy, the god gave up on humans and buried himself in the ground, according to traditional beliefs. Those who performed the dance of Tyi Wara kept the memory of the ancient god alive and encouraged diligent farming.

Only initiates of the Tyi Wara society—one of the most important of six secret initiation societies found in the villages of the region—were permitted to witness the annual rite, performed by dancers wearing headdresses and veils of braided fiber. In each village, the ceremony was conducted on a large field and accompanied by an orchestra of drums and bells. The society's chief was usually the village blacksmith, who together with other older men directed the ritual. The headdress was a stylized rendering of an antelope hewn from hardwood with hatchets and chisels.

The dance invoking Tyi Wara was just one manifestation of the African belief in a spirit world that existed side by side with the visible world. Although the rural people believed in one almighty deity, they also believed that lesser spirits or deities existed and resided in objects. Each deity was identified with a particular aspect of life and could intervene either to help or to do harm. Thus, having once lost Tyi Wara's favor, Songhai farmers took great care to appease him.

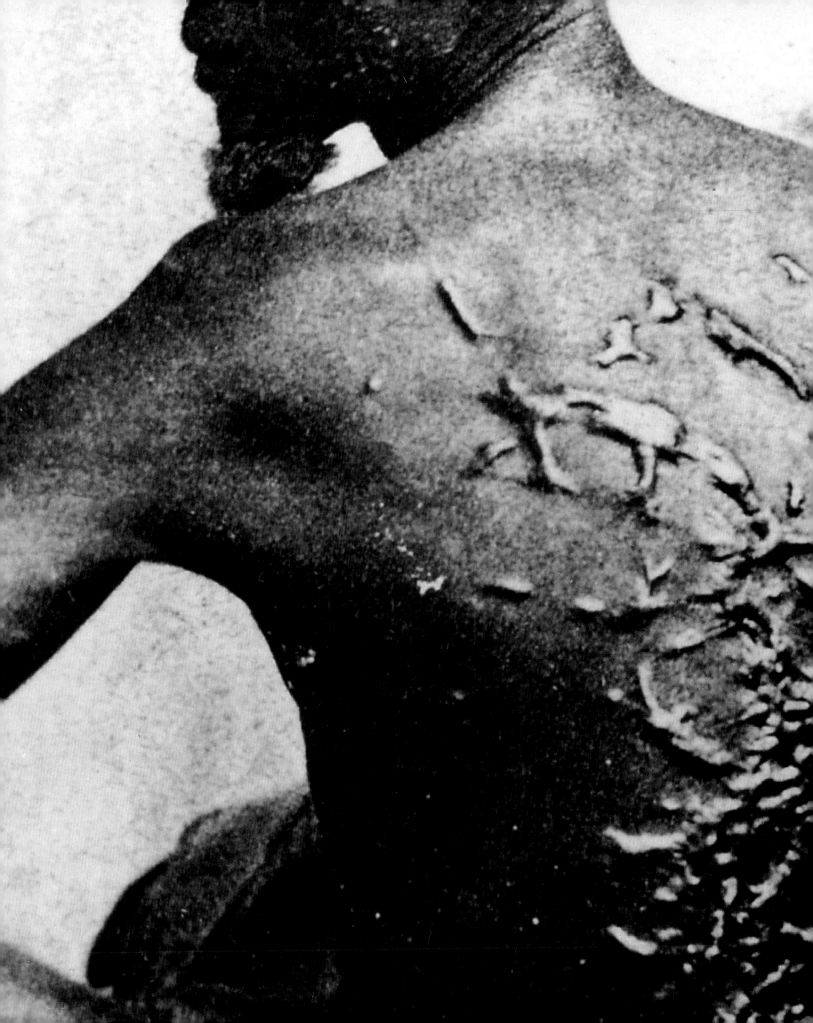

FREEDOM DENIED, FREEDOM WON

Savage whipping left the back of this former slave gruesomely disfigured. The photograph was taken after the man escaped during the Civil War to become a soldier in the Union army.

uring his childhood in the 1750s in what is now eastern Nigeria, Olaudah Equiano spent many days as a lookout, helping to guard his father's village-kingdom of Essaka, Benin, from other Africans raiding for slaves. Several times, Equiano and his companions captured slave hunters and brought them before his father. The boy was preparing for his own future as a leader, and these incidents were exciting previews of what real warriors did. But all his training was not enough to protect the 11-year-old on the fateful day in 1756 when three kidnappers stormed his home.

"One day, when all our people were gone out to their work as usual, and only I and my sister were left to mind the house, two men and a woman got over our walls, and in a moment seized us both," he wrote 33 years later, in elegant English prose. "Without giving us time to cry out, or to make any resistance, they stopped our mouths and ran off with us into the nearest wood. Here they tied our hands, and continued to carry us as far as they could." The kidnappers and their victims rested that night in a small house, then set out again the next morning, each step through the thick woods taking the two children farther from Essaka.

When Equiano's captors risked traveling a road to make better time, the youth saw some people at a distance and yelled desperately for help. The kidnappers quickly gagged the children again, bound their hands, and threw them into sacks until the danger of discovery had passed. That night, the frightened brother and sister huddled together for comfort; the next day they were separated. "She was torn from me and immediately carried away," Equiano wrote in remembered anguish, "while I was left in a state of distraction not to be described."

In the months that followed, Equiano was sold and resold from trader to trader. He managed to escape once, but within hours was overcome with the cold realization that, no matter how hard he tried, it was unlikely that he could ever retrace his steps to his now-distant home—or avoid the slave catchers his new owners would send to find him. "If possibly I could escape all other animals, I could not those of the human kind," he wrote. "Thus was I like the hunted deer." The hunt ended when Equiano reluctantly returned to the slave trader who owned him.

Seven months after his initial capture, Olaudah Equiano finally arrived on Africa's west coast, where a large slave ship rode at anchor, awaiting him and others who shared his fate. Once on board, Equiano saw Europeans for the first time. He also noticed a furnace, and concluded that he was to be broiled in it and eaten by "those white men with horrible looks, red faces, and long hair."

Author and former slave Olaudah Equiano holds an open Bible in this portrait from his 1789 memoir.

Soon the boy joined "some of my own nation, which in a small degree gave ease to my mind." But even that bit of comfort vanished quickly amid the horrors that awaited the Africans. Chained together, they were packed into the hold, where "the air soon became unfit for respiration," Equiano wrote. "This wretched situation was again aggravated by the galling of the chains, now become insupportable, and the filth of the necessary tubs, into which the children often fell." The unlucky boy yearned for death.

Death did bring release for those slaves who succumbed to disease or flung themselves overboard rather than endure the floating hell. But Equiano survived, and when the ship finally reached land, he was taken first to a slave market in Barbados and then to a plantation in colonial Virginia. For most African captives, the journey ended with the plantation. But Equiano's owner subsequently sold him to a British naval officer whose duties took him from Halifax, Nova Scotia, to the Mediterranean. With deliberate irony, the officer named the powerless young slave Gustavus Vassa, after a famous Swedish king. The boy learned to read and write English; and from a later master, a slaveholding Quaker named Robert King, he learned European-style business skills. Permitted to earn extra money when an opportunity presented itself, Vassa bought his freedom in 1766 and went on to a series of adventures that included a polar voyage. In 1789, he wrote a memoir titled *The Interesting Narrative of the Life of Olaudah Equiano, or Gustavus Vassa, the African*, which remains one of the few first-person accounts of the brutal transition from Africa to slavery in America.

The practice of owning human beings as property is at least as old as civilization itself. The ancient Egyptians enslaved whomever they captured, whether the prisoners were Semitic, Mediterranean, or Nubian. Slavery was also an economic pillar of the ancient Greek and Roman empires, and the practice of international trading in human beings, of whatever color, became firmly established in antiquity. A loose association between race and slavery began to emerge as 11th-century Islamic traders shipped North African captives to Arabia, Persia, and other Islamic countries. Forms of slavery also existed in early Europe, sub-Saharan Africa, and other regions.

But at no time did the slavery practiced on other continents ever equal in scope or human degradation the slave system that arose in the Americas. In one of the largest forced migrations in history, about 11 million Africans—and some historians consider this to be a conservative estimate—crossed the Atlantic from the 16th to 19th centuries, ultimately transforming the physical, social, and economic fabric of the cultures of both South and North America.

Slavery took a particularly vicious form in the Americas, and created deep-seated tensions and strained relationships between blacks and whites that have carried over to the present. In early Europe and in many other cultures, slaves were essentially servants owned by wealthy people who had acquired their fortunes in ways unrelated to slavery. In the Americas, it was the slaves, through their back-breaking toil, who made the owners rich. Traders, investors, and settlers regarded a large, stable, depersonalized labor force as the quickest means of capitalizing on rich natural resources.

Although little exists in the slaves' own words describing their circumstances or feelings, especially for those enslaved African Americans who lived and died long before the Civil War, scholars have been able to construct a picture of slavery in North America through legal and commercial documents, archaeological finds, memoirs composed by former slaves in the years just before or after the Civil War, and interviews with former slaves, many of which were conducted in the 1930s as part of the Federal Writers' Project. Limited as the record may be, it clearly reveals that slavery was a varied institution. In the North, at one time nearly 50,000 slaves labored in the cities and on farms and sailing vessels. In the South, the overwhelming majority of slaves worked on tobacco, rice, and cotton plantations. Slaves also staffed many of the early ironworks of Virginia, the cotton mills of North Carolina, the rope works of Kentucky, and the salt mines of Louisiana. In both North and South, a small but significant number worked as house servants and artisans.

From the colonists' point of view, there were many practical reasons for choosing to enslave African laborers. Native Americans were too susceptible to European diseases, and indentured servants—usually poor Europeans who pledged several years of service in return for a fresh start in the colonies—were too few and had too many legal protections. Africans had none of these disadvantages, and they had an added benefit—if they tried to escape, they could easily be identified by their skin color. With time, white slaveholders would also develop racist theories about the inherently subhuman character and intelligence of their "property," which in their minds helped to justify the racially based social system.

The Atlantic slave trade (*pages 42-47*) that supplied the colonists with laborers grew and evolved over time, beginning on a very small scale in the early 1500s with Portuguese traders. Like the merchants who followed them, the Portuguese considered slaves among Africa's riches, as desirable—and as devoid of human rights—as gold or elephant ivory. Portugal yielded supremacy in slave trading to the Dutch in the early 1620s; after about 1700, the lead was assumed by Great Britain. Traders for each successive European power fanned the flames of African tribal and national conflicts by encouraging local kings to take prisoners of war and sell them as slaves.

The first recorded Africans in the North American colonies arrived in Jamestown, Virginia, in 1619, on a Dutch man-of-war. Of the 20 Africans who stepped off the ship, at least three were women, but little more is known for certain. By the mid-1600s, the colony also included at least some black indentured servants who came by way of England. Once their period of servitude had expired, they were, like white indentured servants, given plots of land, clothing, or a small amount of money to help make the

transition to freedom. But as time elapsed and the colony was unable to fulfill its labor needs, the idea of permanent servitude for black workers gained popularity among white colonists. Nowhere was this made clearer than in a 1640 Virginia case involving three runaway indentured servants—a black and two whites. As punishment for their escape, the judge extended the white servants' period of service by four years. But the black runaway, John Punch, was ordered to "serve his said master or his assigns for the time of his natural life here or elsewhere."

During the 1600s, racially based slavery gradually took hold throughout the North American colonies. A Massachusetts enactment of 1641 refers to the practice, and the Dutch colony of New Netherland had made use of black slaves for almost 40 years by 1665, when it was brought under British control and renamed New York. Virginia made slavery legal in 1661 and ensured its perpetuation the next year with passage of a statute declaring that children born to a slave mother would also be slaves. Still another Virginia act, passed in 1667, established that a slave baptized as a Christian would remain a slave—a departure from the previous English practice, in which baptism ensured a release from enslavement.

Although the work of clearing forests and growing the crops that were the colonies' exports created the need for slave labor, the slave population of the colonies grew slowly. Then, in 1672, the British government chartered the Royal African Company as a slave-trading monopoly, assuring a consistent supply of African labor. By the end of the century, more than 1,000 Africans a year were being imported by Virginia alone to work the region's tobacco fields, and more than three-fourths of the white families in the colony owned slaves.

Slavery was so firmly entrenched in Virginia that its detailed slave codes, which were first brought together in a single statute in 1680, served as a model for the other colonies. Although each of the original 13 colonies had its own variations, the laws were very similar. All declared, for example, that slaves were property rather than people, and were subject to sale at any time. Slaves were generally forbidden to hit a white person, even in self-defense; to sue or to testify in court; to marry; to leave their plantations or homes, even briefly, without written permission; to hold unauthorized religious services, or to assemble for any reason without permission; to visit, or to be visited by, whites or free blacks; or to learn how to read or write.

Such laws, including the literacy ban, were at times ignored by lenient masters. But for the most part the codes held the African American slave in an iron grip for life. "For Gods sake don' let a slave be catch wit pencil an' paper," recalled 94-year-old former South Carolina slave Elijah Green in an interview in the late 1930s. "That was a major crime. You might as well had kill your master or missus." The laws restricting mobility were enforced off the plantation by county and state officers known as patrollers—"patterollers," in the plantation dialect—who whipped, and sometimes killed, slaves caught on the road without their masters' written consent.

During the Revolutionary War era, such restrictions obviously clashed with the ideal of individual liberty. Enslaved African Americans protested slavery's injustices with formal petitions for freedom, written by slaves who had illegally become literate or by anonymous free helpers. In January 1773, for example, a group of Boston slaves

From 1858 to 1861, the firm of Price, Birch, and Company—self-proclaimed "Dealers in Slaves"—operated this slave-trading house in Alexandria, Virginia. Captives were held in the large, heavily guarded room—men in one section, women and infants in another, and older children and teenagers in another—while whites wandered through to look the slaves over. Prices ranged from a high of $2,500 to $2,800 for a healthy, strong young man to about $250 for a small child.

petitioned the Massachusetts governor and legislature for "such relief as is consistent with your wisdom, justice, and goodness." Five months later, another petition stated that slaves were "praying that they may be liberated from a state of Bondage, and made Freemen of this Community." At the time, neither the governor nor the state legislature answered those prayers. But in the years ahead, the northern states gradually eliminated slavery, which was not suited to their trading and industrial economies. Rural, maritime Vermont became the first state to abolish slavery outright in 1777. Fifty years later, New York was the last northern state to outlaw the institution. That state had dragged its feet so long because Hudson Valley farmers, like southern planters, put a high value on slave labor. Individual exemptions for some New York slaveholders, primarily invalids, permitted the retention of a few slaves until the mid-1850s.

As the northern states released their slaves, the South became ever more dependent on theirs, in part as a result of the invention of the cotton gin in 1793. This device, which removed seeds from wispy cotton bolls 10 times faster than slaves could, sped up cotton production and made it far more profitable to grow. And as more fields were devoted to raising cotton, increasing numbers of slaves were needed to plant, tend, and harvest the crop. The slave population in the South grew from less than 700,000 in 1790 to more than 2 million by 1830. At the time of the 1860 census, the number of enslaved African Americans had nearly doubled to 4 million, out of a total southern population of about 12 million. Other southern cash crops, including tobacco and indigo, also fueled the slavery boom. In South Carolina, known for its labor-intensive rice plantations, black slaves outnumbered white residents. Yet the bulk of the slaves in the South were concentrated in the hands of only about 385,000 planters.

Slavery expanded even further as settlers pushed into such new southern states as Mississippi, Alabama, Arkansas, and Texas, and the demand for slaves soon outstripped the supply. This shortage in slave labor was a direct—albeit delayed—result of the framing of the U.S. Constitution in 1787. At the time the document was written, many colonists feared that a slave insurrection might result from what was perceived as an increasing racial imbalance in the population, and argued that the importation of additional slaves should be stopped. The Founding Fathers agreed, but as a concession to southerners included a section in the Constitution that postponed outlawing the international slave trade until 1808.

Because slaves could no longer be legally obtained from abroad after January 1

of that year, slaves within the United States became an interstate export crop, sold from the more settled states such as Virginia, Maryland, and Kentucky to owners in the new states. Eager to cash in on a booming business, slave owners in the older states apparently pushed slaves to reproduce. Census figures from the time show a sharply increased birthrate among slaves in the more settled states, followed several years later by a distinct rise in the number of slaves in the new regions.

Such forced breeding was typical of slaveholders' attitudes toward the slaves, who were made to endure every kind of personal degradation. Many former slaves' memoirs speak bitterly of having to witness the mistreatment of a family member and being unable to stop it. In his 1897 autobiography, *Thirty Years a Slave*, former Mississippi slave Louis Hughes recounted watching as his wife, Matilda, caught trying to run away, was alternately beaten by their master and their mistress. "I was trembling from head to foot, for I was powerless to do anything for her," he wrote. "My twin babies lived only six months after that, not having had the care they needed, and which it was impossible for their mother to give them while performing the almost endless labor required of her, under threats of cruel beatings."

For slave women, the lack of power often translated into sexual abuse by white men. In one reported South Carolina incident, a slave named Charlotte at first fought off her master's demands for sex. He then stripped her naked and forced her to sit on a heap of manure until she gave in. Some time later, after giving birth to his child, Charlotte was handed on to the master's cousin. She bore his child too.

While the manure torture may have been unusual, the pregnancies were not—white men were frequent visitors to the slave quarters. And the offspring of such liaisons were usually held in the same low regard as their mothers. But in other, comparatively rare, cases, sexual relations between master and slave evolved into a union of genuine affection. A number of well-known planters publicly acknowledged their black mistresses, and an inspection of slave owners' wills shows that a few even left their estates to women who had once been their slaves.

Most slaves found their only joy and comfort in their families. In Africa, where family members spanned a number of generations and totaled in the hundreds, the family was central to every aspect of life. But as Olaudah Equiano's kidnapping illustrates, slavery had no respect for African families, on either the old continent or the new. Slave owners could sell a child or parent or spouse whenever the urge struck or the price was right. In his 1858 autobiography, former slave Charles Ball remembered being sold as a small boy. Ball's mother pleaded with her owner not to sell her son. "Without making any

Slaves laboring on plantations and in factories during the early 1800s either went barefoot or wore cheap brogue-style shoes like the tattered one below, unearthed by archaeological volunteers at the site of an old canal in Richmond, Virginia. The lack of good shoes meant slaves often suffered from frostbite, infected cuts, and insect bites on their feet.

reply," Ball wrote, "he gave her two or three heavy blows on the shoulders with his raw-hide, snatched me from her arms, handed me to my master, and seizing her by one arm, dragged her back towards the place of sale. My master then quickened the pace of his horse; and as we advanced, the cries of my poor parent became more and more indistinct—at length they died away in the distance, and I never again heard the voice of my poor mother."

Even when slave children remained with their parents, owners often neglected the children's most basic needs. "The cotton planters generally, never allow a slave mother time to go to the house, or quarter during the day to nurse her child," wrote Henry Bibb, a former slave who, after several escapes, became permanently free in 1842. "Hence they have to carry them to the cotton fields and tie them in the shade of a tree, or in clusters of high weeds about in the fields, where they can go to them at noon, when they were allowed to stop work for one half hour. This is the reason why so very few slave children are raised on these cotton plantations, the mothers have no time to take care of them—and they are often found dead in the field and in the quarter for want of the care of their mothers."

On other large plantations, children were left in the care of elderly slave women who were assisted by an older child or two. These women often were in charge of as many as 100 children, from month-old babies to four- and five-year-olds. Because food was sometimes in short supply, young children would rush in to grab for their share, in a scene slaves compared to that of feeding pigs. Childhood was short for slaves, however, and by age five or six, girls and boys would begin work, running errands in the fields or doing simple tasks in the "big house," where the master's family lived. By age 10, they were working full-time.

Slaves performed most of the jobs on the plantation. At the bottom of what amounted to a slave hierarchy, field hands worked at raising crops, herding livestock, and slaughtering animals. A notch higher were the house slaves, who kept the master's household running smoothly. On the same footing with house slaves were carpenters, blacksmiths, and other skilled slave laborers.

Field slaves toiled nearly all of their waking hours, and were routinely pushed to exhaustion by white overseers, who often had a financial stake in how productive they were. On many cotton plantations, slaves were whipped for not picking their share of the crop, usually 250 pounds a day. Henry Bibb wrote of some overseers who instituted so-called contests in which the slave in each group who picked the most cotton would receive the equivalent of a dollar or two in valuables. "After making them try it over several times and weighing what cotton they pick every night, the overseer can tell just how much every hand can pick," Bibb recounted. "He then gives the present to those that pick the most cotton, and then if they do not pick just as much afterward they are flogged."

The work of slave artisans, such as those on the John Burry plantation near Shreveport, Louisiana, who made this wool suit for their master's son-in-law during the Civil War, kept large plantations self-sufficient and profitable.

The work didn't stop when the slaves left the fields at sundown. As part of a 15- to 16-hour day, enslaved men and women also had to perform other chores, such as feeding the mules and cutting wood, before they could return to their quarters. At night, field-slave families crammed into small one- or two-room cabins, each of which might be home to as many as 12 people. The cabins were swelteringly hot in summer; in winter, when the cold winds whistled through the walls, slaves huddled together for warmth. Furniture—or what passed for it—consisted mainly of wooden benches and chairs. Slaves made mattresses of straw or moss, and every third year or so they would receive a new light cotton blanket from their masters. Slave owners sometimes provided crude knives and wooden spoons with which to eat; otherwise, the slaves carved wooden utensils and bowls and made jugs out of dried gourds. Most slaves received meager amounts of food. Their weekly rations were dispensed on Saturdays and usually included a small supply of cornmeal, lard, meat, molasses, peas, greens, flour, and milk.

While their lives were strictly regimented during the workday, at night, on Saturday afternoons, and on Sundays slaves were free to do personal chores, tend their own gardens, go hunting and fishing to supplement skimpy rations, and get together with other slaves. With a proper pass—although some slaves risked leaving without one—they could visit friends on nearby plantations to converse, worship, dance, or sing—pastimes that gradually laid the groundwork for a distinctively African American cultural style. Saturday night was the big social night, when slaves played music and danced. Weddings among slaves, although not legally recognized, were also cause for celebration. Couples stood up before a gathering of friends and jumped over a broomstick to symbolize their union. The most festive time of the year, however, came at Christmas, a special season when slaves were given a few days off, the patrollers eased up, and masters allowed greater freedoms.

The flurry of Christmas parties and visits at the big house made the holidays a busy time for house slaves, a relatively privileged group that included about 10 to 12 percent of southern slaves. Clothed in uniforms or hand-me-downs from the white family, fed on rations much like the family's, and living in or near the big house, these servants generally led a less grueling life than field hands.

The most exalted among the house slaves was the butler, usually a tall, imposing figure who exuded quiet dignity. The butler was in charge of all male house servants, including the carriage driver, the gardener, and the waiters. A slave woman, often the butler's wife, supervised all female helpers in the household. Working as a house servant was typically a family honor passed down from one generation to the next. Life under the watchful eyes of the slaveholders and their families was not always enviable, however, as numerous slave memoirs attest. In her

Although slaveholders were notoriously unwilling to have their slaves photographed, some of them did permit staged, sentimental portraits like the one below, in which an anonymous slave nursemaid holds her young white charge.

Metal occupational tags identify 19th-century black residents of Charleston, South Carolina, as (*top to bottom*) a porter, a general servant, and a fruiterer, or dealer in fruit. Until 1848, only slaves were required to wear such tags; after that date, free blacks were placed under the edict as well.

1861 book, *Incidents in the Life of a Slave Girl*, former slave Harriet Jacobs, a house servant in a southern town, described scenes as abusive as many that took place in the fields. "If dinner was not served at the exact time," Jacobs wrote, the mistress "would station herself in the kitchen, and wait till it was dished, and then spit in all the kettles and pans that had been used for cooking. She did this to prevent the cook and her children from eking out their meagre fare with the remains of the gravy and other scrappings." As for the master, Jacobs continued, "the cook never sent a dinner to his table without fear and trembling; for if there happened to be a dish not to his liking, he would either order her to be whipped, or compel her to eat every mouthful of it in his presence."

On the larger, wealthier plantations, the skilled slaves who worked as carpenters, blacksmiths, spinners, seamstresses, bricklayers, and shoemakers shared equal status with the house slaves. Southern slave owners often boasted that they had "civilized" black "savages" by teaching them useful trades, but the truth was considerably different. Many West Africans brought very specific skills to America, from metalworking to handicrafts to rice farming. During an economic decline in the late colonial period and following the American Revolution, which placed limitations on imports, slave owners were forced to depend more heavily on goods produced by skilled black artisans than on foreign products. On their own plantations, some of the country's Founding Fathers put their slaves to the task of manufacturing: George Washington attempted to produce iron with slave labor at his Mount Vernon, Virginia, plantation; and with the services of several slaves, Thomas Jefferson built a nail factory at his Virginia birthplace, the Shadwell plantation.

From time to time, the highly valued craftsmen were hired out to less affluent farmers. Depending on local custom and the decisions of their masters, the slave artisans might also be allowed to hire out their services and keep a portion of the profit—one way that some slaves were able to save enough money to buy freedom for themselves and family members. The price for a slave, like any other commodity, was based on the going rate, but slaves and owners sometimes negotiated the sale.

The practice of hiring out slaves spread beyond the plantations and into factories in the first half of the 19th century, sparking a protracted debate between slave owners and those who wanted to limit such employment to white laborers, barring even free blacks. Ironically, slaves often cost more to use than white workers. Factory owners rented slave labor at full factory wages, but also had to provide the slaves with room and board—expenses ordinary employees paid out of their monthly wages. Even so, many mill owners found slaves to be ideal workers, and in the late 1830s slaves came to dominate employment in the manufacture of rope and bagging in Kentucky and in the tobacco- and salt-processing factories of Virginia.

Like their counterparts on the plantations and in the factories, those slaves who worked for masters in cities and towns lived under the constant threat of being sold or beaten. City masters often sent slaves out to specialized businesses that whipped them for a fee. In between masters, Mississippi slave Louis Hughes was housed for a time at a slave yard that did just that. "The yard I was in had a regular whipping post to which they tied the slave, and gave him 'nine-and-thirty,' as it was called, meaning thirty-nine lashes as hard as they could lay it on," he recalled. "Men were stripped of their shirts in preparation for the whipping, and women had to take off their dresses from the shoulders to the waist."

Nevertheless, city living was in many ways less repressive for slaves than life in the country. Urban slaves often lived in the homes of their owners, in the attic area or in a room at the back of the kitchen, rather than in poorly built cabins. If city slaves were skilled in a trade, they were more likely to be hired out, and to have the opportunity to hire themselves out in slow times. Slaves in the cities were also more likely to come in contact with free black men and women—a source of inspiration for the enslaved, and of constant worry for their masters.

A small population of free blacks had existed in the colonies before slavery was formally inaugurated, and others constantly joined their ranks. Some slaves saved enough money from hiring out their services to purchase their freedom; others were released at their owner's death through a clause in the slaveholder's will or were granted liberty as a reward of some kind. Still others escaped to freedom. By 1860 there were almost 500,000 free black men and women in the United States, more than half of whom lived in the South. But the racial basis of slavery made free black people something of a legal anomaly—not enslaved but not truly free, either. Limitations imposed on them varied from place to place. In the South, free blacks had to carry a certificate of freedom with them at all times or risk being kidnapped into slavery. Unlike whites, they could also be enslaved for bad debts or failure to pay taxes. In most states, North or South, free blacks could not hold public office or vote. They were not allowed to bear arms, and they could not testify in court against whites except in Delaware and Louisiana. Moreover, they were in constant danger of being sold into slavery by unscrupulous slave traders—a fate that befell Solomon Northup, a freeborn resident of Saratoga Springs, New York, one day in 1841.

A proficient violinist, Northup was lured first to New York City and then to Washington, D.C., by two itinerant white performers who promised him work. Soon after his arrival in Washington, Northup experienced strange symptoms that suggested he had been drugged. Eventually he passed out. "When consciousness returned," he later wrote, "I found myself alone, in utter darkness, and in chains." Held in a slave pen "within the very shadow of the Capitol," Northup argued for his legal rights, only to be beaten and whipped until he could not speak. He was sold soon thereafter and in time became a field hand on a Louisiana plantation named Bayou Boeuf. After 12 years of servitude, Northup managed to have a letter written to some northern friends, who secured his freedom a few months later. He went on to write a damning account of slavery from the perspective of one raised in freedom.

Despite such very real hazards and other less dramatic but more constant restrictions, some free black Americans prospered, even in the slave states. In New Orleans, real-estate investor Thomy Lafon amassed property amounting to $500,000—an enormous sum by the standards of the day. In 1860, that city's 18,000 free blacks owned a total of $15 million in taxable property—including slaves. The number of free African Americans who owned slaves is unknown, but it is clear that

some blacks purchased their relatives to lift them out of slavery. By holding their kin as slaves rather than freeing them, the new owners got around restrictive laws that in some cases required newly manumitted slaves to leave the area. Other black slaveholders, a distinct minority, owned slaves for the same reason as whites—to make money. Black bricklayers, carpenters, tailors, butchers, and shoemakers sometimes purchased slaves to serve as apprentices, as domestic servants, or as workers to hire out. In 1850, nineteen percent of the black tailors in Charleston owned slaves.

No matter who owned them or where they worked, enslaved African Americans never fully accepted their situation. The spirituals and folk songs they sang revealed their longing for liberty. But protests against the conditions of slavery extended well beyond singing. Every day slaves resisted in subtle, little-noticed ways—by pretending to be sick, by killing their master's livestock, by damaging crops or tools, and by working inefficiently or pretending not to catch on to a task. Farmers found they needed to provide slaves with special, heavy-duty shovels and plows, since ordinary farm implements were broken so often. Barns full of grain were likely to catch on fire. Slave men and women also fought back against the hated patrollers by establishing lookouts, installing trapdoors in the floors of their cabins to hide slaves without passes, and even extending ropes across roads to trip approaching horses. "It needs no great probing of the literature of slaving to become aware that, from the beginning, vast numbers of Negroes refused to accept the slave status without a struggle," wrote one historian in 1941. "Contemporary accounts are so filled with stories of uprisings and other modes of revolt, cases of voluntary starvation and more direct forms of suicide, that it is surprising that the conception of the compliant African ever developed."

A more daring form of protest was running away. Generally, a slave decided to take to the woods in reaction to a particular event, such as an expected beating or rumors of being sold. Slaves in the Deep South usually did not flee north because of the great distances involved. Instead, they sought refuge in the wilderness, where some formed societies of runaways that came to be known as maroon communities (*page* 40). Escapees from the Upper South—Virginia, Delaware, Maryland, Kentucky, Tennessee, and Missouri—were more likely to reach the North, where some were aided by the Underground Railroad (*pages* 68-69), as regional fugitive-aid efforts were known. But successful escapes remained a rarity. Census reports for the two decades leading up to the Civil War show that 1,000 slaves—a tiny fraction of the total held in bondage—were reported to have fled each year.

The slave owner's greatest fear was

A "freedom paper" from a justice of the peace attests to the free status of the Rev. John F. Cook of Washington, D.C., his daughter Mary, and his son George. Like other free southern blacks, Cook kept the paper in a watertight tin (*below, right*) that he probably carried with him at all times.

armed slave revolt. Southern landowners watched in horror from a distance in 1791 when Haitian slaves wrested control of their island nation from the white slaveholders there. Within the United States, the best-known revolts were Gabriel Prosser's aborted attack on Richmond in 1800, Denmark Vesey's planned rebellion in Charleston in 1822, and Nat Turner's 1831 uprising in Virginia (*pages 54-55*). But scholars have documented scores of other slave revolts or planned uprisings; and after each rebellion, slave codes were made more stringent and punishments became more severe, in a seemingly endless cycle. The states and the federal government built military forts in the South, in part to hold off Native Americans but also to help contain the slaves in case of mass rebellions.

Although revolts and conspiracies were reported as far back as the 1600s, the first major slave uprising in North America took place in 1739. In the early morning hours of September 9, approximately 20 slaves massed on the banks of the Stono River at a point about 20 miles from Charleston, South Carolina. Their first destination was a local store, where they killed two storekeepers and secured arms and powder. Shouting "Liberty!" and beating on drums, the rebels marched along the main road, torching plantation homes and killing more than 20 whites. Their numbers grew to 100, by some accounts, and they marched for more than 10 miles without significant opposition. The band of slaves then came to a stop in a field, apparently hoping to be joined by other slaves as word of their accomplishments spread. In the late afternoon, however, the rebels were surrounded by armed white colonists. Many blacks were shot, and, according to one account, the planters "Cutt off their heads and set them up at every Mile Post they came to."

Decapitation was a common practice in dealing with revolts; it was meant to discourage those slaves whose religious beliefs held that the body must remain intact for Judgment Day. A similar fate befell those who took part in the Louisiana uprising of 1811. The biggest slave rebellion in U.S. history, it involved 300 to 500 slaves in St. John the Baptist Parish, just outside New Orleans. Beginning at the plantation of a slave owner called Major Andre, the rebels marched toward the city, burning plantations and killing either two or three whites. The slaves displayed military organization to the extent that they were divided into companies, each commanded by an officer. But they had no experience in battle. Confronted by federal troops summoned from New Orleans combined with free black forces directed by slaveholders, the rebels' ranks soon broke. The soldiers killed 66 of the rebels immediately. Sixteen other leaders were later tried and executed. Then, as at the Stono River, the 16 heads were placed on spikes along the road back to the plantation where the rebellion had begun.

A less violent means to freedom was the individual legal appeal, sanctioned by many states' slave codes. Such "freedom suits" did not challenge the institution of slavery but simply alleged that the person in question was being

The lash of braided leather on this wood-handled whip sliced open the flesh of its victims—a common punishment some particularly brutal overseers or slave drivers would follow with a dousing of salt water to intensify the pain.

Some slaves who attempted—and failed—to escape were made to wear this heavy metal collar. Jangling bells revealed the slave's whereabouts. If the wearer tried to run away again, the prongs became entangled in low branches or thick brush.

$100 REWARD!

RANAWAY

From the undersigned, living on Current River, about twelve miles above Doniphan, in Ripley County, Mo., on 2nd of March, 1860, A NE GRO MAN, about 30 years old, weighs about 160 pounds; high forehead, with a scar on it; had on brown pants and coat very much worn, and an old black wool hat; shoes size No. 11.

The above reward will be given to any person who may apprehend this said negro out of the State; and fifty dollars if apprehended in this State outside of Ripley county, or $25 if taken in Ripley county.

APOS TUCKER.

This poster offering a reward for a 30-year-old Missouri slave who escaped in March 1860 reveals the characteristic attitude of the slave owner: Although it describes the man's scarred forehead and "very much worn" coat, it does not bother to give his name.

unlawfully held in bondage. Nevertheless, the suits constantly brought the human reality of slavery before the courts. In a typical case, *Re Negro James*, brought in 1735, a slave named James petitioned a Massachusetts court for his future emancipation—his master's will had provided that he would be freed upon the death of his owner's wife. But the deceased man's son, who had laid claim to James, vigorously contested the petition. At one point he even threatened James's life, prompting the slave to request a writ of protection, which the court granted. James was finally declared to be "absolutely free" in 1737, after his mistress died.

Other slave suits addressed the legal question of whether residence in a region where slavery was illegal would make a slave free. Missouri judges caused considerable confusion on this point by ruling yes in one case and no in a similar one 16 years later. The first case, involving a slave named Rachel, was decided in 1836. An army officer stationed at Fort Snelling, just north of Missouri Territory, purchased Rachel in St. Louis in 1830. She remained with him at Fort Snelling until the following year, when he took her to the free territory of Michigan. In 1834, he took her back to St. Louis to be sold. Rachel's case was tried in a Missouri court, which found in favor of her owner. Later, the state supreme court overturned that decision and ordered a new trial, which resulted in her freedom.

Dred Scott would not be so lucky. In 1833 the Virginia-born slave was transported by his master from Missouri into the free state of Illinois, and later into the free territory of Minnesota. Scott lived away from Missouri for four years. In 1846, aided by a white friend named Henry Taylor Blow, Scott sued for his and his family's freedom, on the grounds that they had established residence on free soil. A lower court upheld his position, but this time the Missouri Supreme Court did not agree and overturned the ruling. Scott's friends then secured his sale to a New Yorker, an interstate transaction that allowed the case to go to the U.S. Supreme Court.

On March 6, 1857, the Court ruled against Scott on several grounds. It stated not only that slaves held on free soil remained enslaved—the key point at issue—but that Scott, simply because he was black, was not qualified to bring suit at all: Since the founding of the original colonies, wrote Chief Justice Roger B. Taney, a Marylander, black men and women had been "considered as a subordinate and inferior class of beings" who "had no rights which the white man was bound to respect." Moreover, the Court went on to declare, the Congress itself could not outlaw slavery in any territory, since that would be an unconstitutional confiscation of slaveholders' property. The ruling thus cast in doubt decades of congressional decisions about

"free" and "slave" territories. The decision elated southerners, but its extremism helped to drive northerners one step closer to condemning slavery altogether.

Arguments between the North and the South over the Dred Scott case reflected a growing split between the once-dominant agricultural South and the increasingly powerful industrial North. Slavery, the most obvious difference between the two regions, became the symbol of that division for politicians on both sides, who battled over whether each new state from the American West should be admitted as free or slave. The debate was further inflamed by a group of reformers known as abolitionists. These advocates, including many free black men and women, some of whom are depicted on pages 62-67, called for the outright end, or abolition, of slavery throughout the United States.

Increasingly on the defensive, southern slave owners pushed hard for concessions from the North to protect their "peculiar institution," as they preferred to call slavery, and secured passage of the Fugitive Slave Act in 1850. The new law provided that escaped slaves had to be returned to the South with a minimum of legal processing—and with stiff penalties for northerners who had aided them. In effect, it exported the practice of slavery to free soil.

The slavery question figured prominently in the 1860 presidential election, which placed Abraham Lincoln in the White House on a moderate antislavery platform and helped establish Lincoln's party, the Republicans, as a major force in American political life. Lincoln, although never one to be out front on the slavery issue, had already observed in an 1858 speech that "this government cannot endure, permanently half slave and half free." Within six weeks of his inauguration, that prophecy came true with the outbreak of civil war.

Although more than 180,000 black Americans served on the side of the Union in that conflict, during the war black men and women continued to be treated as inherently unequal. Lincoln himself at first favored freeing slaves gradually over a 30-year period, with slave owners being compensated for their losses out of the national treasury. Free blacks, he felt, should volunteer to be sent to a nearby colony, preferably Haiti or Panama. But as the Civil War dragged on, Lincoln came to realize just how crucial slaves had become to the Confederate war machine. Military leaders on both sides acknowledged the important role of slave labor in southern armories and munitions plants, in constructing fortifications, and in providing the staple foods that kept the Confederacy fed. On January 1, 1863, Lincoln issued a presidential order, the Emancipation

Vast, unsettled, and overgrown with vines and other dense cover, the Great Dismal Swamp, situated on the border of Virginia and North Carolina, offered sanctuary to runaway slaves— including the man pictured above, about whom little else is known. So many escapees gathered in the swamp that by the late 1700s it was home to one of North America's largest communities of permanent fugitives, or maroons. (The term is a corruption of the Spanish word cimarrón, *meaning wild.) Like the residents of the other 50 or so maroon societies hidden in the southern wilderness, those in the Great Dismal Swamp built homes, farmed small crops, raised pigs and chickens, raided nearby plantations for supplemental food, and traded, illegally, with local whites. The swamp, with its nearly impenetrable vegetation, provided a natural defense from slave catchers. "The chivalry of Virginia has never yet ventured on a slave hunt in the Dismal Swamp," commented an abolitionist newspaper in 1852, "nor is it probably in the power of the state to capture or expel these Fugitives from it." A few years later, however, slaveholders launched several punitive expeditions. The Dismal Swamp community, which had numbered about 2,000 residents, shrank under the assaults—but was not vanquished.*

Proclamation, freeing slaves in the rebel states. It was a bold and unapologetic attempt to weaken the Confederacy as well as to generate favorable world opinion.

At first the proclamation had no real impact, since it applied to rebellious states outside of federal control; the document exempted any slaveholding border states still loyal to the Union. But its words became a reality as federal troops swept through the South. In an interview conducted after the war, two former slaves named Mill and Jule recounted a last conversation with their soon-to-be-former mistress that took place as the Yankees arrived. "Mistress got wild-like," said Mill. " 'Now, Mill you won't go with them, will you?' I felt safe, and said, 'I'll go if I have a chance.' 'Jule, you won't go, will you?' 'I shall go if Mill goes.' She began to wring her hands and cry. 'Now, 'member I brought you up. You won't take your children away from me, will you, Mill?' 'Mistress I shall take what children I've got lef'.' 'If they fine that trunk o' money or silver plate you'll say it's you'n, won't you?' 'Mistress, I can't lie over that,' " Mill replied. " 'You bo't that silver plate when you sole my three children.' "

Mill's words on the eve of real emancipation symbolized the new psychological freedom of former slaves. A hard road lay ahead—harder than some, in the glow and promise of first freedom, might have imagined. But never again would black American men and women be taken against their will, sold at market like livestock, and subjected to the many other degradations of slavery. After more than two centuries of institutionalized servitude, African Americans were, in the words of the Emancipation Proclamation, "thenceforward, and forever free."

Tents provided by the Union army in this Richmond camp in 1865 were a welcome haven for many newly freed slaves with no money and nowhere else to go.

Three and a half centuries of slaving forged the trading pattern shown on the map below. Slave ships followed the routes depicted in red, sailing from West Africa to Caribbean and American ports where men, women, and children were traded for sugar, cotton, grain, and other raw materials. Those supplies flowed to Europe (*light blue routes*), where they were exchanged for rum, guns, and textiles. Traders took the finished goods south to Africa (*dark blue routes*) to pay for slaves.

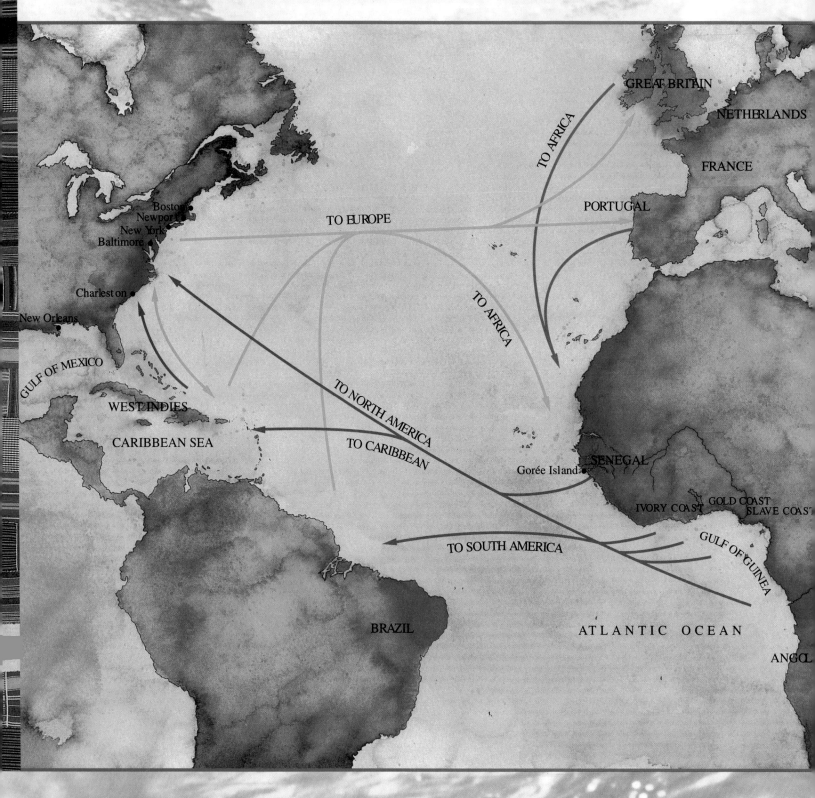

THE TRADE IN HUMAN FLESH

"What a glorious and advantageous trade this is," wrote an employee of Great Britain's Royal African Company stationed on the Guinea coast in 1725. "Put a stop to the slave trade, and all the others cease." The man's remark held a grain of truth. For centuries the Atlantic slave trade played a vital role in the world economy, forming the basis of a vast commercial network linking Britain and the nations of western Europe with their overseas colonies.

This trading of material goods for human flesh began in the early 1500s, but it was in the years between 1700 and 1850—during the growth of plantation economies in North America, the West Indies, and Brazil—that demand for slaves soared. To the traders, the captives were commodities, in principle no different from a hundredweight of cotton. The human "property" was acquired by merchants in

various ways. Some slaves were prisoners captured in African wars; others were kidnapped from their villages; still others were sold into slavery for violating African law. Although most captives came from near the coast, some lived inland, and millions died on forced marches to the sea like the one depicted here. The survivors—about 12 to 13 million Africans over the whole history of the slave trade—took the nightmare voyage across the Atlantic, most of them destined for the West Indies or points south. Perhaps half a million were brought directly to North America.

Traders paid for the Africans with finished goods from Europe. They then sold the slaves in the Americas for raw materials—sugar, cotton, indigo, tobacco, and rice. To complete the cycle, merchants went to Europe to exchange American staples for manufactured goods. The constant demand at all points of the trading triangle created wealth, spawned new industries, and helped make possible the Industrial Revolution. Yet in 1807, partly in response to growing religious and moral objections, Britain became one of the first European nations to outlaw the slave trade. The economic development partially funded by slaving enabled the country to prosper without it.

A BRUTAL INTRODUCTION TO SLAVE LIFE

Most captured Africans were taken to a coastal fort, where they were held until a shipload of slaves could be assembled. Some 50 slaveholding sites, constructed by European traders with the permission of local rulers, formed an archipelago of misery that stretched for 300 miles along the West African coast. Ruins of one of those forts still stand on Senegal's Gorée Island, depicted above in an 18th-century engraving.

A number of slave houses once dotted the island as part of a moderate-size operation controlled at different times by the Portuguese, French, Dutch, and British. Historians estimate that about 60,000 captives passed through its dungeons, a fraction of the total Atlantic trade. But for those prisoners, Gorée offered a savage preview of what was to come. Made to work while they awaited the slavers who would purchase them, the chained captives broke up the island's basaltic rocks into building stones

using cannonballs for hammers, moved barrels containing water, crushed shells to make lime, and did chores for the traders who lived in the upper level of the slave house. They also loaded and unloaded the vessels on which they would later travel as cargo. At night, the captives crowded into dark, damp cells with little air. Many succumbed to diseases that spread quickly in the quarters; the dead and the dying were thrown to the sharks.

Despite a close watch by slave merchants, Gorée's captives sometimes rebelled. In October 1724, fifty-five Africans armed with knives and axes attacked their captors, to no avail. And in 1755, a planned revolt was betrayed by a child. Two of the leaders were killed, and the other rebels were hustled aboard a French ship for immediate export. As that reaction suggests, revolts did not slow the processing of captives at Gorée, which continued to be an active slaving center until 1848.

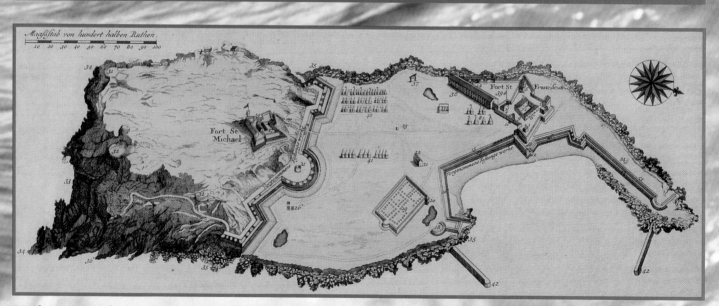

Fortifications are the key feature of this 18th-century Dutch map of Gorée, which emphasizes the island's role as a military base. The slave house shown at right was built somewhat later, to the left of the harbor.

The ruins of Gorée's "House of Slaves" (*above*), built about 1780, offer a grim reminder of the trade in human beings that once flourished on the island.

Daylight beckons beyond the so-called Door of No Return (*above*), which opens onto the sea. Captives may have been led through the door to ships moored in the Gorée harbor. In the small cells where slaves were kept (*right*), some estimate that children were packed 50 to 60 to a room.

This 19th-century engraving, published by English Quakers, depicts captives in a slave ship's hold. Nearly naked and in chains, slaves were made to lie on the bare wood of a ship's deck, which sometimes scoured the flesh from their bodies.

THE ORDEAL OF THE MIDDLE PASSAGE

Given the restrictions of slavery, few survivors of the horrific "Middle Passage" to the Americas ever had a chance to write about it. One who did was the Nigerian captive Olaudah Equiano, who gained his freedom years later. "The closeness of the place, and the heat of the climate, added to the number in the ship, which was so crowded that each had scarcely room to turn himself, almost suffocated us," he wrote. "The shrieks of the women, and the groans of the dying, rendered the whole a scene of horror almost inconceivable."

The captives, chained hand to hand and foot to foot, were held belowdecks, with men, women, and children occupying separate areas. In what was called tight packing, the captives were wedged together with little room to sit up or even to shift their bodies. So-called loose packing, which allowed each slave a bit more room, saved lives and profits. But for those crammed onto the slave decks, the two systems differed only in degree.

During the journey, which lasted between five and 12 weeks, the slaves saw daylight only when they were taken on deck and forced by the lash to "dance" for exercise. Then it was back to the filthy decks, which were ripe for smallpox, dysentery (then known as flux), and other diseases. A British ship's surgeon who served on at least four 18th-century crossings recalled those areas as "so covered with the blood and mucus which had proceeded from them in consequence of the flux, that it resembled a slaughter-house." One Spanish slaver lost 545 of its cargo of 733 slaves to disease and overcrowding. On average, about 13 percent of all African captives died en route. The total death toll is estimated at one to two million people.

Causes of death also included suicide and outright murder. In a notorious 1781 case, Captain Luke Collingwood of the British ship *Zong* ran low on drinking water and ordered 130 slaves thrown overboard. After the slave trade became illegal, captains sometimes jettisoned their human cargo to avoid being caught by naval patrols. Attempted slave revolts usually ended in still more executions.

Contemplating the three and a half centuries of the slave trade, George Francis Dow, an early-20th-century author and historian, despaired of finding adequate words to convey what took place aboard the ships. "The cruelty and horror of the 'Middle Passage'—the voyage from the Guinea coast—can never be told in all its gruesome detail," he wrote. "It is enough to recall that the ships were always trailed by man-eating sharks."

The log from a 1728 crossing of the British slaver *Katherine* lists causes of death among African captives ranging from "flux" to "mellancholly."

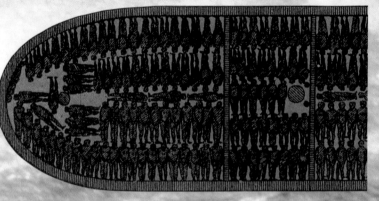

African captives lying side by side cover a ship's deck in the loading plan above. Abolitionists documented the slave trade's inhumanity with diagrams like this one and the four-tiered cross section of a slave ship at right.

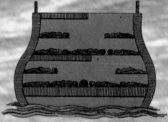

Painted figures reveal how slaves were packed on the decks of the slave ship *Brookes* in this four-inch-tall model. British abolitionist William Wilberforce used the model during a 1789 parliamentary debate on banning the slave trade.

"DE STRENGTH OF DESE ARMS"

When a new owner arrived to take possession of a plantation in Georgetown County, South Carolina, in the early 1900s, he informed an aging field hand named Morris that he no longer needed his services. The former slave, summoning his dignity, replied that he had no intention of leaving. "I was born on dis place before Freedom. My Mammy and Daddy worked de rice fields. De strength of dese arms and dese legs and of dis old back," he said quietly, "is in your rice banks." Chastened, the new owner let Morris stay.

Morris was not alone. At the turn of the century thousands of former slaves still lived and worked in South Carolina's coastal regions, where they and their ancestors had built the rice plantations that enriched generations of white owners. At one time, in the 1850s, the plantations in Georgetown County alone exported more rice than any other seaport in the world. But as Morris and the other former slaves who made that possible passed away, so did most cultivation of rice in the region.

The prosperity rice brought to South Carolina depended on several factors, among them the labor of slaves. As shown here and on the following pages, for many decades slaves planted, tended, and harvested the crops almost entirely by hand, often working in 90- to 100-degree heat. The rice business also relied

10 LBS. NET

This Rice WAS GROWN AT MANSFIELD PLANTATION GEORGETOWN, S. C.

on African know-how. Unable at first to make rice growing succeed, white farmers of the 1700s imported Africans from what is today Senegal and Gambia, regions long known for rice cultivation. Turning snake-infested South Carolina lowlands into plantation rice paddies required a complex system of canals, banks, and floodgates—all of which were constructed, operated, and maintained by slaves.

Rather than following the "gang system" of labor, in which slaves worked in groups, rice plantations ran on the "task system"—an equally exhausting scheme in which each slave was given an individual assignment calculated to last the entire day. Most tasks involved planting, hoeing, weeding, or threshing a specified acreage. A few trusted slaves, like the figure in the engraving below, were sometimes armed with rifles or other noisemakers to frighten away birds that ate into a planter's profits.

Once their tasks were done, the slaves could then tend their own gardens or, depending on their master, earn a little money for doing additional tasks. But for slaves who could not complete a given day's work, the penalty could be cruel. As Hagar Brown, a former slave on The Oaks plantation in Georgetown County, recalled, "Don't done you task, driver wave that whip, put you over the barrel, beat you so blood run down."

Slaves on the Kinloch plantation, located on the North Santee River in Georgetown County, South Carolina, tended rice paddies designated on this land plat by such names as Sister 1, Sister 2, Don't Care Corner, and Swamp Square. While waiting for the rice to sprout, most slaves worked in fields where other crops were grown.

In a sketch (*right*) made to illustrate the 1914 memoir of a Georgetown County plantation mistress, slave women thresh the harvested rice crop with long wooden flails like the one inset here. To gather the rice for threshing, workers cut off the tops of the plants and tied them into bundles.

Using baskets woven from salt-marsh grasses, slaves winnow rice (*above*) by tossing it into the air and allowing the wind to blow away the chaff. Both the winnowing basket (*left*) and the wooden mortar and pestle (*right*) used to grind off the outer husk of the grain were tools employed by rice-cultivating peoples on the West Coast of Africa.

A steam-driven mill (*right*) for threshing and pounding rice, once maintained and operated by slaves, still stands amid live oak trees on the Chicora Wood plantation, a center of rice production in Georgetown County. Inside the nearby shipping barn, milled rice poured through a wooden trough into a chute (*inset*) that deposited the grain on a river barge docked at a wharf on the Pee Dee River.

This two-room slave cabin stands on the grounds of the Arundel plantation, located on the Pee Dee River in Georgetown County. The peaked roof, doors, and windows and the saw-toothed trim are typical of 19th-century slave cabins in the area.

LIFE AND DEATH ON SLAVE ROW

During the long, hot growing season, from March to September, every available slave on a rice plantation labored in the fields. But slaves also worked as engineers, butchers, nurses, and stable hands. Slave carpenters built the "big house" where the master lived, as well as kitchens, barns, rice mills, and chapels. Slave ironworkers created functional items like farm implements as well as graceful accessories like the fireplace andirons opposite. Such artisans were also hired out to other plantations, paying their masters most of the money they earned.

In the evening, slaves returned to their quarters—small, stuffy shanties like the ones in the background image. There they kept more or less to themselves, although never too far from the watchful eye of the driver, a privileged slave who often lived at the end of the row. Stories and songs were passed down through the generations while families did their chores. As one former slave explained, "Mudder and Father tell you story to keep you eye open" while the family worked into the night.

Food was sometimes in cruelly scarce supply. One particularly mean planter gave each slave household a peck of sweet potatoes—about eight dry quarts—and a dozen salted fish each week. Slaves with children also received a peck of grits and a piece of fatback bacon. On another rice plantation, two slaves who had been sold dictated a letter home praising their new provisions. "What we have to trow away now," they wrote, "it would be anough to furnish your Plantation for one season."

Although many enslaved families supplemented their diets by raising vegetables and livestock, malnutrition was a common problem. Rice plantation slaves were also prey to respiratory ailments, parasites, and poisonous snakes. Malaria plagued the slaves as well. Some, who had inherited a trait for sickle-shaped blood cells, had a genetic resistance to the disease. But those without the trait risked death every summer, when plantation owners fled to healthier climes and left their black workers, under an overseer, to endure the scourge.

Slaves in South Carolina receive their weekly food rations in this engraving from the 1860s. As one slave recalled, on Saturday each slave would "line up at smokehouse to draw he share."

An outdoor, or summer, kitchen (*far right*) at the Chicora Wood plantation houses a brick hearth (*inset*) from which food was carried to the main house for the master's meal.

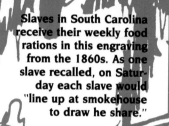

The hand-carved molding on the mantelpiece above and the wrought-iron andirons at right reflect the talents of slave artisans.

This tombstone, on a South Carolina plantation, marks the grave of a slave who died nearly 40 years after the Civil War.

SARAH PYATT
BORN
SEPT. 27, 1846
DIED
APR. 15, 190

REVOLT!

Enslaved African Americans responded in different ways to their life sentence of oppression. Some seemed resigned to their fate. Others quietly resisted by deliberately "misunderstanding" instructions or by being careless with farm equipment. Still others ran away. Perhaps the most daring reaction—and the one most feared by slaveholders—was armed revolt. The slaves were hopelessly outgunned, however, and every North American slave rebellion was soon crushed. Worse yet, as word of an attempted rebellion spread, the event was usually followed by a savage backlash against all slaves.

Although advocates of slavery tried to present armed insurrection as the rarest of rare occurrences, historical research has turned up documented accounts of hundreds of revolts and conspiracies. Indeed, such events took place in waves, with a number of violent episodes followed by relative calm. Each of the famous rebellions presented here, for example, culminated a period of slave unrest. These and similar acts, wrote one historian, "were firebells in the night; cries from the heart; expressions of human need and aspiration in the face of the deepest testing."

Gabriel Prosser

In August 1800, Virginia slave Gabriel Prosser set in motion a plot to attack and seize portions of the city of Richmond, killing as many white residents as possible. Inspired in part by the biblical story of Moses leading the Israelites out of bondage, Prosser spread word of his plan to well over 1,000 slaves. As his followers gathered on the appointed night, however, a thunderstorm erupted. Their progress crippled by the heavy rain, the rebels disbanded. But three slaves had alerted their masters to the revolt. Troops dispatched by Governor James Monroe captured at least three dozen of the insurgents; Prosser eluded searchers for a month. All were tried and hanged. "I have adventured my life in endeavoring to obtain the liberty of my countrymen," said one doomed defendant, "and am a willing sacrifice to their cause."

Denmark Vesey

A carpenter who had purchased his freedom in 1800 with the winnings from a lottery ticket, Denmark Vesey was passionate in his hatred of slavery. He argued boldly with whites on the streets of Charleston, South Carolina, and his eloquent readings and sermons urged other blacks to demand equality. In 1822, talk among Charleston's black population turned to action. More than 9,000 slaves and free blacks were attracted to a plot, promoted by Vesey, to "liberate" the city. Several slaves betrayed the conspirators, however, and Vesey was forced into hiding as 130 others were arrested. Just one man broke—under torture—but his confession led to Vesey's arrest and hanging. Many of the other rebels also were hanged. Panic-stricken South Carolina legislators subsequently barred free blacks from entering the state's ports, in part because Vesey had once been a sailor.

Nat Turner's rebellion

A gifted preacher who saw visions from an early age, Virginia slave Nat Turner believed himself destined for a great purpose. After a solar eclipse in February 1831, which he took as a divine signal, the 31-year-old Turner devised what he later described as a plan of "terror and devastation" that led to the most famous slave revolt in American history.

Instead of risking discovery by organizing a large band of rebels, Turner began with just six slaves, who met as a group on August 21. The next morning they went to the plantation of Turner's master and killed the entire family. By daybreak on August 23, the small force had moved through Southampton County, gathering more than 60 supporters and slaying at least 57 white men, women, and children.

Police and military units captured or killed many of the rebels, but Turner escaped arrest until October 30. During that time, panic spread among southern whites. Hundreds of blacks with no connection to the revolt were killed, and slave codes were harshened and strictly enforced.

As Turner awaited execution, his calm impressed his court-appointed attorney, Thomas Gray. Nat Turner, Gray said, had a "mind capable of attaining anything" and a "spirit soaring above the attributes of man."

Sheltered by darkness and vine-draped trees, a sinister-looking Nat Turner confers with other rebels in the artist's conception at top. Turner's actual appearance is depicted more accurately in the likeness inset above.

In the composite scenes at right, taken from an account published in New York City months after the revolt, Turner and his companions attack a white woman and her children (1); a man identified as Turner's master, Mr. Travis (2); and Captain John T. Barrow, who wields a sword (3). In the final scene (4), troops search out and capture the rebel force.

The Scenes which the above Plate is designed to represent are—Fig. 1, a Mother intreating for the lives of her children.—2, Mr. Travis, cruelly murdered by his own Slaves.—3, Mr. Barrow, who bravely defended himself until his wife escaped.—4. A comp. of mounted Dragoons in pursuit of the Blacks.

A RARE VICTORY AT SEA

In June 1839, on a humid Havana night, 49 men and four children—all just arrived from Africa—were hustled into the steaming hold of the slave ship *Amistad*. Most of the captives were of the Mende people of West Africa. One was a born leader—Cinque (*right*), a rice farmer and the 25-year-old son of a prominent Mende family. Allowed on deck for some air at one point, Cinque used sign language to ask the ship's cook what was to become of the Africans. He was told they would be slaughtered as meat for the Spanish crew. In reality, they were destined for a grim enough fate: resale into slavery in another part of Cuba.

Like many slaves on many slave ships before them, the imprisoned Africans began planning an insurrection—something most traders guarded vigorously against. But on the *Amistad* (ironically, the name is Spanish for "friendship"), the crew was lax, offering the Mende captives a rare chance. Using a nail he had found on deck and hidden under his arm, Cinque broke a padlock, releasing the chain that linked the captives at the neck. The men then grabbed sugarcane knives they found in the hold and crept up on deck under cover of a nighttime storm.

Led by Cinque, the Africans discovered Captain Ramón Ferrer fast asleep on a mattress; the ship's cook slept nearby in a dinghy. They killed both men. Two other sailors escaped by leaping overboard, leaving behind only the slave cabin boy and the two Spanish slave traders who had chartered the vessel.

Cinque ordered the Spaniards to sail the *Amistad* back to Africa, toward the rising sun. By day, they obeyed. But at night, the traders headed northwest, toward the United States. Two months later, the schooner reached waters off New York. By then at least eight Africans had died, succumbing to thirst and illness.

Cinque gave the order to drop anchor at the tip of Long Island, and he and eight others rowed ashore for provisions. The black men created quite a sensation

Draped in traditional Mende garb and holding a staff, Cinque, leader of the *Amistad* insurrection, adopts a regal pose for this portrait by New Haven painter Nathaniel Jocelyn, completed while the *Amistad* case made its way through the courts. Below, in an 1840 engraving from an abolitionist publication, the *Amistad* captives dispatch Captain Ramón Ferrer.

among the people they encountered as they used gold doubloons found on the schooner to buy food and drink. Cinque was uneasy about the attention and eager to be under way the next morning. Before the *Amistad* could head back out to sea, however, it was seized by an American naval ship and escorted to Connecticut, beginning an 18-month legal battle over the Africans' fate. Accused of murder and mutiny, the captives were also in danger of being returned to Cuba as slaves—a course of action demanded by the Cuban and Spanish authorities and favored by U.S. president Martin Van Buren to avoid a diplomatic crisis.

The *Amistad* captives had support from two important sources, however: Spanish law and American abolitionists. In 1817 Spain had prohibited the importation of slaves into any of its territory, including the colony of Cuba. Africans such as the *Amistad* group were imported illegally and sold

with false papers. Once the fraud was exposed, it fell to the American courts to determine whether the *Amistad* Africans could be considered slaves.

While that debate raged, American abolitionists publicized the *Amistad* case, feeding the enormous curiosity the incident excited in the northern United States. By publishing likenesses of the captives (*below*), they gave human faces to the abstract miseries of slavery. They also raised money for a legal defense and managed, against all odds, to find an interpreter for the Mende-speaking Africans. Josiah Gibbs, an enterprising Yale professor, learned a few of the prisoners' words, then chanted them over and over as he strode along the New York City docks. Eventually, he met James Covey, a Mende sailor on a British ship. Covey's translating skills proved vital to the case, enabling the *Amistad* defendants to testify and to follow the proceedings. The prisoners were already famil-

iar with lawsuits: In the Mende system of law, trials were popular public events.

After an initial verdict in the Africans' favor, the case went to the U.S. Supreme Court in February 1841, with former president John Quincy Adams representing the prisoners. At 73, frail and nearly blind, Adams claimed the day. To the astonishment of both sides, the Court agreed that the Africans had been illegally sold and were not slaves.

But the long odyssey of Cinque and his companions was not yet over. Despite their legal victory, the Court offered the Africans no funds for the voyage home. Abolitionists eventually raised the money; but the wait was too long for one of the group, whose homesickness apparently led him to drown himself in a New England river. A few months later, the 35 surviving *Amistad* defendants finally returned to Africa, among the very few African captives out of millions ever to return home.

Taken from wax casts, the silhouettes at left and below offer enigmatic glimpses of the *Amistad* captives. Fabanna (*near left*) told interviewers he had left behind in Africa two wives and a child; similarly, Tsukama (*left, center*), whose name means "a learner," was separated from his parents, three sisters, and four brothers. Middle-aged Berri (*far left*) had been sold by soldiers to an African king, who traded him to a Spanish merchant.

Teme (*far right*), a young girl, had last seen her widowed mother, older brother, and sister when some men broke into their home at night, captured the family, then sold her separately. Margru (*right, center*), had become a slave after her father pawned her as security for a debt. Grabeau (*near right*), whose name meant "Have mercy on me" in Mende, was Cinque's second-in-command. A rice farmer before capture, he spoke four African tongues.

A DARING FLIGHT THROUGH THE SOUTH

In border states such as Maryland, Kentucky, and Tennessee, enslaved men and women sometimes slipped away to freedom, but in the Deep South—hundreds of miles from free soil—escape was far more difficult. Pursued by slave catchers and hunting dogs fast after a scent, fugitive slaves in Georgia or Alabama, for example, were almost sure to be caught, savagely whipped, and, in many cases, sold away from family and friends. Among the exceptions to this grim scenario were a resourceful couple named William and Ellen Craft.

As William Craft later recounted in his 1860 book, *Running a Thousand Miles for Freedom*, the two first met as slaves in Macon, Georgia. Cruelly separated from their own families in childhood, Ellen and William did not want to bring children into the world as slaves. They began thinking of a way to flee to the North, and one day in December 1848 William hit on a plan. "It occurred to me that, as my wife was nearly white, I might get her to disguise herself as an invalid gentleman," he later wrote, "while I could attend as his slave." William did not need to explain to his readers why Ellen would have to impersonate a white man; no southern lady would have ever traveled alone with a male servant.

Less than a week later, the Crafts left their cabin "like persons near a tottering avalanche," as William put it, "afraid to move, or even breathe freely, for fear the sleeping tyrants should be

aroused." Dressed as a man, with dark glasses, a poultice in a handkerchief covering her beardless cheeks, and her right hand in a sling so that she would not be asked to write, Ellen assumed her role of slaveholder. She boldly purchased two train tickets with William's savings, and the couple headed for Philadelphia.

For the next four days, the Crafts' fate depended on Ellen's ability to act like a white man. She played her role of sickly young man to the hilt, politely declining liquor and cigars and attracting the friendly concern of several fellow travelers. One even warned her to keep close watch over William, explaining, "I can see from the cut of his eye that he is certain to run away."

In Baltimore, with the journey nearly over, the Crafts had their worst moment (*opposite, below*). Despite the protests of other passengers, a railroad official balked at letting the "young gentleman" take William on the northbound train without proof of ownership. "Neither of us dared to speak a word," William wrote, "for fear of making some blunder that would tend to our detection." Just then a conductor entered the station; joining the group that had gathered, he vouched that the couple had been on his train earlier in the day. As the final boarding bell rang, the official grudgingly made an exception for Ellen, "as he is not well." Hours later, William and Ellen stood on free soil.

The Crafts moved from Philadelphia to Boston, and then, after the passage of the Fugitive Slave Act in 1850, escaped to England. There they learned to read and write, and William published his classic account of their journey. After the Civil War ended, the couple returned to Georgia, where they bought a plantation and converted it to a freedmen's school.

In this 1851 letter, William Craft urges others not to buy the couple's freedom, likening such an act to "recognizing us as property and being willing to pay our oppressors for enslaving us."

83

In the 1851 engraving above, Ellen Craft wears the masculine disguise that allowed her and her husband, William, shown at top in later years, to make their escape from Georgia.

"I AM YOUR FELLOW-MAN"

Settled with his wife and five children in Rochester, New York, in 1848, Frederick Douglass—an escaped slave who was now an internationally known abolitionist and orator—sat down to write a public letter to a former master, Thomas Auld. "Just ten years ago this beautiful September morning, yon bright sun beheld me a slave, a poor degraded chattel," he wrote, "lamenting that I was a man and wishing myself a brute." After chastising Auld for past wrongs, Douglass ended his letter simply, "I am your fellow-man, but not your slave."

Douglass had journeyed a long way from the plantation on Maryland's Eastern Shore, where he was born Frederick Bailey in 1818. Rumor had it that his father was Aaron Anthony, Thomas Auld's father-in-law and the plantation manager who owned the Bailey family. Such parentage made little difference in the life of a slave. When Frederick was taken into Anthony's house at age six, he slept on the floor of a kitchen closet and ate from a wooden trough.

When Frederick was eight, he was sent to Baltimore to work as a houseboy for Thomas Auld's brother, Hugh. His new mistress, ignoring the laws against slave literacy, taught him to read. Hugh Auld warned that such study would render the boy unfit for slavery—and he was right. Frederick Bailey secretly began reading abolitionist texts, and spent time with lay preachers and others who talked of freedom.

Perhaps to purge any thoughts of escape from the young man's mind, the family returned Frederick to Thomas Auld when he was about 15. Perceived as sullen, the youth was hired out to Edward Covey, a notorious slave breaker, in 1834. After six months of wretched treatment, he rebelled, wrestling Covey to the ground. For Bailey, the incident "rekindled the few expiring embers of freedom," he later wrote, "and revived within me a sense of my own manhood." In 1836 he went again to Baltimore, and two years later he escaped to freedom, disguised as a sailor.

Finding refuge in the New York home of black abolitionist David Ruggles, Bailey was joined by Anna Murray, a free black woman he had courted in Baltimore. The two married, then departed for the greater safety of New Bedford, Massachusetts, a port that had a large Quaker population. There Bailey took a new last name, Douglass, and worked at odd jobs. He soon became a lay preacher, with strong abolitionist leanings. By 1841 he was traveling across New England, speaking tirelessly against the evils of slavery.

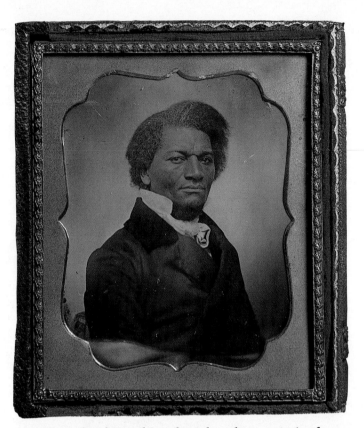

A young Frederick Douglass adopted a sober expression for this photograph, likely taken during the height of his early fame as an abolitionist writer and lecturer.

In 1845 Douglass published the first of three autobiographies. The book was a best seller—and made his whereabouts dangerously clear to his former master. Douglass hurriedly left the country for a lecture tour of Great Britain; while he was there, British friends raised funds to buy his freedom. On his return to the United States two years later, Douglass founded an influential abolitionist newspaper, the *North Star*, and became an Underground Railroad agent.

Douglass's efforts in the abolitionist cause continued unabated to the Civil War, a conflict he urged free blacks to join. "Let the black man get upon his person the brass letters, U.S.," he wrote, "and there is no power on earth which can deny that he has earned the right to citizenship." Although that prediction proved too optimistic, Douglass himself prospered after the war. He served as marshal of Washington, D.C., and as the city's recorder of deeds, and was consul general to Haiti from 1889 to 1891. A reformer to the end, Douglass died of a heart attack February 20, 1895, just hours after delivering a speech on women's rights. Wrote black former congressman and war hero Robert Smalls, "The greatest of the race has fallen."

With his dog Ned asleep on the rug beside him, Frederick Douglass (*above*) works in the book-filled study of his house in the Anacostia district of Washington, D.C., in the late 1800s. Douglass's violin, which he learned to play as a young man in Baltimore, rests at his right elbow.

An inscription on the gold head of this elegant cane notes that it was presented to Douglass in 1890 by the Wayman Grove Camp Meeting Association. Douglass was showered with such honors and memorabilia in his later years.

Purchased in Ireland in 1846 during his first lecture tour abroad, this pocket watch was Frederick Douglass's first timepiece. It cost him $40—a considerable sum in those days—and he carried it with him all his life.

BLACK LEADERS IN THE ANTISLAVERY CAMPAIGN

"Remember that we are one, that our cause is one," wrote former slave Frederick Douglass in 1847, addressing black readers in the first issue of his abolitionist newspaper, the *North Star*. "We have sighed beneath our bonds, and writhed beneath the bloody lash;—cruel mementoes of our oneness are indelibly marked on our living flesh." Shaped profoundly by his experiences as a former slave, Douglass (*pages 60-61*) was among many 19th-century African Americans deeply committed to the eradication of slavery. In abolitionist societies throughout the North, black Americans contributed their time, money, writings, and oratory, often at great personal risk. Some also helped to found new organizations dedicated to freedom. Boston's African Baptist Church served as the first home of the New England Anti-Slavery Society, for example; and the American Anti-Slavery Society, founded by members of both races in 1833, included many black leaders.

As African American freedom fighters joined forces with their white counterparts, the partnerships were not always congenial. Even among abolitionists, racial prejudice kept many whites from fully supporting economic or social equality for blacks. Disagreement also raged over colonization—the notion that freed slaves should relocate to Africa. Although African American shipowner Paul Cuffe sponsored the emigration of 38 black Americans to Africa in 1815, most other black abolitionists resented the repatriation idea, since they considered themselves as American as any white. Blacks and whites alike could be found on both sides of abolition's other debates, such as whether to include temperance and women's rights on their agenda for change.

These and other issues were freely aired in the abolitionists' meetings and public orations, which became increasingly common after proslavery president Andrew Jackson encouraged postmasters to remove abolitionist materials from the mails. Some of the most powerful speakers were former slaves like Douglass. Abolitionism was also remarkable for its female orators, black and white, who braved ridicule and sometimes violence—even from members of their own race—in an age when "respectable" women did not speak in public.

So many African Americans fought in the antislavery crusade that the prominent black abolitionists depicted here and on the following pages can be only a sampling. History records many more black activists who worked tirelessly against slavery, vigorously engaging in tasks that ranged from aiding fugitive slaves to fund-raising for the abolitionist cause through quilting bees and fairs. Ultimately, the movement rested on the efforts of countless others, black as well as white, whose names may never be known.

James Forten (1766-1842)
Born a freeman in Philadelphia, James Forten made a handsome living servicing ships in his own dry dock and gave generously to the antislavery cause. Among the first to proclaim that the races were biologically equal, he also advocated women's rights, temperance, and universal peace.

When the Pennsylvania senate considered banning the emigration of free blacks from other states, Forten opposed it in a fiery 1813 pamphlet. "Has the God who made the white man and the black left any record declaring us a different species?" he asked. "And should we not then enjoy the same liberty and be protected by the same laws?" By 1817 he had become an equally vigorous opponent of colonization.

Forten provided funds and rounded up subscribers for white abolitionist William Lloyd Garrison's newspaper, the *Liberator*, and is credited with turning Garrison against colonization. In 1833 Garrison, Forten, and other abolitionists of both races met in Forten's home to organize the American Anti-Slavery Society. Forten's death in 1842 was mourned as a great loss to the abolitionist cause.

David Walker (1785-1830)

An early advocate of black nationalism, Walker was born in North Carolina to a free mother and an enslaved father. He witnessed slavery's evils before moving to Boston, where he joined the Massachusetts General Colored Association, one of the first African American political organizations. In 1829 he published his *Appeal to the Colored Citizens of the World*, a call to overthrow slavery with violence. "Will you wait until we shall, under God, obtain our liberty by the crushing arm of power?" he asked white readers.

Distributing such literature was a capital offense in many southern states, and in Georgia a price was put on Walker's head—leading some to attribute his early death to poison.

Sojourner Truth (c. 1797-1883)

A woman of keen intellect, Sojourner Truth was an inspired orator, yet she never learned to read or write. Born Isabella Baumfree, a slave, in Hurley, New York, she was forced to marry an older slave and bore five children, three of whom were sold. At about the time New York's 1828 emancipation law would have freed her, Baumfree escaped. She remained nearby, however, and on learning of the illegal sale of her only son, she sued for the boy's return—and won.

Baumfree became known as a preacher while working as a domestic in New York City. In 1843 she dedicated her life to preaching, taking the name Sojourner Truth. "The Lord gave me *Truth*," she said, "because I was to declare truth unto people."

A feminist as well as an abolitionist, Sojourner Truth delivered her best-known speech at an 1851 Ohio women's rights convention. In a deep voice that resonated with her first master's Dutch accent, she rumbled, "Look at me! Look at my arm!" and held up her muscular right arm. "I could work as much and eat as much as a man—when I could get it—and bear the lash as well! And ain't I a woman?"

After slavery ended, Truth continued to work for black suffrage and helped former slaves find homes and gainful employment.

William Watkins (c. 1801-1858)

A schoolteacher born in Baltimore and largely self-educated, William Watkins wrote scathingly about both slavery and colonization. The phrase "philanthropic slaveholder," he once observed, made no more sense than "sober drunkard." And as a keen opponent of colonization—some 20 years before Frederick Douglass took up the cause—Watkins insisted that blacks in the United States were Americans, and that their place was in America, not Africa. Free blacks, he wrote, "had rather die in Maryland, under the pressure of unrighteous and cruel laws than be driven like cattle to the pestilential clime of Liberia."

David Ruggles (1810-1849)

Born free in Norwich, Connecticut, David Ruggles helped hundreds of fugitive slaves to safety on the Underground Railroad, among them Frederick Douglass. He also traveled as a journalist, lecturer, and agent for an abolitionist weekly, arguing that "our hope for victory, under God, is in the power of the *press*." As the first known African American bookseller, Ruggles paid a high price for his antislavery views when his New York City shop was burned by a white mob.

William Whipper (1805-1885)

The son of a white Pennsylvania businessman and his black servant, Whipper inherited his father's lumber business and, with a free black partner, made it one of the state's leading lumberyards. He was dedicated to nonviolence and rational persuasion, helping to found the antislavery American Moral Reform Society in 1835 and financing and editing its journal in the belief that "moral elevation" would entitle blacks to their freedom. Later, however, he came to regard freedom as an inherent right. An Underground Railroad activist, from 1847 to 1860 Whipper donated $1,000 a year to aid fugitives passing through Pennsylvania.

Maria Miller W. Stewart (1803-1879)

A Connecticut orphan, Maria Stewart was bound as a servant to a white clergyman's family. At age 23 she married a Boston seaman; he died three years later, and the white executors of his will cheated Stewart out of a substantial inheritance. Undaunted, she took up "the cause of God and the cause of freedom" and in 1832 became one of the first American-born women to speak publicly to mixed audiences of men and women. She railed against slavery and injustice, racism and sexism. In her last public address, in 1833, Stewart defended what some considered her immodest behavior: "Men of eminence have mostly risen from obscurity; nor will I, although a female of darker hue, and far more obscure than they, bend my head or hang my harp upon the willows."

Sarah Mapps Douglass (1806-1882)

Most Philadelphia schools did not encourage blacks to attend; so Douglass, the daughter of a prominent black Quaker family, was educated by tutors and at the "colored" school founded by her mother and James Forten. She went on to open an academy for black children and later trained many of the city's public school teachers at the Quaker-sponsored Institute for Colored Youth.

An early member of the biracial Philadelphia Female Anti-Slavery Society, Douglass became friends with Sarah and Angelina Grimké, the white abolitionist daughters of a slaveholding South Carolina judge. The three women challenged the deep-seated racial segregation in Philadelphia public life, which could be found even in Quaker meetings.

William C. Nell (1816-1874)
A former law student from Boston, William Nell never applied to the bar: He could not swear to uphold a national constitution that supported slavery. Instead, he became an abolitionist and helped to desegregate Massachusetts public schools. Nell also was active in the abolitionist press, serving at one time as a writer on the staff of the *Liberator* and later as publisher of the *North Star*. Nell's 1855 book, *The Colored Patriots of the American Revolution*, remains an important source in documenting early African American military service. Six years after its publication, he was made a postal clerk—one of the first black federal appointees.

Robert Purvis (1810-1898)
One of several wealthy black abolitionists, Robert Purvis grew up in Philadelphia, inheriting a fortune at the age of 16 from his father, a white South Carolina cotton broker. As co-founder of the American Anti-Slavery Society, Purvis gave much time and money to helping runaway slaves. In his home, which a fellow abolitionist dubbed Saints' Rest, a trapdoor concealed a secret room in which fugitives could hide.

He and his wife, Harriet (a daughter of James Forten), as supporters of the Free Produce movement, used no foods or other products brought to market by the toil of slaves.

In 1838 Purvis protested in vain against a provision in the Pennsylvania constitution that rescinded the right of blacks to vote. But when school officials decided to exclude black children from public schools, Purvis withheld his sizable tax payment. The policy was reversed.

Charles Lenox Remond (1810-1873)

One of eight children, Charles Remond was the oldest son of a successful Curaçaoan merchant and his wife living in Salem, Massachusetts. At the age of 28, he was named the first African American lecturer for the Massachusetts Anti-Slavery Society. This tireless freedom fighter often traveled for three weeks at a time, sometimes speaking twice a day. When meeting houses were unavailable, he convened groups outside. Disregarding white mobs that sometimes appeared, he appealed for "immediate, unconditional emancipation for every human regardless of tongue or color." Remond also protested sexual discrimination: At the 1840 World Anti-Slavery Conference in London, to which he was forced to travel in steerage because he was black, he declined his seat on the main floor when he learned that the women delegates had been refused theirs. In 1842 Remond became the first person of color to address the Massachusetts legislature, where he appealed against the "odiousness and absurdity" of segregated seating on railroads.

Sarah Parker Remond (1826-1894)

When a white school refused to admit Sarah Remond, her family moved from Salem, Massachusetts, to Newport, Rhode Island, so she could attend a black private school. From then on, Remond protested the segregation of churches, theaters, and even an ocean liner. At 16 she joined her brother Charles (*left*) on the lecture circuit; to avoid the "heartless and vulgar prejudice" of hotel owners, they stayed with friends. Remond began lecturing for the American Anti-Slavery Society when she was 30. During a tour in England, she told one audience that if Englishwomen "knew the unspeakable horrors to which their sex was exposed on southern plantations" they would "demand for the black woman the protection and rights enjoyed by the white." Remond later practiced medicine in Florence, Italy.

Henry Highland Garnet (1815-1882)

Second only to Frederick Douglass in stature and fame, Henry Highland Garnet was, like Douglass, a former Maryland slave. He escaped to New York City at the age of nine with his family. In 1835 Garnet enrolled at New Hampshire's Noyes Academy, an integrated institution. Shortly after his arrival some 300 white men, opposed to the presence of black students, hitched 90 yoke of oxen to the school building and dragged it into a swamp. Garnet, in fear for his life, left the academy. He completed his studies at Oneida Theological Institute, near Utica, New York, then became the minister of a black Presbyterian congregation in Troy, New York, in 1842. His early ex-periences, however, had left their mark: He became convinced that armed resistance was the only answer to slavery and the next year delivered a ringing "Call to Rebellion" at the National Negro Convention. "Strike for your lives and liberties," he urged the nation's slaves. "Rather die freemen than live to be slaves. Remember that you are FOUR MILLIONS!" Douglass condemned that stance as dangerously impractical. But Garnet was not alone: The convention fell just one vote short of adopting his remarks as its official resolution. Four years later, a similar meeting unanimously adopted another of Garnet's appeals for rebellion, reflecting the increasingly militant views of black abolitionists.

In the fall of 1859, Garnet ex-pressed hope that the end of slavery was near: "I believe the sky is brightening, and though I may not live to see it, the day is not distant when, from the Atlantic to the Pacific, from Maine to California, the shouts of redeemed millions shall be heard." Active in politics after the Civil War, he worked for a time with the Freedmen's Bureau, and in 1881 accepted an appointment as U.S. minister to Liberia.

Margaretta Forten (1808-1875)

The eldest of James and Charlotte Forten's eight children, Margaretta Forten taught in the Philadelphia school run by Sarah Mapps Douglass before founding her own private grammar school for black students in 1850. Forten was an astute businesswoman who also helped manage her father's estate after his death in 1842. She completed real-estate transactions he had begun and pursued legal means to protect the interests of his heirs.

Influenced by her parents and the other abolitionists who regularly visited their home, Margaretta Forten was drawn to the antislavery cause. In a poem, she hailed the "blessed few" of the American Anti-Slavery Society, which her father helped establish. But women were denied full membership in the group—a fact that led Forten and others to found the integrated Philadelphia Female Anti-Slavery Society. They not only opposed slavery but also advocated social equality between the races.

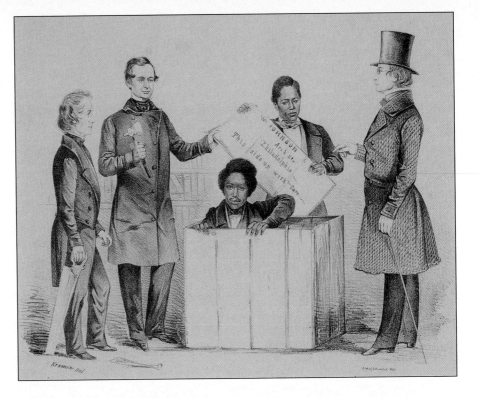

Surrounded by Underground Railroad agents, Henry "Box" Brown (*right*) emerges from a two-by-three-foot shipping crate. William Still, who holds the lid, wrote that Brown sat up, "saying, 'How do you do, gentlemen?'"

When its lantern was lit, this "Faithful Groomsman" hitching post welcomed fugitives to the Underground Railroad station in New Hope, Pennsylvania.

REAL-LIFE EXPLOITS ON A LEGENDARY "RAILROAD"

The Underground Railroad, a secret network of safe houses and sympathetic hosts who helped escaping slaves, is the stuff of American legend. But the facts behind the legend are hard to pin down. No one really knows, for example, how many slaves used the "railroad," or how many even knew of it. And there was never just one Underground Railroad; the term actually referred to a number of unrelated escape routes through the North as well as some that led south to other countries. Historians agree that on each route a few "stations"—often private homes or black churches—offered the fugitives shelter. Getting the refugees from one station to the next was the job of "agents" of both races—although, understandably, the slaves tended to trust the black agents more than the white ones.

Secrecy was usually the rule. Some agents transported passengers in false-bottomed carts; others offered sanctuary in hidden rooms. Depending on the local mood, however, the Railroad could be a somewhat public affair. In Indiana, prominent white abolitionist Levi Coffin, a Quaker bank director, flaunted his 35-year role in the Midwest arm of the Railroad. Black antislavery activists had to be more circumspect, but in some Pennsylvania communities agents bought tickets for fugitives and openly sent them by train to Philadelphia, to be met by a member of that city's Vigilance Committee, founded in 1838 by black abolitionist Robert Purvis (*page 65*) and others.

Some Railroad passengers were rescued from slavery by black conductors such as Harriet Tubman, who ventured south to lead them

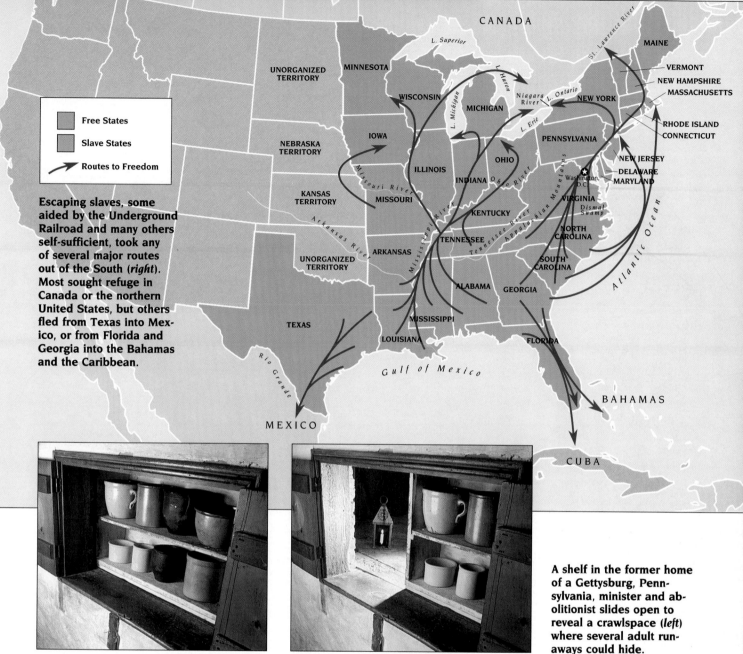

Escaping slaves, some aided by the Underground Railroad and many others self-sufficient, took any of several major routes out of the South (right). Most sought refuge in Canada or the northern United States, but others fled from Texas into Mexico, or from Florida and Georgia into the Bahamas and the Caribbean.

A shelf in the former home of a Gettysburg, Pennsylvania, minister and abolitionist slides open to reveal a crawlspace (left) where several adult runaways could hide.

out. But for the most part the Underground Railroad was a refuge for slaves who had completed the most dangerous part of their journey alone. That fact is overlooked in many postwar accounts of the secret network, which often depict runaway slaves as passive and helpless. Black abolitionist William Still's enormous 1872 memoir, The Underground Railroad, is one of the few books to recognize the bravery of the fugitives.

As chairman of the Philadelphia Vigilance Committee, Still recorded the names and histories of about 100 fugitives a year from 1850 into the next decade. The account includes slaves "guided by the North Star alone, penniless, braving the perils of land and sea," and others fleeing "secluded dens and caves of the earth, where for months and years they had been hidden away."

Still also documented the case of Henry "Box" Brown (opposite), who was shipped in a crate from Richmond, Virginia, to Still's office. Brown nearly died when the box was transported for hours upside down. Lear Green, a female fugitive, traveled from Baltimore to Philadelphia inside a chest. But such escapes could also fail. Samuel Smith, the white man who shipped Brown, later boxed up two slaves who were caught before reaching safety. Smith was imprisoned; the runaways, Still wrote, were "dragged back to hopeless bondage."

A LIFE DEVOTED TO FREEDOM

When Harriet Tubman was a 13-year-old field slave in rural Maryland, she tried to protect another slave from a whipping by placing herself between him and the overseer. A two-pound weight thrown by the overseer struck her in the head, knocking her unconscious. Confined to bed for months, the deeply religious child thought hard about the idea of slavery. At first, she later recalled, she prayed that her master would realize it was wrong to own another human being. Then she heard that he might sell her and her brothers to a chain gang in the Deep South, and she prayed for him to die.

As it happened, her master did die shortly thereafter, and the slaves became his son's property; the rumored sale did not occur. Harriet recovered, although she suffered from headaches and seizures the rest of her life, and was hired out as a laborer for a nearby timber operator. In 1844, at about age 23, she married John Tubman, a free black man, and moved to his cabin. But she was still a slave, a situation she was coming to find unendurable. So, in 1849, when Harriet Tubman learned again that she and her siblings might be sold, she decided to escape. Leaving her husband behind—he may have been reluctant to jeopardize his own freedom—Tubman slipped away, walking north by night through a

A neatly made bed is visible through the doorway of a room in the Harriet Tubman Home (*left*) in Auburn, New York. Now a museum, the home was founded by Tubman, shown at far left in 1906, as a haven for elderly or poor patients. She died there in 1913.

hundred miles of unknown territory. When she reached Pennsylvania, she recalled, "I looked at my hands to see if I was the same person, now I was free."

Tubman found work as a domestic in Philadelphia, where she met William Still, a leader in the Underground Railroad. She soon became the Railroad's best-known conductor. Making at least 15 trips south, Tubman helped an estimated 300 slaves to escape, including her parents and six of her 10 brothers and sisters. Cool-headed and fearless, she carried a rifle for protection against slave catchers and also to discourage any runaway who had second thoughts about escaping. Slave-holders offered the huge sum of $40,000 for Tubman's capture, but she was never apprehended. She also never lost a passenger.

During the Civil War, Tubman served as a nurse, worked with freed slaves, and acted as a spy, scouting out warehouses, ammunition depots, and other sites inside southern territory. After the war she married Nelson Davis, a young black veteran. (John Tubman, who had taken another wife, had since died.) Keeping the name Tubman, she worked for aid and schooling for free blacks, transforming her home in Auburn, New York, into a cooperative farm for the poor and the aged. She also sought a pension for her Civil War work, but it was denied. Her only financial reward from the U.S. government was a small widow's pension, given to her after the death of her second husband.

SURVIVORS OF THE WANDERER

Although millions of African Americans remained in bondage, the importing of new slaves into the United States was outlawed in 1808. Rather than eliminating the traffic in human flesh, however, the ban merely drove up the prices slave traders could command. Dodging naval patrols along the African coast, some traders continued to smuggle native Africans into the South almost to the start of the Civil War.

Among the last of the illegal slave ships, and the best known in its day, was the *Wanderer*, shown at right in a 1931 oil painting. Built in New York as a sporting yacht, the swift, roomy vessel was purchased by William Corry, the agent for an aristocratic Georgian named Charles Lamar; it was then secretly refitted as a slave ship.

In September 1858, Corry and his crew reached the mouth of the Congo River, then cruised the coastline to buy kidnapped Africans, most of them teenage boys. By the time the ship turned toward America, it held between 500 and 600 people in appallingly crowded conditions. About 400 of them survived to reach Jekyll Island, Georgia, in late November. Sick, naked, and shivering in the autumn chill, the Africans crowded around bonfires on the sand. There they ate a porridge akin to cattle feed and received a cursory look from a local doctor.

The Africans did not stay on Jekyll Island long; fearing federal prosecutors, Lamar rapidly dispersed his human chattel into several states. Throughout the South, the "*Wanderer* Negroes" attracted interest from whites and blacks alike, not only because of rumors about their illegal status but also because of their African names, language, and customs, which many of them retained after slavery ended in 1865.

Early in the 20th century, anthropologist Charles Montgomery interviewed and photographed several ex-slaves who had come over on the *Wanderer*. Most still had an African name as well as an American one, and they readily shared memories of African laws and practices. Some of them spoke a form of Kongo, one of the tongues of modern Zaire; in this language, they told Montgomery, *zola* meant "love," *tucka* was "young man," and *ndoomba* was "young women." For most of those he interviewed, however, Africa itself had become an unattainable dream. "I'm gittin' so old," said one man, "I'm 'fraid I couldn't git back."

Among the *Wanderer* survivors were (*above, left to right*) Cilucängy, who was given the American name Ward Lee; Pucka Geata, or Tucker Henderson; and Tahro, or Romeo. All three came from a mountainous region beyond the Congo.

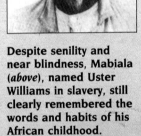

Eyeglasses askew in the portrait above, Katie Noble, whose African name was Manchuella, said she came "from deep in Africa." Older than most of the others when captured, she had to leave a child behind.

Despite senility and near blindness, Mabiala (*above*), named Uster Williams in slavery, still clearly remembered the words and habits of his African childhood.

Zow Uncola (*above*), given the name Tom Johnson, recalled growing up on a treeless plain on Africa's East Coast. "Where I come from," he said, "you can see the water just drippin' out o' the sun."

African Americans who fought beside John Brown included (*clockwise from near left*) Shields Green, nicknamed Emperor for his confident bearing; John Copeland and his uncle Lewis Leary; author Osborne Anderson, who later served as a Union soldier; and blacksmith Dangerfield Newby.

UNSUNG HEROES OF HARPERS FERRY

"I am not terrified by the gallows," wrote 23-year-old John Copeland in a last letter to his parents, "upon which I am soon to stand and suffer death for doing what George Washington was made a hero for." A former Oberlin College student, Copeland was one of five black volunteers who joined white abolitionist John Brown for his failed raid on a federal arsenal at Harpers Ferry, Virginia (*background image*). Intended as the first blow in a war of liberation, the 1859 attack led to heated debate between proslavery forces, who regarded Brown as a terrorist, and antislavery advocates, who deemed him a martyr. Both sides, however, focused primarily on John Brown. Contemporary accounts paid little notice to Copeland

and the other black members of Brown's 22-man force.

The black participants were a diverse group, with backgrounds suggesting the full range of the African American experience of their day. Shields Green, who was hanged with Copeland, was a runaway slave from Charleston, South Carolina; he was in his mid-twenties. Dangerfield Newby, a former slave who had been freed by his white master and father, hoped to liberate his wife and seven children, all still enslaved. A third volunteer, 29-year-old Osborne Perry Anderson, was a freeman born in Pennsylvania who had emigrated to Canada. There, in 1858, he attended a meeting at which John Brown previewed his bold plan. A printer by trade, Anderson

would later write the only memoir of the raid by one of its participants. As for John Copeland, he had been recruited to Brown's cause by his 24-year-old uncle, Lewis Sheridan Leary, a saddle maker who volunteered after hearing the fiery abolitionist lecture in Ohio.

Brown had originally hoped to gather many more recruits of both races. A friend of such notable black abolitionist leaders as Frederick Douglass, Henry Highland Garnet, and Harriet Tubman, Brown had believed that free blacks would rally to his call; Tubman, indeed, hoped to join him but fell sick. Other influential African Americans were less enthusiastic about the plan, however. More familiar than Brown with the conditions of slavery in

the South, they viewed the Harpers Ferry strike as foolish and doomed to failure. Frederick Douglass clearly expressed his own lack of interest in notes he made following a meeting: "Brown for Harpers Ferry and I against it."

A last-minute change in timing also limited the number of volunteers for the Harpers Ferry attack. Recruits were still secretly gathering at Brown's farmhouse headquarters outside the town when curious neighbors became suspicious about the unusual level of activity. Rather than run the risk of discovery, Brown decided to go forward with the raid at least a week earlier than he had planned.

And so, on the rainy night of October 16, the tiny army sprang into action. In the battle that followed, the band of 22 killed several bystanders and seized the town, then held out against federal troops for a day and a half. Ten of Brown's men were killed or fatally wounded, including Newby and Leary. Brown himself and six others, among them Copeland and Green, were captured and hanged.

Five others escaped, including Osborne Anderson, the only black survivor. His book about the raid, A *Voice from Harper's Ferry*, is one of the few sources to describe the role of local slaves in the attack, though the extent of their involvement remains unclear. According to Anderson, slaves in Harpers Ferry had rallied to Brown's cause, offering prayers and stepping forward to fight "without impressing or coaxing." Historians agree that a number of slaves gave their lives during the assault, but the local black population did not rise as one in revolt—in part because the raid was over so quickly.

Yet life at Harpers Ferry would never be the same. Local observers reported that slaves "burned with anxiety to learn every particular" of the raid, and several slave owners were reported beaten "by their servants." Newspapers noted widespread arson, with "the heavens illuminated by the lurid glare of burning property." In time those fires were eclipsed by the conflagration of the Civil War—which broke out a year and a half after John Brown's raid, sparked in part by the martyrs of Harpers Ferry.

RECONSTRUCTION: A FALSE DAWN

In 1865, hope of equality for the nation's four million slaves rose on the horizon like daybreak after an eternal night. On February 1, President Abraham Lincoln signed the Thirteenth Amendment, putting Constitutional backbone into the words of the Emancipation Proclamation, which two years earlier had granted freedom to slaves in any state, or part of a state, held by the Confederacy. Next, on March 3, Congress created the Bureau of Freedmen, Refugees, and Abandoned Lands, charged with providing relief to impoverished blacks and whites and with helping slaves on the brink of liberation begin their transition to independence. Indeed, a month later, on April 9, 1865, the ravaged Confederacy laid down its arms at Appomattox, Virginia, and in effect surrendered any legal claim to keeping its black citizens in bondage.

The end of the war brought reform—political, social, and economic—as African Americans grasped the rights held out of their reach for two and a half centuries. However, as the country struggled to put itself back together over the next 12 years—a period aptly named Reconstruction—freed slaves would find their dreams of equality evaporating like mist. By 1877, despite initial good intentions, the North had abandoned black Americans to the will of southern whites, whose campaigns of violence and sabotage succeeded in reestablishing the power imbalance of the antebellum era. The result would be nearly 100 more years of oppression.

Slaves greeted the news of their freedom with a full range of responses. Some immediately left their former masters, eager to start a new life. Others, confused and uncertain about their new status, stayed with what they knew. "Folks dat ain' never been free don' rightly know de *feel* of bein' free," explained James Lucas, one of Jefferson Davis's former slaves. "Dey don' know de meanin' of it." Still others, reflecting on the choices now before them, approached their liberation with restraint—and some trepidation. "Jes like tarpins or turtles after 'mancipation," said a former North Carolina slave. "Jes stick our heads out to see how the land lay."

Initially, though, it was a time to rejoice. In towns and cities, blacks joined together for parades, lined the streets to hail Union soldiers, or gathered at churches to sing their thanks to Jesus. "Wagon loads o' people rode all th'ough de place a-tellin' us 'bout bein' free," recalled one slave. "Never was no time like 'em befo' or since," said another, describing the jubilation in a village near Appomattox. There was "shoutin' an' clappin' hands an' singin'! Chillun runnin' all over de place beatin' tins an' yellin'. Ev'ybody happy."

Those who had always toiled to enrich others now saw the opportunity to strike out on their own, to come and go as they pleased, to work their own land or ply a trade for their benefit alone, to learn to read and write, and to live together in families, married in the eyes of God and the law. Couples who had "jumped the broom" in slavery sought to formalize their unions. "We had a big wedding, and she wore a white dress with two frills on it. I wore a dove-colored suit and a high brim hat with a small crown," reminisced a freed plantation worker named Milton Marshall. Never again would he and other African Americans lose their wives, husbands, and children through sale. Of those whose families had vanished to distant plantations, many took to the road, hoping to find them. "I was fifteen years old when I left Beaufort, at the time Freedom was declared," recalled Rebecca Jane Grant of Lena, South Carolina, in an interview conducted nearly 70 years later. "We were all reunited then. First, my mother and the young chillun, then I got back." To help former slaves locate their families, the Freedmen's Bureau formed what amounted to a missing persons agency. But relatives were difficult to trace. Slaves often lacked surnames to link them together, had been sold more than once, or

Newly freed slaves wave copies of the Emancipation Proclamation in this 19th-century engraving. The release from bondage allowed blacks to travel freely for the first time in their lives.

had been separated too long. "I never did know my pa," said a woman from Luray, South Carolina. "He was sold off to Texas when I was young."

As the bleak reality of the war's aftermath became apparent, the euphoria of freedom soon gave way to pangs of hunger and cold. The bare necessities—food, clothing, and shelter—once provided by a master, were in scarce supply in the depleted South. According to a former Charleston slave, "The colored people lived on cornmeal mush and salt water in the week, and mush and vinegar for Sunday. I don't see how we live, yet we is." By August 1865, the Freedmen's Bureau was delivering rations to 100,000 starving ex-slaves every day, each allotment intended to last an adult one week.

Despite the hardships they now faced, the freed slaves possessed great faith and determination. But few had the experience or skills needed to forge an independent life. "All that us slaves know how to do was to work hard," declared a woman who had cooked and cleaned in the house of a large plantation, tended its garden, and milked the cow. The vast majority were illiterate and had no working knowledge of money. "Never had any money, didn't know what it was," said one former slave from South Carolina. Another, who had been given $35 by a passing Union soldier, lamented that he could have used it to his advantage if he had only known its value: "I been so fool, had never seen no greenback. Throwed it away eating crackers and peanuts."

It was clear that the support offered by the Freedmen's Bureau would not be enough to help the millions of displaced blacks construct new lives. During the first year of freedom, Frederick Douglass spoke out on the need for blacks to begin participating in government—to organize, to vote, and to serve as elected officials. But soon after the war's dust began to settle, southern states put together governments that deliberately excluded black citizens from the democratic process. Guided by the very same men who had led the states out of the Union in the first place, state legislatures enacted notorious Black Codes that blocked African Americans from claiming nearly all the rights accorded other citizens. Such actions were made possible by North Carolina-born Andrew Johnson, who had stepped into the presidency following Lincoln's death on April 15, 1865. One month after assuming office, Johnson offered pardons to virtually any southerner who took an oath of allegiance to the United States and issued proclamations to seven Confederate states instructing them to convene constitutional conventions. According to Johnson's directives, only white voters could take part in the conventions, and they in turn had the power to determine who in their state was qualified to vote.

Leaders in the United States Congress were incensed, and responded in March 1866 by pushing through—over Johnson's veto—a civil rights bill that defined a citizen as anyone born on American soil, with the exception of Native Americans. The bill guaranteed equal rights to all citizens regardless of race and permitted the federal government to intervene when states declined to protect those rights. A month later, the legislature drafted the Fourteenth Amendment to the Constitution, which decreed black citizenship and forbade the states to deny any citizen "equal protection of the laws." Outraged, southern legislators refused to ratify the amendment—but Congress ultimately sidestepped procedure and simply declared the law to be in force.

The Congress also extended the tenure and scope of the Freedmen's Bureau. In addition to feeding the poor and building hospitals, orphanages, and communities for the old and the infirm, the bureau could now set up its own courts, make arrests, and even act as judge in locales that were particularly lax in upholding the rights of blacks. Of all its works, though, perhaps the bureau's most important achievement was in education. African Americans, thirsting for the knowledge that had been denied them, sought schooling by the tens of thousands. Responding to demand and assisted by black churches and many philanthropic organizations, the Freedmen's Bureau established more than 4,000 schools, including two dozen colleges and uni-

versities, and recruited 9,000 teachers, more than half of them from the North. With nearly 97 percent of the black population unable to read or write at the end of the Civil War, "it was a whole race trying to go to school," observed ex-slave Booker T. Washington, a future educator himself. "Few were too young, and none too old to make an attempt to learn." From his North Carolina home, one particularly determined boy known as "little Moses" walked 200 miles to attend a school at St. Helena Island, South Carolina.

Across the South the black community rallied enormous support for itself, raising money to pay for buildings, supplies, and teachers' salaries. In South Carolina, during the school year 1866-67, freed men and women donated nearly $17,000 to education. In Jefferson City, Missouri, a group of discharged soldiers contributed $6,325 to the founding of the Lincoln Institute. And in Nashville, former slaves sold scrap metal—leg irons from the city's slave pen—to purchase books for the new Fisk University.

But the one thing most ex-slaves felt could truly make them free was the thing they found most difficult to obtain. "Gib us our own land and we take care ourselves," declared one, "but widout land, de ole massas can hire us or starve us, as dey please." In fact, before the war's end, thousands of freed slaves had been given land abandoned by Confederate planters. General William Tecumseh Sherman, searching for a way to divest himself of the ex-slaves who had fallen in with his troops on their march to the sea, reached an agreement in January 1865 with the secretary of war to settle the freedmen on 40-acre plots carved from a strip of land between Charleston, South Carolina, and Jacksonville, Florida. Although this was a special order, meant to solve a military problem, it perpetuated a persistent rumor that the federal government had promised every freed slave 40 acres of land and a mule to help work them. After grim years of tending the plots of others and reaping none of the profits, impoverished blacks believed they would soon be rewarded for their sacrifices. A bold handful of former slaves even took over the plantations on which they lived, claiming that, under the new laws, the people who did the work and

Children of all ages assemble for their teacher outside a freedmen's school in North Carolina. In its seven years of operation, the Freedmen's Bureau helped educate nearly 250,000 pupils.

created the wealth were entitled to the property.

Those dreams were dashed on May 29, 1865, when President Johnson ordered that land confiscated by Union armies during the war or abandoned by fleeing southerners be returned to the owners. Although many ex-slaves vigorously resisted returning the land they had already worked and improved, they were eventually forced to comply with the policy. Perhaps in an attempt to make amends, in June 1866 the federal government opened up 44 million acres of public land in Arkansas, Mississippi, Alabama, Louisiana, and Florida. The Southern Homestead Act offered black farmers and southern whites who had pledged their loyalty to the Union 80-acre tracts plus one-month subsistence grants to get started. Unfortunately, the land was generally poor, the grants were too small to finance the necessary equipment and supplies, and the whites were loath to accept their colored neighbors. Of the 4,000 homesteaders—2,500 in Florida alone—most failed altogether or scratched out only a marginal subsistence.

Finding themselves without means of support, most of the freed slaves were forced to work for their old masters, many of whom behaved as though slavery still existed. "Freedom wasn't no difference I knows of," remarked a former slave. "I works for Marse John just the same." The Freedmen's Bureau helped negotiate labor contracts between farmers and their employees to ensure some measure of fairness and humane treatment, but the wages stipulated often fell substantially short of those paid in the North. Although some whites simply refused to pay reasonable wages, many others just didn't have the money themselves. Mourned one ex-slave, "We thought we was going to be richer than the white folks, 'cause we was stronger and knowed how to work. We soon found out that freedom could make folks proud, but it didn't make them rich." As a result, nearly all newly freed black Americans labored in positions of economic servitude. A few rented fields from landowners, but such arrangements were rare: Whites did not want to give up control of their property, especially to blacks. Ultimately, most of the white agricultural South turned to sharecropping to get the work done.

Under this system, which blacks were forced to accept to survive, landowners provided fields, tools,

seeds, and other supplies to the worker, or "cropper," in return for a share of the proceeds. Typically, they also extended credit to the sharecropper to pay for food and other necessities—purchased at the plantation commissary—then collected on the debt after the harvest. However, landowners were likely to charge exorbitant prices and interest rates, with the result that sharecroppers ended the year just breaking even or actually in debt—certainly in no position to accumulate enough capital to invest in land of their own.

With conditions for freed men and women still bleak in 1867, Congress passed the most sweeping of the laws designed to improve their plight: the Reconstruction Acts of 1867 and 1868, which awarded blacks full participation in the political process. The legislation abolished the legal authority of existing governments in the southern states and placed the states, divided into five military districts, under the rule of the army. It also required district commanders to register all eligible voters, regardless of color, to elect delegates to state conventions for the purpose of drafting new constitutions.

In cities and towns across the South, voting registrars responded to their congressional mandate, signing up new black voters and conducting public meetings to instruct them in American government and the benefits of citizenship. By the end of 1867, nearly every black voter had joined a political organization such as the Union League or the Loyal League, which were promoted by the Republican party and the Freedmen's Bureau. Local chapters served as "a political school for the people," in the words of a North Carolina teacher, and as a vehicle for rising black political leaders. The vote was restricted to men, but women and children participated enthusiastically at most political events.

Roughly 735,000 blacks registered in the southern states—100,000 more than the white names on the roster—and in the constitutional conventions that convened in 1867 and 1868, a third of all delegates, and a majority of those at the South Carolina convention, were black. Despite attempts by whites to intimidate or manipulate black voters and persuade whites to boycott the polls so that the required majority of registered voters could not be met, one by one the former Confederate states ratified new constitutions. These documents often included provisions even more progressive than those in the North, such as universal public education, care for the disadvantaged, suffrage for black males—a proviso that would become the Fifteenth Amendment to the U.S. Constitution in 1870—and the elimination of rules for voting and holding office that excluded non-landowners.

With the doors now open to public office, prominent blacks filled many local posts, both elected and appointed, including those of sheriff, mayor, and prosecuting attorney, as well as justice of the peace and county superintendent of education. Others took office in state legislatures: In South Carolina's first Reconstruction government, black legislators held 87 of the 127 seats in the lower house. Also in South Carolina, Jonathan J. Wright sat on the state supreme court, and Francis L. Cardozo filled the posts of secretary of state and, later, treasurer. Mississippi, Louisiana, and South Carolina each elected African American lieutenant governors; and in Mississippi, John Roy Lynch served as Speaker of the House and in 1873 went to the U.S. Congress as one of the state's representatives.

Eight southern states sent a total of 22 black congressmen and senators to Washington, D.C., between 1869, when Joseph H. Rainey of South Carolina became the first black to be seated in Congress, and 1901, when the last black Reconstruction-era congressman left the House. In 1870, Mississippian Hiram R. Revels, the first black elected to the U.S. Senate, stepped into the slot vacated by Jefferson Davis nearly a decade before. Mississippi also sent Blanche K. Bruce to Washington in 1874, the only other black American to serve in the Senate until Massachusetts elected Edward Brooke in 1966. Of the African Americans in the House of Representatives, South Carolina's Rainey and Rob-

An 1868 broadside celebrates the accomplishments of Oscar J. Dunn (*center*), Louisiana's first black lieutenant governor, and 29 of the 50 black convention delegates who helped rewrite the state's constitution in 1868.

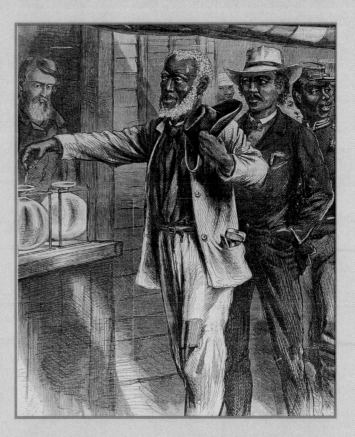

A former slave casts his first ballot in this 1867 engraving. During black voter registration in the South, army guards were dispatched to prevent whites from intimidating the ex-slaves into staying away from the polls.

ert Smalls (*page* 82) served the longest, with five terms each, while Mississippi's Lynch and Florida's J. T. Walls each had three terms.

Seated during an administration plagued by scandal and corruption, most African Americans proved to be admirable leaders who took their responsibilities seriously. At no time did they—or, for that matter, the black community as a whole—seek vengeance for their 250 years of oppression. Yet most southern whites remained opposed to equality for blacks. Early, nonviolent methods of circumscribing black progress included petitions, court actions, and passive resistance, such as refusing to sell or lease buildings for schools. Another tactic was boycotting prominent black businesses. "I always had plenty of work before I went into politics," said Henry Johnson, a South Carolina bricklayer and plasterer who became a state legislator, "but I never have got a job since. I suppose they do it merely because they think they will break me down and keep me from interfering with politics."

White southerners found a number of ways to sabotage black efforts to get ahead in the business world. Refusing to patronize black-owned businesses was among the mildest methods—but effective nonetheless. The Mississippi River Packet Company, owned by black leaders in Louisiana, failed for lack of white patronage, as did a Charleston streetcar company founded by black politicians and under charter from the state. A more blatant abuse of power involved a ship owned by the black-led Liberian Exodus Joint Stock Company, which sought to establish trade and travel routes to Africa. First, white officials in Charleston refused to let the ship sail until expensive repairs had been made to the already seaworthy vessel. Then they refused to grant passage to some travelers booked for a journey. Finally, white business leaders—who did not want to lose their cheap labor force—had the ship stolen and sold in England. Crowning the ordeal, the U.S. circuit court in South Carolina refused to admit a suit brought by the blacks to reclaim their property.

African Americans in the South had few illusions about protecting their civil rights against the prevailing hostility. Blacks arrested for petty theft sometimes received harsher sentences than whites who had committed murder, and crimes against black victims typically went unpunished altogether. Attempting to rectify the worst injustices, the Freedmen's Bureau appealed some cases to state governors, tried others in its own courts, and even had martial law declared in counties on the verge of anarchy. But the bureau could not change underlying attitudes toward black citizens, and its efforts brought limited results.

Increasingly, restive white southerners from Virginia to Texas resorted to violence. The Ku Klux Klan was only one of many quasi-military groups that used intimidation and physical abuse, including murder, to achieve their goal: to "kill or drive away leading Negroes and only let the humble and submissive remain," as a Klan paper in Alabama put it.

Many of those terrorized refused either to flee or to submit to the white supremacists. Instead, they attempted to fight back by forming local black militias for self-protection. But the Ku Klux Klan and its ilk often intercepted weapons shipments or raided the state arsenals. As racist groups gained momentum, state governments passed antiterrorist laws and activated their militias. Nevertheless, the violence continued unabated. Even the Enforcement Act and the Ku Klux Klan Act, passed by Congress in 1870 and 1871 to protect black citizens from "a carnival of murders, intimidation, and violence of all kinds," brought little relief. When cases against

ROBERT SMALLS

In the predawn hours of May 13, 1862, 23-year-old Robert Smalls, a seaman and slave from Beaufort, South Carolina, executed one of the most daring maritime maneuvers of the Civil War—and demonstrated the leadership that would mark his later career as a U.S. congressman. Smalls and the rest of the slave crew of the Confederate ship *Planter*, docked in Charleston Harbor, had been left on board while the captain and the white crew members went ashore for the night. Pulling anchor at about 3:00 a.m., Smalls, wearing the captain's distinctive straw hat, sailed unmolested past the guns of three Confederate forts, stopping once to pick up his wife and two children and the families of other slave crewmen. He then ran up a white flag and delivered the boat to a Union blockade ship in the Atlantic, explaining, "I thought the *Planter* might be of some use to Uncle Abe." The U.S. military gratefully accepted the ship, valued at $60,000, and appointed Smalls its pilot.

A year and a half later, on December 1, 1863, when the *Planter's* captain deserted his post under heavy Confederate shelling, Smalls again displayed nerves of steel. Taking the helm, he returned fire and led the gunboat out of danger. For his actions, the seaman received a promotion to captain and command of the ship until it was decommissioned in 1866.

Back home in Beaufort, Smalls was respected for his intelligence and good humor as well as his heroism, and he achieved political prominence during the Reconstruction years. He served in the state militia until 1877, attaining the rank of brigadier general, and was elected a delegate to South Carolina's constitutional convention in 1868, where he drafted a resolution for the state's first free educational system. That same year, Smalls was elected to the lower house of the state legislature. He rose to the state senate two years later, and in 1875 was elected to the U.S. House of Representatives, where he served five terms.

Congressman Smalls claimed some key legislative victories for his state, among them the development of naval facilities in Port Royal and the erection of a number of government buildings in Beaufort. But his most notable accomplishment was the introduction and support of civil rights legislation that clarified the rights of former slaves to own property, make contracts, and benefit from full protection of the laws. He failed, however, to garner support for an amendment that was likely close to his heart: It proposed that in the enlistment of men in the army "no distinction whatever shall be made on account of race or color."

Smalls left Congress in 1887, and in December 1889 was appointed customs collector for the port of Beaufort, a position he held for nearly 24 years. He continued to be politically active, however. In 1895 he was one of six black delegates to South Carolina's state constitutional convention, where he attempted—unsuccessfully—to salvage the voting rights of the state's black citizens. In his remaining years, he saw all of the former Confederate states pass restrictive election laws and witnessed the backlash against blacks that came with the end of Reconstruction. One of Smalls's last public acts was to prevent a lynching in Beaufort in 1913. When rumors circulated that a mob planned to lynch two black men jailed for the murder of a white man, he spread the word that the city's black citizens would torch the homes of whites unless the mob was turned back. The sheriff took Smalls at his word and kept the mob at bay. Smalls spent his last years at the black school in Beaufort, talking to the children about politics and history and counseling them on the value of education. He died in February 1915.

white raiders actually came to trial, fearful witnesses seldom agreed to testify, and when they did, juries would not convict.

Clearly only the most vigorous intervention on the part of the federal government would stem the brutality. However, by 1872 the Grant administration was turning its attention to problems of rampant political corruption and a worsening national economy. As the problems of the South faded into the background on the national level, many militant whites grew bolder still, conducting drills and parades in open mockery of the law. Incidents of mob violence occurred more and more frequently, one of the most vicious taking place in April 1873 in Colfax, Louisiana. There, a mob of whites murdered 105 black citizens during an attack stemming from a dispute over election results. Ninety-eight persons were indicted in the massacre, and nine went to trial. Three men were convicted of violating the blacks' civil rights, but the convictions were later overturned by the U.S. Supreme Court, which—incredibly—ruled that the mob constituted a private army and thus the federal government had no authority in the matter.

Pressing their advantage, white groups brazenly harassed black voters in Alabama during the 1874 election. "We will carry the state or kill half of you on election day," a black campaign worker was warned. When Mississippi, on the brink of anarchy, requested federal aid to combat violence at the polls, the U.S. Attorney General refused, remarking that Americans were "tired out with these annual autumnal outbreaks in the South"—outbreaks clearly orchestrated by white terrorists during election time.

Two years later the Supreme Court laid waste to the racially protective aspects of the Fourteenth and Fifteenth Amendments. In *United States v. Cruikshank*, Court justices charged individual states, rather than the federal government, with protecting the voting

A Ku Klux Klan member, wearing the black hood and clothing that helped him blend into the night, palms a small gun he used to threaten blacks in Mississippi. Captured by federal troops in 1871, he revealed to authorities the group's secret passwords and signals.

rights of their citizens. Ruling on *United States v. Reese*, the Court determined that although the Fifteenth Amendment, which guaranteed black suffrage, prohibited discrimination on the basis of "race, color, or previous condition of servitude," the denial of voting rights might be permissible on other grounds, such as one's grandfather's voting eligibility.

By 1876, state governments that adhered to Reconstruction policies survived only in South Carolina, Florida, and Louisiana. The presidential election that year—pitting Republican candidate Rutherford B. Hayes against Democrat Samuel J. Tilden—came to turn on the electoral votes of these three states, which were in dispute. While Democrats, who counted among their ranks the white supremacists, asserted that the votes numbered in their favor, Republicans pointed out that most of the black voters had been frightened away from the polls.

The two sides assembled in Washington, D.C., in February 1877 at the Wormley House— a hotel owned by James Wormley, an African American—to confirm an informal agreement worked out beforehand. The Democrats agreed to the election of Hayes if, in return, the new president would withdraw all remaining federal troops from the South, support a federal subsidy to complete a railway system, name a southerner postmaster general, and guarantee that the states could rule themselves as they pleased. Known as the Compromise of 1877, the agreement effectively restored white southerners to most seats in both local and national governments. Black suffrage declined as voting rights ceased to be protected, though in some states blacks able to fulfill certain requirements—such as interpreting a portion of the state's constitution—remained on the election rolls into the early 20th century.

The era of Reconstruction came to a halt. Yet despite continued white domination, changes in society and politics had been set in motion that would play out over the coming generations. As abolitionist Henry Highland Garnet vowed in 1866, when the country was taking its first reluctant steps toward recognizing African Americans as full citizens, "We are engaged in a stubborn war with unrelenting foes, which we mean to fight to the end on our native soil, aiming to complete the establishment of our rights and liberties."

TWO

THE SURGE WESTWARD

Seated proudly in front of their Nebraska homestead in 1887, the Shores family achieved the dream of many African Americans who went west—land of their own and a chance to prosper.

pirits were high in Cleveland in 1874, the year that the Women's Christian Temperance Union was founded. And in Philadelphia that same year, the city proudly celebrated the opening of the nation's first zoo. But far to the west, the gold-mining hamlet of Yankee Hill, Colorado, was in the grip of more pressing concerns. The citizens of this boom town were living under a reign of terror imposed by renegades and drifters. Desperate to bring an end to the rampant violence and lawlessness, the town fathers advertised for a marshal in Denver's *Rocky Mountain News*.

One man who responded was 42-year-old Willie Kennard, a former trooper in the all-black 9th Cavalry Regiment. Kennard rode into town packing a pistol on each hip and looked up the Yankee Hill mayor, Matt Borden. "I'm puttin' in for your marshalin' job," Kennard announced.

Borden, lingering over his morning coffee with the four men who sat with him on the town council, could hardly believe his ears. For a black man to ride into a place as wild as Yankee Hill and apply to be the lawman made no sense at all. Surely he would provoke hostility simply by being in town; as marshal, he would be lucky to live long enough to draw his first pay.

But Kennard would not be put off. Faced with his persistence, the mayor devised a way to get rid of the unwelcome applicant while having some cruel fun at his expense. Kennard would first have to pass a test, Borden told him, by bringing in Barney Casewit, a cold-blooded criminal no one wanted to tangle with. Casewit had raped a 15-year-old girl and then shot her father dead when he tried to avenge her.

The mayor and councilmembers, eager to see the uppity black man taken down a peg, scurried after Kennard as he strode to Gaylor's Saloon, a rowdy establishment where Casewit and other ruffians hung out. After sizing up the desperado, Kennard walked up to his table and announced that he was under arrest. The outlaw sprang from his chair, reaching for his Colt .44s. But Kennard outdrew him, firing directly at the gunman's holsters. As the story goes, the bullets shattered the cylinders of Casewit's six-shooters, leaving him so dumbstruck that he quietly shuffled off to jail.

Mayor Borden, apparently more pleased to have Casewit put away than to see the black stranger humbled, gave Kennard a tin star. Barney Casewit was tried, convicted, and ultimately hanged. For the next three years the black marshal enforced the law in Yankee Hill, quelling the violence and putting many more desperadoes behind bars. Then, in typical western fashion, Kennard pulled up stakes in 1877 and moved on; little is known of his life after that.

Although the tale of Willie Kennard's triumph is unusual for its high drama, it has one thing in common with the stories of other African Americans in the Old West: They are nowhere to be found in conventional history textbooks, novels, movies, or television horse operas. For all the world knows, the experiences of countless thousands of black pioneers, who headed west with other Americans in search of a better life, never happened.

But blacks did play a large—and early—role in the settling of the West. According to current research, the first black Africans to set foot in the North American West were mariners on the ships that brought Spanish explorers, a decade or so after Columbus first sailed to the New World. For the next several centuries, most of the black Africans in the West would be slaves transported to Mexico to toil for the Spaniards. Not until the growth of European colonies on the Eastern seaboard in the 18th century would men and women—white and black alike—begin to penetrate the West from a new direction.

As the American frontier swept westward between 1840 and the start of the Civil War, the number of blacks entering the new territories increased. But the greatest wave of black emigrants in the 19th century came after the war ended. African Americans, both freeborn and ex-slave, looked to the frontier for the economic betterment that would come with owning their own land and the greater social justice that might be hoped for in a place where everybody was starting afresh.

White Mountain Apache scouts, shown here in about 1883, exemplify the complexity of black-Indian relations in the Old West. The man on the right, identified only as "a renegade Negro," may have sought refuge with the White Mountain tribe decades earlier as a runaway slave. Ironically, all three now helped the U.S. Army suppress other Indian tribes.

African Americans fanned out all over the Southwest, the Pacific Northwest, the mining regions of California, Colorado, Arizona, and the Dakotas, the sod-house frontier of the Great Plains, and even into Canada. Black men worked side by side with other men of all colors and backgrounds as scouts, fur traders, cowboys, prospectors, farmers, ranchers, seamen, oilmen, merchants, bankers, and lawmen. Black women tended their homes and their families and tilled the land right alongside the men. Some women started up businesses that catered to the pioneers—laundries, restaurants, hotels, and stores.

Many black adventurers, male and female, realized their dreams; others met with frustration and bitter disappointment, stymied by bad luck, harsh conditions, or a racism as vicious as any they had left back east. But whatever the outcome for individual African Americans, the sum total of their experiences was full and active participation in the building of the West.

The black sailors who came to North America with the earliest explorers were followed in short order by much larger numbers of black African slaves. Starting in 1501, Spanish conquistadors, who purchased slaves in the thousands from Portuguese,

Dutch, British, and French traders, put these bondsmen to work digging for gold and silver in South America, Central America, the islands of the Caribbean, and the viceroyalty of New Spain, as modern-day Mexico was then called.

One of these slaves, a black man named Estevanico, became the first non-Indian to set foot in the present-day American Southwest. Originally from Azamor, Morocco, Estevanico had sailed to Florida with a 300-man expedition led by a Spanish nobleman named Pánfilo de Narváez. The Narváez party landed near Tampa Bay in April 1528 and within a few weeks had plunged recklessly into the dense subtropical forest. Aiming north and west toward what is now Texas, the proud conquistadors, decked out in their glistening armor and colorful brocades, soon found themselves in a struggle for their very lives. Desertion, disease, storms, starvation, and Indian attack took a dreadful toll on the explorers. Ultimately, only four men were left in the party; one of them was Estevanico.

For an incredible eight years the four wandered across the Southwest. Several times they were captured and enslaved by Indians—one of history's rare instances in which slave masters learned firsthand what it meant to be in bondage. Escaping captivity, they encountered other Indians, who thought the outsiders were supernatural beings and ascribed to them strange powers of healing. Of the four men, Estevanico coped best with the ordeal; he adapted more quickly than the others to the harsh and varied terrain over which they traveled, and he learned to communicate with the Native Americans, picking up at least six Indian languages.

The explorers finally reached Mexico City, where they related their adventures to astonished Spanish officials. Because he had a special gift for dealing with Indians, Estevanico, after recovering from his odyssey, was chosen to lead the Franciscan friar Marcos de Niza and a small party in search of what the Spaniards believed was a fabulous treasure-trove—the legendary Seven Cities of Cibola. Starting out by retracing some of the route he and his three companions had taken, Estevanico led the expedition to the area of present-day Arizona. Ranging far ahead of the main party, he found not seven cities of gold but one of a group of unimpressive-looking pueblos of the Zuni people. At this point Estevanico apparently lost his deft touch with Native Americans; the Zuni, taking him for a spy, promptly killed him.

Though their quest for Cibola failed, the gold-hungry Spaniards spent another half-century futilely searching for treasure in the lands north of New Spain. Finally, in 1598, they got down to the business of settling the territory, which they called New Mexico. Establishing settlements there involved a considerable degree of intermarriage. Before long, the colonial population reflected the fruits of these unions. Living alongside pure Africans, Indians, and Spaniards were a variety of racial mixtures: Those of combined African and Spanish ancestry were called mulattoes; mulattoes with Indian blood mixed in were pardos or color quebrados; people of mixed Indian and Spanish blood were mestizos.

Some of these mixed-blood people took leading roles in helping establish and operate missions in the north. In 1781 a group of 12 poor farm families—46 people of mixed ancestry—made a grueling trek from Sinaloa, Mexico, to the southwestern part of the province of Upper California—then a vast territory extending eastward all

the way to the eastern boundaries of present-day Utah and Arizona. Eleven families survived the ordeal to found El Pueblo de Nuestra Señora la Reina de los Angeles (the Town of Our Lady the Queen of the Angels), known to later generations simply as Los Angeles. One of the city's first mayors was Francisco Reyes, a mulatto.

Although civil and military authority in Spanish-held lands lay chiefly in the hands of white men, some pureblood Africans and mulattoes began moving into leadership positions in colonial affairs about the time Mexico staged a revolution against Spain that ended successfully in 1821. Men of color continued to rise in the newly independent nation, ranged on both sides of sometimes-violent debate over a number of political issues, including what form of government it should have— monarchical or republican.

One prominent personality was Manuel Victoria, a black man who advanced through the military ranks to become first a lieutenant colonel in the province of Lower California, then its principal commander. In 1831 Victoria was appointed governor of Upper California. He aroused hostility among advocates of republican rule in the province when he tried to undo a plan put forth by the previous governor to secularize the Catholic missions and give their land to baptized Indians, whom the priests were keeping as virtual slave laborers. Then he attempted to impose military rule and ordered the death penalty for minor offenses.

Just a year after assuming office, the increasingly despotic Victoria was ousted and replaced by Pio Pico, a member of a distinguished mulatto family of landowners, government officials, and military officers. Pico tried to promote republican principles, but his luck in office was no better than Victoria's. To succeed he needed the support of José María Echeandía, Victoria's liberal-minded predecessor as governor, who was still a power in Upper California politics. But when Echeandía rejected Pico's proposed policies and threatened to use force to remove him from office, Pico, too, gave up after just a year.

Pico took office again in 1845, however, and made a serious effort to return Upper California's government to republican ideals. His aim was to improve the general welfare of the population, but the liberal measures he espoused, such as granting mission land to propertyless Californians to promote the growth of private enterprise, only served to create a well-off class of ranchers and merchants. Pico's second administration also ended after a year. The main problem this time was a general collapse of Mexican authority in Upper California following the so-called Bear Flag Rebellion, an insurrection by American settlers coinciding with the eruption of war between the United States and Mexico in 1846.

Far from the tropical intrigues of Mexican politics, in the wintry upper reaches of the American West other black men and women were making their mark as explorers, fur traders, and homesteaders. As early as 1673, several blacks had sailed with Louis Jolliet and Father Jacques Marquette down the Mississippi River to the mouth of the Arkansas River, although nothing is known of their roles in the expedition. And Haitian-born fur trader Jean Baptiste Pointe du Sable (*pages* 100-101) explored his way up the Mississippi from New Orleans and built a trading post beside a rushing

Awestruck Indians watch as a Hidatsa chief tries to rub the color off the chest of the first black man they had ever seen, in this painting by Charles Russell. York, a slave owned by William Clark of the Lewis and Clark expedition, won the friendship of Indians all along the route of the trek. He returned from the expedition a hero in 1806 and was given his freedom a few years later.

river in Northwest Territory; the settlement eventually grew to be the city of Chicago. Black men also took part in government-sponsored expeditions to explore new United States territories in the West in the early 19th century. A notable member of the Lewis and Clark expedition to survey the Louisiana Purchase was a slave named York, who was owned by William Clark.

Black frontiersmen shared all the adventures and dangers of their vocation with such white contemporaries as Daniel Boone, Davy Crockett, Kit Carson, and Jim Bridger, but enjoyed none of the enduring fame accorded their white counterparts. Some African American pioneers were famous in their own time, however, as intrepid pathfinders. Edward Rose, an early interpreter, guide, and hunter, had a reputation as one of North America's leading mountain men, as these pioneers were called. Moses "Black" Harris was a well-known trapper in the 1820s who also explored new routes across the Cascade Mountains and into California. George Bonga, a fur trader who combed the backwoods with his brother, Stephen, was so skilled at picking up the languages of the Indian peoples he encountered that Lewis Cass, the governor of Michigan Territory, named him an official territorial interpreter. Jim Beckwourth (*pages* 102-103) made his presence felt across the continent, serving as a U.S. Army scout in the Seminole Wars in Florida and later blazing a new trail through the towering Sierra Nevada to the California coast.

But the exploits of these early African American heroes had already begun to

fade from public notice by 1840, when the first waves of emigrants headed west on the Oregon and Santa Fe trails, raising the curtain on one of the great dramas of human history. Over the next two decades about 300,000 people journeyed in their Conestoga wagons across the dry, featureless, wind-swept Great Plains to the fertile lands of the Pacific Coast. There they hoped to start life anew, to better their political and economic stake in the nation, or to answer a call to adventure. Among the 300,000 were an undocumented but substantial number of black people, moving west for the same reasons.

Although every westward step took these African American emigrants farther and farther away from the hurly-burly of life back in the States, they could not escape the issue that was inflaming the American body politic during this period—whether the new territories would come into the Union as free or slave states. And when the United States annexed the Republic of Texas in 1845—and then, three years later, acquired even greater expanses of western land in the treaty ending the Mexican War—the fevered debate only became hotter.

Propertyless families wanted the chance to obtain cheap land and own their own farms. In their eyes, the westward expansion of slavery meant that they would be thrown into an unfair contest with slaveholders, who controlled a large unpaid labor force. Unable to compete, small farmers would be driven off their land and reduced to penury. The question, according to one orator in 1848, was "not whether black men are to be made free but whether white men are to remain free." On the other side, southern slave owners recognized that their system could not survive if it did not spread. Unless more territories came into the Union as slave states, the growing number of free states would soon give the North enough votes in Congress to abolish slavery.

Stephen (*above*) **and George Bonga, sons of an African father and a Chippewa mother, made up the second generation of a fur-trading family renowned throughout Minnesota Territory. George, who also married a Chippewa, gained wealth as a fur trader and won a reputation as a gentleman. By 1850 the Bonga family in Minnesota was said to number over 100. Bonga Township in Cass County is named for the family.**

The Missouri Compromise of 1820 represented the best solution the Congress could come up with to address the question of slavery in the territories. It allowed Missouri to enter the Union as a slave state but made the latitude of 36°30'—the state's southern boundary—the dividing line between future slave and free territories in the rest of the Louisiana Purchase, most of which lay on the northern, or free, side of the line. But the acquisition of Texas and the former Mexican territories—all of present-day California, Nevada, and Utah, most of New Mexico and Arizona, much of Colorado, and a corner of Wyoming—again raised the question of whether slavery would expand westward.

To meet the new situation the Congress enacted a package of legislation called the Compromise of 1850, which admitted California as a free state and organized the New Mexico and Utah territories without restrictions on slavery. But the compromise also included a harsh new fugitive slave law that allowed southerners to recapture runaway slaves even in free states and made it a crime for anyone to aid a runaway. Some of the black people dragged back into slavery under the new law had been living free for years.

For several centuries, escaping slaves had risked whipping, branding, mutilation, and even death at the hands of slave hunters to strive for freedom, belying southern propaganda about how well cared for and content slaves were. Many run-

aways made their way north and others fled to the West or to Mexico, but a number of slaves who escaped from plantations in the Deep South headed for the Seminole Indian encampments in Spanish Florida.

The Seminole were originally a band of Indians who had broken away from the Creek Nation and other tribes. They left their various homes in Georgia, Alabama, Appalachia, and the Carolinas in about 1750 and took refuge in Florida. But the Indians soon found themselves in the path of British and, later, American designs on that territory. Facing increasing hostility from the U.S. government in the early 19th century for defending Spanish territory—and their own homes—against American incursions, the Seminole were disinclined to turn over escaped slaves to their enemies. Instead, they received runaways as allies in their campaign of resistance to American pressure.

News of the friendship offered by the Seminole and the welcome extended by Spanish colonial officialdom attracted more fugitive slaves. For their part, the escaped slaves offered the Indians, who were mainly hunters and fishermen, their expertise in farming and raising livestock. They also drew on their knowledge of the white man's ways to advise the Indians in their dealings with whites. In return, the Seminole wholly accepted blacks into their communities. Blacks dressed in Seminole clothing and married into Seminole families (*page* 109).

In an effort to eliminate Florida as a haven for runaways, to recapture the escaped slaves, and to force the Indians to emigrate to reservations in Arkansas and Indian Territory (present-day Oklahoma), the United States waged two costly wars against the Seminole between 1817 and 1842. In these campaigns, which set the U.S. government back $20 million and cost 1,500 soldiers their lives, blacks fought alongside Indian warriors, motivated by loyalty and by the fear that they would be returned to bondage if the federal forces won.

By 1843 their cause was lost, however, and most of the Seminole—red and black—were forced to give up their homes and make the agonizing trek westward—a journey into exile that had come to be called the Trail of Tears by the Cherokee, Chickasaw, Choctaw, and Creek nations that preceded the Seminole to Indian Territory. On the new lands, the black Seminoles became the targets of slave hunters. Some of their pursuers were white men, but others were Creek Indians. The Creeks, like some other tribes in the South, were slaveholders, and thus had no scruples about recapturing runaways. Now, despite having been driven into exile themselves by white America, they sometimes hunted escaped slaves to return to their white owners for rewards.

Although a declaration issued by the U.S. Attorney General in 1848 held that blacks on Indian Territory were free, it also decreed that U.S. military power could not be used to protect them from the raiders. As a result, hundreds of black Seminoles fled to Mexico and did not return until slavery had been abolished.

Before the Civil War, many of the western territories prohibited slavery and had few laws discriminating against black people. Accordingly, African Americans venturing west hoped to find a more tolerant climate in the new lands. Instead, they saw more

and more restrictive laws being passed against them, despite contributions made by black mountain men and explorers to the development of the western territories. Three black scouts, for example, were part of a government expedition led by Captain John C. Frémont in 1842 to map out the best wagon route to Oregon. Yet Oregon Territory extended no welcome to these trailblazers or to any other black emigrant.

In the two decades before the Civil War, when African Americans never exceeded one percent of Oregon's total population, the presence of blacks in the territory sometimes dominated debate in the legislature. Between 1840 and 1860, Oregon passed three pieces of legislation specifically aimed at blacks. The first law, passed in 1844, barred blacks from settling in the territory and gave any black residents a deadline by which they had to leave. Men were given two years to vacate the area; women three. The law was repealed a year later, but similar laws were enacted in 1849 and again in 1857; these allowed blacks living in the state to stay but prohibited others from moving in. When Oregon joined the Union in 1859, it was the only territory to enter as a free state with a black-exclusion provision in its constitution.

Despite the legislature's efforts, two African American men were able to overcome the antiblack laws; not by subterfuge but by their merits, by their ability to win steadfast white friends and supporters, and by a little good timing. The first, George Washington Bush, had lived in several midwestern states before settling and prospering as a farmer in Missouri. Soon racial prejudice began permeating the state, however, and in 1844 he lit out for Oregon Territory. He figured he had only two years to make good under the 1844 exclusionary law, but luck was with him, and the law was repealed not long after he arrived.

Bush's traveling companion on the trek west was a white man named Michael T. Simmons, who, within a short time after establishing himself in Oregon, became a member of the territorial legislature. In the meantime, Bush had settled on a 640-acre site on Puget Sound. He soon found, however, that the Donation Land Act of 1850, which granted 320 acres to a settler who obtained the land before the end of 1851 and cultivated it for four years, benefited whites only, and he could not claim his property. Simmons sponsored and pushed through the legislature a special exemption for Bush, and in 1855 the black homesteader gained title to his land, which is today called Bush Prairie. Before his death in 1863, Bush earned a civic reputation of his own, becoming known as a generous man who would share his crops with neighbors during hard times.

The second man who won exemption from Oregon's antiblack laws was George Washington, the son

By the mid-19th century, as shown on the map below, the United States had come into possession of the entire West through purchase, annexation, mediation, and conquest. (States show the year in which they were admitted to the Union.) The vast area was open to settlement by all comers—provided they were white. African Americans were excluded by law from Oregon Territory and proscribed from filing land claims in other states and territories, but by pluck and determination they eventually made their mark in every corner of the new land.

of a slave father and a white mother. Formally adopted by a white family, Washington, too, lived for a time in Missouri, where, upon reaching adulthood, he was granted by the legislature all the rights of a citizen except that of holding public office. In 1850 he and his adoptive parents moved to Oregon, and Washington staked out a parcel of land. But because of the territory's antiblack laws, his adoptive father had to file the claim. White settlers who supported Washington circulated petitions on his behalf, which were sponsored by a local representative of the government. As a result, in 1852 the Oregon legislature passed a special law enabling Washington to stay in the territory. He then purchased 640 acres in the Chehalis Valley and became a successful farmer. Twenty years later he founded the town of Centralia, in Washington State, and during the financial panic of 1893 saved the town by providing food and jobs for destitute residents.

While Oregon Territory's total emigrant population grew steadily during the 1840s and 1850s, California's jumped more than fifteenfold, from about 14,000 to 223,856, in just the three years after gold was discovered there in 1848. Although this population explosion included only about 2,200 blacks, most of them were slaves, and the slavery issue became a hotly debated topic. California had been admitted to the Union as a free state under the Compromise of 1850; but now, two years later, the state legislature passed its own fugitive slave law, which permitted slave owners to bring slaves into this "free" state and later return them to the South or sell them.

Despite their uncertain legal status, blacks, like hundreds of thousands of other Americans, were caught up in the gold rush. Black forty-niners found that once they were in California, they were welcome at gambling tables in the mining camps and towns but usually had to patronize separate hotels and restaurants. Many slave owners put their slaves to digging, often with the promise that a slave could buy his freedom with his share of the proceeds. Those promises were not always kept. In one particularly shameful case, Alvin Coffey, who left Missouri in 1849 with his master, worked the diggings until he had enough money to buy his way out of slavery; his owner treacherously accepted the money and then sold him to another man. Refusing to lose hope despite the cruel betrayal, Coffey made a deal with his new master and this time succeeded in purchasing not only his own freedom but also that of his wife and three children.

Another African American who made good in California was Biddy Mason, whose rise from slavery to wealth happened in the space of only a few years. In 1848 she traveled from Mississippi to Utah, and then three years later to California, walking alongside the wagons of her master's caravan and tending the livestock during the journey. When her owner decided in about 1855 to move back east to Texas with his slaves, Biddy Mason dug in her heels. She won the support of the local sheriff, who prevented the owner from taking Mason and her three daughters with him. And at a subsequent Los Angeles County court hearing, at which Mason's owner failed to appear, a judge ruled that the owner had lost his property rights in Mason.

Despite laws passed in 1844, 1849 (*above*), and 1857 barring settlement by blacks in Oregon Territory, George Washington (*below*) was specially exempted by the legislature in 1852. He later founded Centralia, Washington.

Now a free woman, Biddy Mason moved to Los Angeles and started working as a practical nurse. Hoarding her skimpy pay, she saved enough to purchase several parcels of land, which soared in value and earned her a fortune when she sold them. She used the money to pay taxes on church property, assist flood victims, and feed the needy in local jails. Mason died, respected and honored, in Los Angeles in 1891.

Although a scattering of black Californians like Biddy Mason beat the odds to achieve success, racism in the state continued to escalate. In 1852, the year the legislature passed the state fugitive slave law, it also enacted a law prohibiting African Americans from testifying in court. A rallying point for many black residents was the court case concerning Gordon Chase, an African American barber who had been murdered by a white man. The prosecution went into court with an eyewitness to the crime, one Robert Cowles. But a group of physicians asserted from an examination of Cowles's hair that he was one-sixteenth black, and on those grounds he was not allowed to testify. (A conviction was secured anyway, based on the testimony of a second witness whose whiteness was apparently unassailable.)

Blacks reacted by establishing the Franchise League, whose purpose was to recapture the right to testify and to win the right to vote. And in 1855, forty-nine black delegates convened the first meeting of the Convention of Colored Citizens of the State of California in Sacramento. Determined to win repeal of all discriminatory laws, especially the testimony law, for three years the members passed resolutions and peppered the state legislature with petitions, all of which died in committee. Not until 1863, the year of the Emancipation Proclamation, did the California legislature repeal the antiblack laws, thus removing not only the ban on black testimony but also the one barring blacks from staking a claim to public land.

California's antiblack laws were tough; and those miners who descended on Colorado in 1859, when a new wave of gold fever swept the West, found a similar situation there. Not only were African Americans unwelcome in mining camps, the territory barred them from filing mining claims as well. But the authorities apparently hadn't reckoned on an ambitious and capable black man named Barney Ford. Ford, a former slave, had done his part to shatter white stereotypes of black people even before coming to Colorado. In 1850 he left Chicago, bound for California with other forty-niners. Traveling by steamship south toward the Isthmus of Panama, he contracted malaria on the part of the route that cut through Nicaragua. While he was laid up in that Central American country to recuperate, his keen business eye saw that a comfortable place of lodging in that part of the world would be popular and profitable.

Using funds he earned as a hotel barber in Chicago, Ford put up a

Black entrepreneur Barney Ford (*below*) opened the lavish Inter-Ocean Hotel in Denver in 1873. A *Rocky Mountain News* article extolling the hotel stated merely that it was "built by Mr. B. L. Ford" before going on to praise the personal qualities of the white manager, the head clerk, and even some of the salesmen who supplied the fixtures and furnishings.

hotel that was a going concern until it burned down in 1854. He then returned to the States, where he heard news of the Colorado strike. The gold bug bit again, and he set out, eager to grab his share of riches. Once in Colorado, he tried to stake a mining claim but ran head-on into the territory's discriminatory statutes. He hardly hesitated before making an end run around the laws by filing a claim in a white lawyer's name in exchange for paying the lawyer 20 percent of the proceeds. Ford and three black companions, two of whom were runaway slaves, struck gold on a hill along French Gulch in 1860. But before they could enjoy their good fortune, a gang of white brigands raided their camp. The black men escaped into the woods with only half a bottle of gold dust, but for a long time the rumor circulated that Ford and his partners had hidden a fortune in gold on the hill. Although no gold was ever found, the place was dubbed Nigger Hill, a name that apparently never troubled the white powers that be until 1964, when they finally renamed the spot Barney Ford Hill.

Ford went on to become a successful businessman, operating restaurants and hotels in Cheyenne and Denver, including the luxurious four-story Inter-Ocean Hotel, which catered to Denver's elite visitors. He successfully lobbied against Colorado's law prohibiting black men from voting or serving on juries, and in 1885 persuaded the state legislature to adopt a civil rights act making it illegal to deny blacks access to hotels, restaurants, and other public facilities.

Ford's victories were welcomed by the thousands of African Americans then living in the West, most of whom had fled there following the Civil War. For most newly freed slaves in 1865, the worsening racism among whites out west and the proliferation of antiblack laws in the territories were only rumors and possibilities, while the racial terrorism and brutal poverty they were experiencing as "free" people in the South was frighteningly real. Though the Confederacy had been defeated and rebellion crushed, the white southerners who had supported secession had managed to hold on to enough power to block attempts at breaking up the old plantation system and distributing the land to newly freed slaves. And without land, blacks had little choice but to return to the plantations and work for whatever their ex-masters were willing to pay them.

The white South fought viciously to hold on to its cheap labor supply. Black farmers working as sharecroppers became mired in debt and tied to the land. New vagrancy laws made it a jail offense for blacks to be unemployed, which left many with the choice of either being bound in feudal relationships with their former masters or serving indeterminate sentences on labor gangs. Blacks who attempted to leave were often harassed—in some cases, murdered—by bounty hunters, who raided their roadside camps and forced them back where they had come from. Black emigrants who managed to elude these predators often saw their hopes crushed at the Mississippi River, where white boatmen refused to take them to the west bank.

But the lure of the West, with its promise of new beginnings for anyone who braved the journey, was too great. All the official and illegal obstacles in the world could not keep great numbers of ex-slaves from getting out; and droves of blacks left Mississippi, Louisiana, Tennessee, and Texas, taking with them a dream of a better life, in which they stood on equal ground with whites.

One contingent of African Americans living and working in the West, particularly in Texas and Indian Territory, were already proving themselves to be on a par with their white counterparts. These were the black cowboys, who were engaged in a line of work where how well you did your job was often more important than what color you were. Before the Civil War many of these black cowboys had learned riding, roping, and branding as slaves on Texas ranches. Ironically, as long as a black man on a ranch was considered a piece of property with substantial monetary value, he was likely to be treated relatively well and spared the more hazardous jobs. If the owner needed some wild mustangs broken, for example, he would probably give the job to one of his Anglo or Mexican cowhands; should a mishap cripple or kill the man, the boss might regret it but he wouldn't be out any money. Needless to say, after emancipation the customary way of doing things took a 180-degree turn. African American cowboys, worth no more to a ranch owner than their Anglo or Mexican counterparts and black to boot, were given the dirtiest and most dangerous jobs on the ranch or on the trail.

The services of all cowboys became more valuable after the war, however, when the price of meat soared. Easterners had developed a preference for beef over pork, and a flood tide of new foreign immigrants coincided with an industrial boom to swell the populations of large eastern cities. The western cattle industry became a major profit-making venture, and cowboys—white ones, at any rate—became the heroes of dime novels and, later, of Hollywood movies.

Of the approximately 35,000 men who worked on ranches and trail drives, about one-quarter were black. A black cowboy might hold any job at a ranch or on a trail drive, but seldom rose to the position of ranch foreman or trail boss, except in an all-black outfit, because it was a rare white cowboy who would take orders from a black man. Many African American cowboys were wranglers, in charge of the *re-muda*—the pool of horses from which trail hands chose their mounts for the day—

William in Action, a sketch by Frederic Remington, shows a black cook at work on a trail drive. Paid as much as $60 a month for their work, cooks were second only to the trail boss or ranch foreman in the cowboy hierarchy.

the lowliest job on a trail drive. Most, however, were ordinary hands, who rode at the sides and back of the herd, or top hands, who rode at the front. This position was one of respect and responsibility, but it was also the most dangerous—the cattle at the front of the herd were unpredictable.

A notch higher in rank than the top hands was the cook, who presided over about a 60-foot circle around his chuck wagon. This was typically the highest position to which blacks could aspire. One extraordinary cook, who has come down through history known only as Sam, worked for an outfit on the Pease River in north Texas in 1878. His meals included such delicacies as buffalo steaks, roast bear meat, pan-fried breast of wild turkey, barbecued antelope ribs, and wild plum cobbler. Such a cook was much appreciated by experienced cowboys, who knew that the usual fare on the trail was some variety of salt meat, beans, biscuits, and thick black coffee.

At the ranch or on the trail, all cowboys—black, Mexican, and Anglo—shared a common life. They rode and ate together, and often slept in the same shack or tent and even under a shared blanket. In the towns, however, racial segregation was more common. Saloons in Texas served whites at one end of the bar and blacks at the other. African Americans were not served in white restaurants (except at the back door) or lodged in white hotels, and they were strictly barred from brothels staffed with white prostitutes. Casinos were more democratic, though, with the color of the cowboys' money being more important than the color of their skin. Black cowhands and white ones were equally welcome to sit down and gamble away their hard-earned wage of $25 or $30 a month.

One of the most colorful of this fraternity of stalwart horsemen was African American Nat Love, who was born into slavery in 1854. He heard about the Texas-to-Kansas cattle drives as a youngster, and when he left home at age 15, on a horse he had won in a raffle, he had his heart set on becoming a cowboy. Love got to Kansas, where he encountered a Texas outfit making preparations to return home. When he asked for a job, the trail boss thought he could dispense with the upstart by declaring that a job was his if he could break Good Eye, the wildest and most dangerous horse in the outfit. Love wore the horse down and won a job. He became one of the ablest cowboys of his time, learning Spanish, becoming an expert reader of brands, and winning several roping and shooting contests. Some of these exploits he pulled off in Deadwood, Dakota Territory, thus winning for himself the nickname Deadwood Dick.

While black cowboys on ranches and trail drives were enjoying a degree

African Americans and whites drink and play cards in the Bertoli Saloon in Freeland, Colorado, in the 1870s. Gambling houses—where professional gamblers applied themselves to the task of separating cowboys from their money—were one of the few integrated venues in the West.

of rough-hewn equality with and respect from their white counterparts, their brothers and sisters in the rural South faced a situation that was shifting from hopeful to horrible. Little more than a decade after the defeat of the Confederacy, the Union troops that had kept the peace in the South and enforced the reforms of Reconstruction were withdrawn, and violence against African Americans exploded all over the South. The nightriders of the Ku Klux Klan and various other hate groups were in full cry, plundering, burning, raping, and murdering.

Many blacks lost all hope when they saw the very men who had held them as slaves regaining control of the state governments in the South. African Americans began looking elsewhere for opportunities, and the West offered something available nowhere else—free land. Under the Homestead Act, passed by Congress in 1862, grants of 160 acres of public land on the Great Plains went to people who would live on and farm the land for five years.

In the 1870s, many former slaves set out for Kansas. The chief catalyst for the movement was Benjamin "Pap" Singleton, a former slave from Tennessee. Although he was 70 in 1879, he was bold and energetic, envisioning a group of black colonies separate from but coexisting with white communities.

Singleton helped promote a westward migration that enlisted so many African American families it became known as the Exodus of 1879. The Exodusters, as the emigrants were called, came primarily from Louisiana, Mississippi, and Texas. Between 15,000 and 20,000 of them moved to Kansas in that one year.

Life in Kansas was not kind to many Exodusters. A good number of them arrived without money or proper clothing. Settlers in Nicodemus, an all-black town founded by W. H. Smith, a black man, and W. R. Hill, who was white, spent their first winter in dugouts, unable to build homes until the following spring. Some emigrants never managed to get their heads above water economically, and others could not save enough money to buy the bare minimum of items they would need to go homesteading—a plow, a wagon, a team of mules or oxen, and seed for their first crop. The weather tended to harsh extremes—windy 110-degree summer days, blinding winter blizzards, tornadoes, dust storms—and the threat of drought was ever present.

Yet it wasn't only the weather or the hard scrabbling to make a living that shriveled the spirit of these new Kansans—it was seeing their hopes of living in peace and amity with their white neighbors evaporate. On occasion there was open hostility. In other instances, it was the quiet rumbling of the whites' racist fears: Many believed that the large numbers of blacks coming into the state would impel white migrants to choose Nebraska or Dakota or Minnesota for their homesteads instead of Kansas. In time, many blacks became discouraged about their lives in Kansas and moved on to Oklahoma Territory, where no fewer than 30 towns with predominantly black populations sprang up between 1890 and 1916.

One of the most successful of those black towns was Boley, Oklahoma, which was established in 1904 in the old Indian Territory. At first,

Former slave Benajmin "Pap" Singleton (*above*) distributed posters like the one below in a decade-long campaign to encourage freedmen to leave the South after the Civil War and emigrate to Kansas. He was inspired by God to do this work, he said, and motivated by his trade: As a cabinetmaker, he made coffins for blacks who had been murdered by nightriders in post-Reconstruction Tennessee.

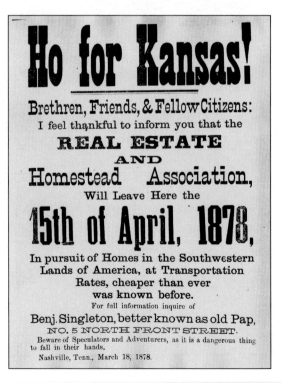

life in Boley, too, was hard. People had only tents and dugouts as shelter. Later they built two-room houses resembling shoeboxes. These structures, with doors at either end and windows on the sides, were jokingly called shotgun houses: One could fire a gun through the front door, it was said, and the shot would go out the back door without hitting a thing.

Within a few years, Boley offered its residents two banks, a sawmill, a cotton gin, three newspapers, two hotels, and a college. Booker T. Washington, one of the best-known black leaders of the day, visited Boley in 1905 and pronounced it "the most enterprising of the Negro towns in the United States." But Boley lost much of its luster during the Depression. When cotton faded as a cash crop in the 1930s, so did the town's economic health. And its population, once as high as 5,000, began to dwindle. Today Boley has fewer than 500 residents, most of whom are retirees or people who commute daily to jobs 90 miles away in Oklahoma City. In an ironic instance of racial equality, virtually all the black towns established out west in the post-Reconstruction era have shared the fate of many other American small towns: They have dwindled in vitality and population or been abandoned altogether as successive generations of young people have gone off to the big cities.

But even before the black towns began to fade, the curtain had rung down on the rich history of African Americans in the Old West, and for a simple reason: By the end of the 19th century there was no more Old West. Virtually all the usable land had been spoken for; towns, farms, and ranches dotted the landscape. With the exception of the cowboys, who joined the Wild West shows and rodeos that showcased their talents, many westerners—black and white alike—had settled into the roles of everyday citizens.

White racism in the West had not abated much. Perhaps its most far-reaching consequence was the complete expurgation from popular culture of any hint that black people had played a part in the story of the West. As Americans pursue their interest in that story, the myth of an Old West without African Americans is being shattered. The all-white cast of characters has been joined by its black counterparts—the heroes and the villains, the wise and the foolish, the rich and the poor, the winners and the losers, the standouts and the plain folks, and, yes, even the cowboys and the Indians.

Jean Du Sable built his home and bustling trading post, crudely sketched in the 1930 aquatint above, side by side with the Potawatomi, near the mouth of the Chicago River. By the time he sold his holdings—for the then-princely sum of $1,200—he had amassed more than 400 acres of land.

THE FIRST CITIZEN OF CHICAGO

When, in the early 1800s, Old Chief Black Partridge of the Potawatomi tribe recounted the settling of the Eschikagou plain—present-day Chicago—he declared that the first non-Indian to settle at Eschikagou was "a black man, a quite black Frenchman named Jean Baptiste Pointe du Sable." More than a century would pass before many Americans would learn the truth in the old Potawatomi's words: The founder of Chicago was Du Sable and not the white man customarily given the credit.

Born around 1745 in Haiti to an African woman and a French mariner, the urbane, Paris-educated Du Sable was an anomaly on the frontier. He had apparently migrated to New Orleans in 1765. He then took up fur trapping and trading, and headed up the Mississippi River to the plains.

Earlier explorers had recognized in the Eschikagou River a critical link between the Great Lakes and such major waterways as the Mississippi and Ohio rivers. But until Du Sable arrived in about 1772, all had been turned back by Indians. Du Sable befriended the local tribes and married a Potawatomi. On the riverbanks, he built a trading post and a substantial house.

Du Sable continued to prosper, rising to such prominence that he drew the attention of the region's British commandant. An official report in 1779 described him as "a handsome Negro, well educated," but "much in the interest of the French." Whether Du Sable took any part in the Revolutionary War is unclear, but the British, suspecting him of partiality to the colonists' French allies, jailed him briefly.

Once Du Sable was back in Chicago, he buckled down to business and family life. He extended his landholdings and remarried his wife in a Catholic ceremony; the couple had a son and a daughter. In the fall of 1796, Du Sable—still bridging two cultures—ran unsuccessfully for election as chief of the local Indian tribes. Four years later, no doubt disillusioned by his defeat, he sold his Chicago properties and spent most of his remaining years in Missouri, where he died in 1818.

Displayed in Chicago's Du Sable Museum of African American History, which opened in 1961, this bronze bust strongly conveys the black pioneer's undaunted spirit. Although grass-roots efforts arose as early as the 1880s to credit Du Sable as the city's founder, he was not officially recognized as such until well into the 20th century.

ADVENTURES OF A MOUNTAIN MAN

Jim Beckwourth was a man with at least nine lives, and not one of them was dull. Born a slave, he became a fur trapper and trader, an Indian fighter, an Indian chief, an army scout, an explorer, a prospector, and a peacemaker. Some of his tales, recounted in an 1856 autobiography, may have been a trifle tall. But judging from reports at the time, there is no doubt Beckwourth had a hot temper, a restless spirit, and a genius for hunting, shooting, and fighting.

Born in Frederick County, Virginia, in 1798, to a black woman and the white man who either owned or oversaw her, Beckwourth moved to St. Louis as a teenager. There he was apprenticed to a blacksmith, an arrangement that lasted five years, until he and his employer allegedly came to blows. Beckwourth fled, joining a party heading for work in the lead mines in what is now Galena, Illinois, then later traveling down the Mississippi to New Orleans.

Beckwourth returned to St. Louis, and in 1823 signed on with General William Ashley's fur-trading company, embarking on the life for which he was made. He brokered horses from the Pawnee for the trappers to take into the Rocky Mountains, hunted for food for the expedition, and learned to trap beaver. He was instantly at home in the rugged terrain, adept with tomahawk, gun, and bowie knife, and unafraid of the Native Americans' arrows. Of one five-hour battle with the Blackfeet, during which he twice galloped through the Indians' line, Beckwourth later wrote, "I now began to deem myself Indian-proof and to think I never should be killed by them."

In 1828, in fact, he was adopted by an Indian tribe—the Crows. By one account, a trapper who hoped to collect more furs from the Indians told the Crows that Beckwourth had been stolen from them as a baby. In his memoirs, Beckwourth admits that an old Crow squaw claimed him as a long-lost son. "What could I do under the circumstances?" he asked. Even if he had denied it, he wrote, "they would not believe me." The tribe named him Morning Star—renaming him Bloody Arm after he led them in combat against the Blackfeet—and married him to the chief's daughter.

Beckwourth stayed with the tribe for about six years and was chosen to be their chief. But the time came for him to move on, and he crisscrossed the country in his wanderings. He set up trading posts in New Mexico and California, served as an army scout

Jim Beckwourth, shown in a daguerreotype taken about 1855, met biographer T. D. Bonner in San Francisco around this time. They collaborated on *The Life and Adventures of James P. Beckwourth*, published in 1856.

against the Seminole in Florida, and in 1844 carried dispatches in the Mexican War. He also prospected for gold. In 1850 he made the discovery that would put his name on the American map forever. Crossing the Sierra Nevada near what is now Reno, he found a pass through the mountains, opening a way for settlers to reach California and the Pacific Ocean.

For a while Beckwourth settled down in the valley below the pass and operated a hotel and trading post. He then moved on to Denver, where in June 1860 the newspapers announced his marriage to one Elizabeth Ledbetter. The marriage was short-lived, however, and two years later, at the age of 64, a restless Beckwourth volunteered to fight for the Union in the Civil War. The army turned him down but in 1866 recruited him to lead a peacemaking mission to the Crows in Montana. Legend has it that his own son welcomed the former chief and that the Crows offered Beckwourth his old place among them. When he declined, they held a tribal feast anyway and poisoned him to keep him from leaving the tribe once more.

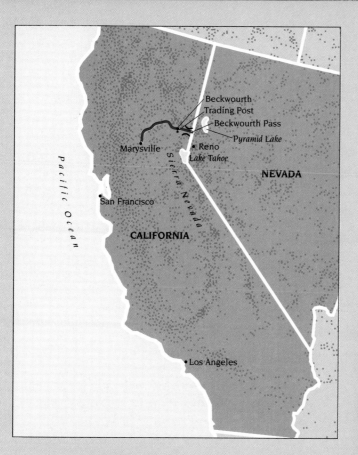

Traveling with gold prospectors in 1850, Beckwourth discovered the pass that now bears his name, leading through the Sierra Nevada into California. He guided the first wagon train through this mountain gateway, later used by the Western Pacific Railroad.

Settling in Beckwourth Valley, near the pass he discovered, Jim Beckwourth built the trading post below for adventurers headed west. "My house is considered the emigrant's landing place," he wrote, "as it is the first ranch he arrives at in the golden state."

Sue Beckwourth, the last of the frontiersman's many wives, was a member of the Crow tribe. The couple lived together in 1864, farming and trapping on the South Platte River.

Despite the historical record, white actor Jack Oakie (*above, left*) was cast to play black scout Jim Beckwourth in the 1951 western *Tomahawk*.

103

A NEW LIFE FOR A PIONEER FAMILY

Sometimes riding, sometimes walking alongside her family's covered wagon as it jolted along the trail to California, Sylvia Estes didn't dwell on the heat or her sore feet, the swarming locusts or the stampeding buffalo, or the occasional Indians the pioneers encountered. She was leaving behind the life of a slave and starting a new adventure.

Born in Clay County, Missouri, in 1838, Sylvia was about 13 when her father earned enough money to purchase his family's freedom and a 40-acre farm. But a peaceful life eluded Clay County blacks, slave or free: One morning a friend of the Estes family found a sign on his gatepost warning, "Don't let the sun go down on you here." So on April 1, 1851, Sylvia's family loaded their wagon and set out for California.

It was a hard six months on the trail. Dried buffalo dung was often the only fuel for their fires, and at times mosquitoes flew so thick they covered the lids of the cooking pots. Coyotes howled at night, and the pioneers sometimes had to slake their thirst in streams fouled by the decaying carcasses of animals.

Once in California, they settled outside Placerville, a mining town near Sacramento. Sylvia's father and brother farmed and panned for gold, and the women took in washing. In 1855 Sylvia married Louis Stark, the son of a slave and a Kentucky plantation owner. The families prospered, but in 1858, when the state assembly passed restrictive laws aimed at blacks, they decided to leave the country. They boarded a steamer bound for British Columbia, where James Douglas, governor of Vancouver Island, promised black settlers "all the rights and protections" of citizenship.

The Estes family settled on Vancouver Island, while the Starks homesteaded on Saltspring Island, a sparsely populated wilderness. In time Sylvia and Louis moved across the island to Fruitville, where they built a larger house for their growing family. But Louis spent much of his time mining on Vancouver Island, and in 1874 Sylvia reluctantly agreed to join him. That arrangement lasted only two years: She moved back to Fruitville and Louis went his own way.

Of their seven children, the oldest son, Willis, remained with his mother until his death in 1943, at age 85. Sylvia Stark died the next year, at the age of 106.

Still sheltered by fields and trees, Sylvia Stark's Saltspring Island home remains in the family. The 260 acres were divided among relatives; one of her granddaughters lives in the house.

Covering nearly 1,800 miles, the rugged trail followed by Sylvia Stark and her family in 1851 took them across plains, deserts, and mountains. Their voyage by steamer seven years later, from California to Washington Territory and then to Vancouver, was rocked by storms. To lighten the ship's load, 40 horses in the hold were brought up on deck and thrown overboard.

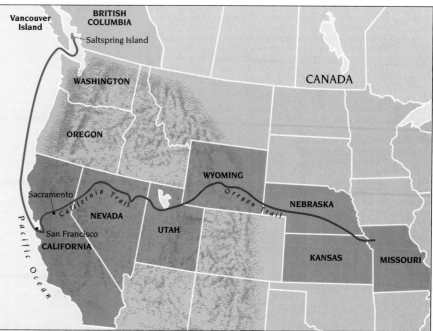

Sylvia Stark was about 93 and still planting her own garden when she sat for this portrait in 1931. Her son Willis, shown here in the early 1900s, was skilled at tracking and killing cougars.

BLACK WOMEN ON THE FRONTIER

The black women who came west in covered wagons never show up in movies about crafty cattle thieves and straight-shooting sheriffs—but they should. According to census records, diaries, letters, and other memoirs, thousands of black women flocked to the West before and after the Civil War and into the early 20th century. They came as slaves, ex-slaves, and sometimes as mail-order brides.

Black pioneer women were twice as likely as white women in the West to have jobs—usually low-paying, back-wrenching ones

as domestics. They scrubbed the dust-grimed shirts of gold miners and soldiers, cooked and cleaned for white families, took care of white children, and then went home to do it all over again for their own families. Some barely scraped by; others turned meager wages into substantial savings, which they used to buy freedom for family members still in slavery, to help the needy, or to purchase land. Many became innkeepers, entrepreneurs, and educators. They were all women who took chances and believed in change. San Francisco land-

owner Mary Ellen "Mammy" Pleasant, for example, suspected of supplying abolitionist John Brown with funds for his raid on Harpers Ferry, was one who made a substantial mark on history, as did Charlotta Spears Bass, who in 1912 served as editor of the *California Eagle*, the first African American newspaper on the West Coast.

Only a handful of these spirited pioneers can be described here. There are countless others who labored quietly and whose names and achievements may never be known.

This unknown elderly woman, photographed around 1900, lived on the Colorado plains in the town of Pueblo.

A pioneer family gathers around their wagon in about 1900.

These black schoolteachers worked in Guthrie, Oklahoma, the capital of Oklahoma Territory from 1890 to 1907.

Biddy Mason. During the gold rush, 32-year-old Biddy Mason walked behind her master's 300-wagon caravan from Mississippi to southern California, where she gained her freedom and invested in real estate. The time and money she spent helping others earned her the nickname Grandmother Mason.

Clara Brown. When newly freed slave Clara Brown rolled into Colorado gold-mining country in 1859 in the back of a covered wagon, she made two vows—to make enough money to live independently, and to locate her children, who had been auctioned away 20 years before. She established a laundry in Central City—charging 50 cents for every grimy shirt—and accumulated enough money to purchase property and travel east. She found 34 of her relatives, but only one of her children. Brown brought her family back with her and later helped other black families make the trip as well. Known as Aunt Clara, Brown opened her home to anyone in need of a bed or medical care, and helped start Sunday schools and churches in the towns where she worked.

Elvira Conley. Elvira Conley was a confident woman, with no fear of wide-open western towns and no regrets about leaving her past behind. Emancipated in 1864 at age 19, Conley at first led a by-the-book life, marrying an ex-soldier and giving birth to a daughter. When the marriage ended in 1868, though, she gave the child to her mother to raise and moved to Sheridan, Kansas. In a town filled with "reprobates, gamblers, horse thieves, murderers and disreputable women," in the words of one eyewitness, Conley set up a booming laundry business patronized by Wild Bill Hickok, among others. In 1870 she became a governess for a wealthy family and for the next 60 years tended four generations of their children.

Annie Neal. Annie Neal ran the Mountain View Hotel in Oracle, Arizona. Built as a wedding present for 25-year-old Annie by her husband, William, in 1895, the hotel catered to travelers and to people suffering from tuberculosis. Neal provided nursing care, a private school for her guests' children, and monthly church services in the hotel's recreation room. But running the inn wasn't her only talent. Her husband operated stagecoach lines between mining towns, and he took her along when he was transporting gold bullion—Neal was a crack shot with her Long Tom rifle, able to mow down any holdup men. Buffalo Bill Cody sometimes stopped at Mountain View and, said Neal admiringly, he was "the only hotel guest to whom I ever lost a shooting match."

Mary Fields. Folks who saw Mary Fields delivering the U.S. mail sometimes spun around for a second, startled look. Better known as Stagecoach Mary, Fields was six feet tall, weighed more than 200 pounds, wore men's clothes, and puffed thick black cigars. She was the only woman in Cascade, Montana, allowed to gulp red-eye whiskey in saloons, and the town would toss her a party whenever she felt like having a birthday. Born a slave in Tennessee in 1832, Fields took her first job in the West at age 52, doing heavy labor and hauling freight for a Catholic mission in Cascade. The bishop fired her, though, after she got into a shootout with a handyman. Next, she briefly ran a restaurant, then landed a job carrying the U.S. mail. By the age of 70 she was running a laundry. She had her own way of making sure nobody cheated her: When one customer refused to pay his bill, she knocked him out with a single blow. That, she said, settled the bill.

TWO PEOPLES OF COLOR

On June 25, 1876, in Montana Territory, warriors of the Sioux Nation and other Native American tribes decisively defeated General George A. Custer at the battle of the Little Bighorn, killing Custer and everyone under his command. Of the more than 200 deaths, perhaps none was more ironic than that of Isaiah Dorman. As a runaway slave in the 1850s, Dorman had found refuge with the Sioux and had taken a Sioux wife. His adopted people called him Azimpi, which means teat but sounds like Isaiah in the guttural Sioux pronunciation. After the Civil War, Dorman traded on his understanding of the Sioux and their language to get work at frontier forts in the Dakotas.

Dorman was 55 when he was appointed interpreter to General Custer, and he probably welcomed the chance to revisit Montana and palaver with the Sioux. But when Custer made his last stand, Dorman fell. Moments before he died, it is said, the Sioux leader, Sitting Bull, recognized the black man and gave him water. Afterward, when Sioux women and children mutilated the soldiers' bodies to deny them passage to the afterworld, they left Azimpi's body intact.

The ironies in the life and death of Isaiah Dorman suggest the complexity of the relationships between African Americans and Native Americans. At various times, blacks such as Dorman fought beside whites to conquer the Indians. In other situations, especially before the end of slavery, African Americans and Native

Americans stood together against a common white enemy.

Soon after North American colonists chose to use black slaves instead of Indians to farm the land, Native Americans began giving sanctuary to runaway slaves and provided support for the small fugitive slave communities that sprang up near them. Although treaties between Native Americans and white colonists stipulated that the Indians had to return runaway slaves, most tribes ignored that proviso.

But the colonists, perhaps with a "divide-and-conquer" strategy in mind, also encouraged the Indians to take black slaves of their own. The Cherokee, Chickasaw, Choctaw, Creek, and Seminole tribes acquired African American slaves by the thousands. But slav-

The Seminole Negro Indian Scouts, shown here in about 1885, were recruited by the U.S. Army to fight Indians refusing to leave their lands.

ery under the Indians could be quite different than under southern white masters. The Cherokee, for example, were so liberal by comparison that black slaves sometimes ran away from white owners to work for them. The Creeks intermarried with their slaves and treated the children of such unions like full-blooded Indians. Most welcoming of all were the Seminole people, who considered African Americans equals. Seminole slaves were expected only to give a small tribute in corn to the chiefs.

Slaves, runaways, and free blacks had much to offer their Native American allies. Unlike most Indians, black men and women understood the whites' language and were familiar with the culture. In addition, they had a rudimentary knowledge of medicine, and could treat such diseases as smallpox, measles, and yellow fever, which usually devastated native peoples. Many Native Americans also thought blacks communed with spirits and were capable of performing supernatural feats. It was partly because of these beliefs that Indians often spared blacks in a massacre.

When it came to courage, Indians were color-blind, and chiefs gladly married off their daughters to brave black men. Similarly, black men, who significantly outnumbered black women in the colonies, were happy to take Indian brides. The children of these marriages were considered free, and sometimes they could buy freedom for their fathers.

The solidarity between blacks and Indians was often seen by whites as a threat, and with good

A black Indian watchmaker from Oklahoma wears a Native American-style vest in this portrait made around 1890 (*left*).

Diane Fletcher (*below*), a black woman who lived with the Kiowa Indians in Oklahoma Territory, wears Kiowa clothing for this photograph taken at the end of the 19th century.

Members of a black Choctaw family gather outside their cabin in Indian Territory (later the state of Oklahoma) in about 1889.

A former slave of the Creek Indians, Paro Bruner posed for this informal portrait around 1900.

reason. Black fugitives swelled the ranks of the Seminole and fought side by side with them against white soldiers in the bloody Seminole Wars of 1817-18 and 1835-42. When the Seminole were defeated and forced to move to Indian Territory, their black kinfolk became the targets of slave hunters, whereupon many Indians and blacks headed out of the country and into Mexico.

For other black men and women, the American West—and the contact with Indians that it brought—offered some economic and social improvement. Whites, believing that blacks had a pacifying effect on the Indians, often had them handle negotiations with wary tribes. As trappers, traders, scouts, and interpreters, African Americans had many opportunities to deal with the various Indian tribes, and some continued to join Native American communities. Around 1800 Pierre Bonga, a slave who represented a Canadian fur-trapping company in negotiations with the Chippewa, married a member of the tribe. His son George, who also married into the Chippewa, was the interpreter for the United States dur-

ing the 1837 treaty negotiations with the tribe.

Not all Indians welcomed African Americans into their tribes, however. The Comanche and the Apache saw little difference between the whites and the blacks who invaded their lands. Sometimes they stole blacks and sold them as slaves to Cherokee or Creek owners. Other times they killed them. In 1871, for example, a Comanche band gunned down Britton Johnson, a rancher and former slave living in Texas. Comanches had earlier abducted Johnson's wife and children, and to reclaim them the black man pretended to join the tribe. Later the rancher and his family escaped, only to be tracked down and murdered by Comanche raiders who disemboweled Johnson and stuffed his abdomen with the corpse of his dog.

After the Civil War, some exslaves joined the U.S. Army, whose postwar priority was to sweep Native Americans off much of western land and into reservations. Black soldiers, whom the Indians dubbed buffalo soldiers as a mark of respect (*pages* 150-152), at one time made up 10 to

John Taylor, shown at left with his Ute bride, Kitty Cloud, at their 1907 wedding, was an ex-slave who could translate Navajo, Ute, Apache, and Spanish. In the family scene above, Kitty (*standing at right*) and the couple's daughter Enterpe are joined by Kitty's sister and her child by a white husband.

20 percent of the western force. They fought the Ute in Colorado, the Cheyenne in Kansas, and the Sioux on the Great Plains.

While the buffalo soldiers were engaged with the Plains Indians, much of the task of dealing with the Comanche went to a valiant band of black Indians known as the Seminole Negro Indian Scouts. Never more than 50 strong, the scouts were mostly the sons of the black Seminoles who had fled to Mexico in the 1850s. Growing up in the borderlands, the young men had learned how to track, trap, and survive in the rugged terrain. In the 1870s the army recruited them as Indian fighters, promising them land as payment. The scouts were housed in Seminole camps on military reservations in Texas.

Serving under a white lieutenant named John Bullis, the black scouts proved to be superb trackers and cool under fire. During one engagement, on April 25, 1875, at the Eagle's Nest Crossing of the Pecos River, Bullis and three of the scouts found themselves in a gunfight with about 30 Comanche warriors. After 45 minutes of constant attack, the four men attempted a retreat. The three scouts escaped, but Bullis was stranded when his horse bolted. Under withering fire, Sergeant John Ward, the black Seminole who was second in command, led his comrades back to rescue Bullis. They were successful, and for their bravery all three scouts received the Congressional Medal of Honor.

The Seminole Negro Indian Scouts became one of the most decorated military units in the United States. But when the Indian threat was over, in the early 1880s, the army reneged on its promise of land. And since the federal government had earlier declared 1866 the deadline to register as a member of the Seminole Nation—and thus be eligible for land grants on the Indian reservation—many of the scouts and their families were left homeless and destitute.

The wars blacks fought with the Indians in the Florida swamps and against them on the Great Plains are long over, but the complex, centuries-old relationship between African Americans and Native Americans has left an enduring legacy. In 1926 Professor Melville Herskovits, a scholar and anthropology professor at Northwestern University, questioned a sampling of 1,551 African Americans about their family histories. One out of every three reported Native American ancestors.

OUTLAWS AND LAWMEN IN THE WILD WEST

The myth of the American frontier is peopled with larger-than-life white villains and heroes, from killers like Jesse James and Billy the Kid to lawmen like Wyatt Earp and Wild Bill Hickok. But probably few can name the equally cold-blooded black renegades who terrorized the Old West, or the black marshals and sheriffs who brought criminals of all races to justice. The crimes of outlaws like Cherokee Bill and Rufus Buck were as vicious as any committed by the Kid or the James Gang, and during the 1870s, black deputy marshals were among the 200 or so appointed to take on bandits in Oklahoma's rough-and-tumble Indian Territory. Vested with the authority to arrest whites and defend themselves while doing it, the black deputy marshals (*overleaf*) pitted their wits and strength against the meanest outlaws in the West in their efforts to safeguard the Plains.

Cherokee Bill. Part Cherokee, part black, and so good-looking that many women hid him from the law, Cherokee Bill (*above, front row, third from right*) sparked such fear in Indian Territory that one town passed an ordinance allowing him to come and go as he pleased. Born Crawford Goldsby in 1876 in Fort Concho, Texas, by the age of 18 he was known for his rapid-fire shooting. When deputy marshals finally captured him at age 20, he had killed a railroad conductor and a station agent, policemen, storekeepers, and even his own brother-in-law. Cool to the end, Cherokee Bill remarked on his way to the gallows in Fort Smith, "This is about as good a day to die as any."

The Rufus Buck Gang. Made up of two blacks and three Creek Indians, the dreaded Rufus Buck Gang set a record for violence in the often-bloody Indian Territory. For 13 horrifying days in the summer of 1895, the outlaws robbed, raped, or murdered nearly everyone who crossed their path. Among their victims were a U.S. deputy marshal, ranchers, shop- keepers, widows, farmers, and even a child. The posse sent after them, which included more than a hundred Creek Indians, finally tracked the outlaws down and, after a seven-hour gunfight, trapped them in a cave. The gang surrendered, and all five—shown above in chains on the day before their execution—were hanged on July 1, 1896.

Ben Hodges. Although his tombstone memorializes him as a "self-styled desperado," Ben Hodges's weapons were fast cards and a silver tongue, not the shotgun he holds in the photo below. A notorious cattle thief, forger, card shark, and confidence man, Hodges operated out of Dodge City, Kansas. He claimed to be from an old Spanish family—a story he made use of in a land swindle—but was actually the son of a black father and a Mexican mother. When he died in 1929, at age 73, he was buried near other cowboys. Explained a pallbearer, "We wanted him where they could keep a good eye on him."

Ned Huddleston. Also known as Isom Dart, Ned Huddleston (*left*) discovered early his talent for thieving. Born a slave in Arkansas in 1849, he was made to forage for Confederate soldiers, and after the Civil War rustled horses and livestock in Colorado. He came close to death or imprisonment several times, but on each occasion was saved by pure luck and, once, by his own kindness. When a deputy sheriff was hurt while transporting him to jail, Huddleston took the man to a hospital and then turned himself in. Impressed, the jury let him go. His luck ran out at age 51, when a gunman shot him in the back.

BLACK MEN OF THE LAW

Bass Reeves. Everything about Deputy U.S. Marshal Bass Reeves was big: He stood more than six feet tall, wore a big hat and sported a bushy mustache, and was known and respected throughout Indian Territory. Polite and courteous, Reeves would sing softly to himself before a gunfight—then coolly take his man. In more than 30 years of service, only one fugitive eluded him, and Reeves himself was never wounded. He killed 14 men during his career—they all drew on him first—but the black lawman relied as much on his wits as on his weapons. He often disguised himself as a cowboy, a tramp, or a renegade to apprehend an outlaw. Reeves died in 1910, at age 71.

Grant Johnson. A former slave of the Creek Indians, Grant Johnson found ingenious ways to keep the peace in Indian Territory. The deputy marshal—seated front and center in this 1907 reunion photograph of lawmen appointed by the famous white "hanging judge" Isaac Parker—once held off arresting a known murderer for three months, figuring he could lure the accused into a false sense of security. The strategy paid off one day in January 1895: When the man came to town to shop, Johnson arrested him at the counter of the general store. Although he packed two pistols and a Winchester rifle, Johnson was loath to use his weapons; he had been on the job 14 years before he killed a man.

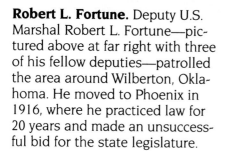

Robert L. Fortune. Deputy U.S. Marshal Robert L. Fortune—pictured above at far right with three of his fellow deputies—patrolled the area around Wilberton, Oklahoma. He moved to Phoenix in 1916, where he practiced law for 20 years and made an unsuccessful bid for the state legislature.

Francis T. Bruce. An early Colorado pioneer and a Denver policeman and civic leader in the 1890s, Bruce went by the affectionate nickname Daddy. He helped organize Denver's black Masonic lodge and in the early part of the decade was appointed a bailiff for the municipal court.

Ben Boyer. The imposing deputy sheriff of Coaldale, Colorado, from 1905 to 1910, Ben Boyer stood six feet two inches tall, weighed 225 pounds, and carried a custom-made Colt .45. A deadly shot who could manage the roughest outlaws, Boyer also served as a prison guard.

THE WEST IN BLACK AND WHITE

Not all the African Americans who ventured into the American West made their living by farming or herding cattle. James Presley Ball, a freeman born in Virginia in 1825 and reared in Cincinnati, wielded a camera. One of the country's first photographers and among the best of his day, Ball produced riveting images that today fetch record prices from collectors. His medium was the daguerreotype, made by exposing a sensitized silver-coated plate to mercury vapor. The technique was ideal for detailed portraiture, but when it was supplanted by print photography, Ball became adept at that method too.

Settling for a time in Richmond, Virginia, Ball opened a one-room portrait studio in 1846 with $100 he earned working in a hotel. The studio was successful, but the entrepreneur soon returned to Ohio as an itinerant photographer. The next year, perhaps tired of life on the road, he landed in Cincinnati and once more took up studio work. Business flourished, and by 1851 Ball's Daguerrean Gallery of the West occupied four rooms and employed nine men. It was known "through nearly every State of the Union," trumpeted a publication of the day, "and there is scarcely a distinguished stranger that comes to Cincinnati but, if his time permits, seeks the pleasure of Mr. Ball's artistic acquaintance."

An active abolitionist as well, in 1855 Ball depicted slavery's horrors in a panorama: Ball's *Splendid Mammoth Pictorial Tour of the United States Comprising Views of the African Slave Trade; of Northern and Southern Cities; of Cotton and Sugar Plantations; of the Mississippi, Ohio and Susquehanna Rivers, Niagara Falls, and Canada.* According to a companion text, the exhibit spanned 600 yards and included sketches, paintings, and photographs.

Ball worked in Cincinnati until about 1871, when he moved to Minneapolis. Nine years later he was in Helena, Montana, and in business with his son. There he broke out of the studio setting and began documenting all facets of life in the burgeoning American West. In 1901 Ball followed his son to Seattle, then moved to Portland, where he died around 1902.

Acclaimed nationally for his photographs, J. P. Ball, shown here in the 1890s, was also active politically. In Helena, Montana, he was a delegate to the 1894 Republican convention.

In this photograph of policeman William C. Irvin, taken around 1888 in Ball's Helena, Montana, studio, the curling of one corner of the image is a visual deception, or trompe l'oeil effect—an innovative style in 19th-century photography.

J. P. Ball's plush Cincinnati studio, located in the heart of the city, had four rooms—including the "great Gallery," depicted above in an 1854 engraving. The huge room could exhibit 187 photographs.

William Biggerstaff, flanked at right by members of the Helena sheriff's department, posed for this gruesome 1896 photograph just minutes before he was hanged for committing murder. Afterward, Ball recorded Biggerstaff laid out in his coffin (far right).

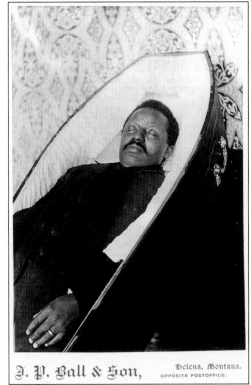

Five dollars bought a settler land in Nicodemus, Kansas, according to this certificate issued by the town's developers—six black men and one white.

State of Kansas, ss:
Graham County.

This is to Certify, That

of   County, State of

has this day paid the sum of FIVE DOLLARS, being the full amount of Membership Fees in the

Nicodemus Town Company of Graham Co., Kansas,

and that said

any vacant Town Lot on the town site of Nicodemus, Graham County, Kansas, at the time said party arrives at Nicodemus; the said Nicodemus Town Company giving their obligation to make Title to said Lot as required by law. And it is further agreed that no Intoxicating Liquors shall be sold on said lot within five years from this date.

Dated at   this   day of   187_

Scattered across the plains and mountains of the West, the all-black towns profiled on these pages and shown on the map at left grew up near other cities and rail lines. Developers studied migration patterns, an area's natural resources, and the accessibility of a site before deciding on a location. To lure potential settlers, they looked to the East and South, advertising through newspapers, handbills, and broadsides.

BLACK TOWNS: HAVENS IN THE WEST

"I always felt I was free here. Nobody, no white man, could come in and order me around," said Sam Wilcots, who grew up in the all-black town of Boley, Oklahoma. His sentiments were shared by thousands of African Americans who emigrated from both the North and the South after the Civil War to settle the dozens of black towns that sprang up from Kansas to California. Black leaders and white entrepreneurs alike helped organize the towns, with the twin goals of offering blacks a life of self-determination and making a profit from residents, who typically paid a small fee for land in the communities. The cheap—and sometimes free—land offered by the towns' promoters was a major draw for many blacks heading west, who were also seeking better work opportunities and freedom from white harassment. Many spent their savings to make the journey, and once they arrived scrambled to make a living. Despite the obstacles residents faced, however, many of the settlements grew and prospered for decades as havens of black culture, until the larger cities began to lure residents and businesses away.

During its heyday in the mid-1880s, Nicodemus bustled with schools, a Baptist church, and three dozen businesses, including Williams General Merchandise (*left, center*). By the 1950s the population had dwindled to 16 families, and most buildings, including the homestead at left, were in ruins.

Distinguished members of the town council of Boley, Oklahoma, assemble for an official photograph in the early 1900s. Formed in 1904, Boley was one of the most successful of the all-black towns. It is still home to about 500 people, many of whom commute to work in nearby Oklahoma City.

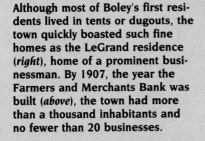

Although most of Boley's first residents lived in tents or dugouts, the town quickly boasted such fine homes as the LeGrand residence (*right*), home of a prominent businessman. By 1907, the year the Farmers and Merchants Bank was built (*above*), the town had more than a thousand inhabitants and no fewer than 20 businesses.

Advertised as a "valley resort" in a pamphlet distributed by town founder Oliver T. Jackson (*right*), Dearfield was the first all-black community in Colorado. Jackson, an Ohio native, dreamed of a place where black farmers would strive and prosper together. Settled by seven families in 1911, the town consisted of little more than a few simple frame houses and a service station (*above*).

Believers in black economic solidarity, Colonel Allen Allensworth, an army chaplain, and his wife, Josephine, organized investors in 1908 to found the central California town named for them.

An Allensworth resident reads a newspaper on the porch of the town's library, and two young men peruse the books inside in the photographs below. The library was dedicated in 1913 to the memory of Josephine Allensworth's mother and eventually became part of the Tulare County library system. The town also offered a school, a church, a civic center, and a park.

COWBOYS
OLD AND NEW

From the Wild West shows of the late 1800s to the dusty arenas of modern rodeos, in a sport that is still mostly white and southern, black cowboys have pitted their skills against untamed bulls and broncos.

Bulldogger Bill Pickett was the most famous of the black rodeo cowboys. Born in Texas in 1870, Pickett wrestled steers using a technique he apparently picked up from watching bulldogs round up errant cattle: He would bite a steer on its tender upper lip to subdue it, then flip the animal on its side. Pickett made a name for himself at county fairs and exhibitions, and in 1905 joined the Miller Brothers 101 Ranch Wild West Show, the only black among the 90 cowhands performing. The popular show's main draw until he died in 1932 from a horse's kick to the head, Pickett was inducted into the National Cowboy Hall of Fame in 1971, the first African American honoree.

Other topnotch black cowboys (*opposite*) followed Pickett onto the rodeo circuit, including Jesse Stahl, who began riding broncos in 1913. But only recently have blacks begun taking rodeo's top honors: Los Angeles-born Charles Sampson was named the 1982 world champion bull rider, and Texan Fred Whitfield took home the calf-roping trophy in 1991.

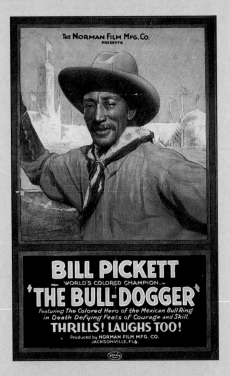

THE NORMAN FILM MFG. CO.
PRESENTS

BILL PICKETT
WORLD'S COLORED CHAMPION—in
'THE BULL·DOGGER'
Featuring The Colored Hero of the Mexican Bull Ring
in Death Defying Feats of Courage and Skill.
THRILLS! LAUGHS TOO!
Produced by NORMAN FILM MFG. CO.
JACKSONVILLE, FL.

Promising "Thrills! Laughs Too!" this poster advertises a silent film from about 1923 in which Pickett demonstrated his steer-wrestling technique.

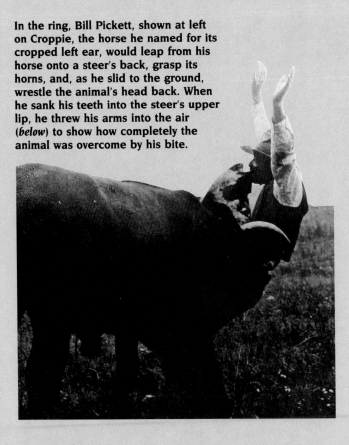

In the ring, Bill Pickett, shown at left on Croppie, the horse he named for its cropped left ear, would leap from his horse onto a steer's back, grasp its horns, and, as he slid to the ground, wrestle the animal's head back. When he sank his teeth into the steer's upper lip, he threw his arms into the air (*below*) to show how completely the animal was overcome by his bite.

Calling on agility and strength, Jesse Stahl dominates a bucking horse in this photograph dating from around 1930. Other riders considered him the best, but Stahl often placed third instead of first because of his race.

Champion bull rider Charles Sampson, shown here in Salinas, California, in 1992, knows about goal setting. He often tells inner-city youth about how he cleaned stalls in a stable as a boy to earn money to ride and learn to rope.

Fred Whitfield, roping a calf at a 1990 Las Vegas rodeo during his first pro season, has the sport "in his blood," according to his mother. As a child, Joyce Whitfield recalled, he would lasso chickens, the mailbox, and "sometimes he'd rope me."

A MOTHER LODE OF BLACK HISTORY IN THE WEST

Like many children, Paul Stewart grew up playing cowboys and Indians. Because black families were few in Clinton, Iowa, in the 1930s, he had white play-mates, and they never let him be the cowboy. "There's no such thing as a black cowboy," they confidently explained. Stewart believed them until one day in the early 1960s when, during a trip to Denver to visit a relative, he spotted an African American man in a 10-gallon hat, chaps, boots, and spurs striding down the street. As Stewart recalled later, "I said to my cousin, 'Who's he trying to fool? Everybody knows there are no black cowboys.' " Stewart had to eat his words, though, when he learned that the man was a rancher. "For the first time, I realized that the history books had deliberately left black people out," he said.

"So that other children wouldn't have to go through what I did, I made a vow to find out everything I could about black cowboys."

Stewart, a barber by trade, moved to Denver and set up shop. As he clipped hair he would ask his customers what they knew about black pioneers, sometimes secretly tape-recording their recollections. Before long people began bringing old boots, photographs, and other keepsakes to display in Stewart's shop—and soon the shop was overflowing. In 1971, realizing he had the makings of a museum collection, Stewart moved the items to a larger space—an old saloon—and the Black American West Museum and Heritage Center was born. Now located in Denver's Five Points district, the museum has more than 35,000 items.

A self-taught historian, Stewart gathered much of his knowledge about black pioneers from oral histories he recorded by traveling throughout the West. Along the way he picked up more photos and such memorabilia as ropes, rifles, saddles, shaving mugs, mailbags, and even the buffalo coat of the first man born in Montana Territory. Since 1975, when he closed the barbershop, Paul Stewart has been the museum's full-time, unpaid curator. Arranging the artifacts by subject, he now has rooms devoted to the buffalo soldiers (*pages* 150-153) and to black pioneers, cowboys, ranchers, farmers, fur traders, and miners.

But Stewart has become his own best exhibit. The same year he devoted himself full-time to the museum, he was hired as a consultant to the Denver public schools, launching a personal crusade to fill what he calls "a void in history." Dressed in full cowboy regalia—just like the cowboy he saw on his first visit to Denver—he enthralls the students with stories of life in the Old West, showing slides from his collection and letting the children examine the ropes, spurs, and other items he brings with him. When he first came to Colorado, Stewart says, he "went up into the mountains looking for gold." He has since found his treasure in "the history of blacks in the West. This is the real gold mine."

A genial man who has gathered the memories—and memorabilia—of more than 800 people, Paul Stewart had no plans to retire when this picture was taken in 1993. "I'll probably drop dead with a microphone in my hand."

A portrait of a family from Nicodemus, Kansas (*pages* 118-119), presides over items used by black pioneers, including, from left to right, a waffle iron; a glass rolling pin; a lantern; a can opener that clamps to a table; a quilt; various personal items; and, on the floor, a wringer for squeezing water from laundered clothes.

Objects in Stewart's corral-like exhibit (*below*) evoke the lives of black ranchers and homesteaders in the Old West: a saddle (*foreground*) and, from left to right, a wagon wheel; a plow; yoke for oxen; a bearskin coat; a corn sheller that deposits kernels in a pail; a canvas bucket; various harnesses; and photographs of black pioneers.

SOLDIERS
IN THE SHADOWS

Buffalo soldiers of the 9th U.S. Cavalry Regiment's E Troop, veterans of the Spanish-American War, pause in San Francisco for a photograph in 1900 en route to occupation duty in the Philippines.

Doris Miller had little reason to love the United States Navy. He had joined a fighting service, and it had stuck him—as it did all black sailors—in the most menial of jobs. He was a mess attendant waiting tables on board the mighty battleship USS *West Virginia*, berthed at Hawaii's Pearl Harbor. Day after day, the 22-year-old Miller served food to the *West Virginia*'s white officers and cleared away their dirty dishes from the wardroom. Once in a while, an officer might have a friendly word for the young black man. But otherwise he was given no more notice than the wardroom furniture, as though, despite having a battle station and an assigned combat function as an ammunition handler amidships, he was not a fighting navy seaman, not a real sailor.

That perception changed dramatically on December 7, 1941. It was a quiet Sunday morning, and Miller was busy with laundry when, at 7:55, the boom of an explosion and the roar of low-flying planes shattered the peace. In came 353 Japanese dive bombers, level bombers, torpedo planes, and fighters, launched from six aircraft carriers, to bring off the greatest surprise attack in naval history. As the *West Virginia* rocked with the blast of the first of seven torpedoes and two bombs that would slam into her that morning, the call to general quarters echoed through the ship. Doris Miller raced toward his battle station but was turned back by wreckage and fire. He then ran up the steel stairs to the bridge and out onto the signal bridge. The skipper, Captain Mervyn Bennion, sprawled there bleeding heavily. Heedless of his own safety, Miller helped drag Bennion to cover, though the captain was done for, disemboweled by a piece of shrapnel. Then, Miller ran out into the open again and grabbed a machine gun mounted forward of the conning tower.

Mess Attendant Second Class Doris Miller had been a crack shot with a squirrel gun back home in Waco, Texas, but as a sailor he had received only a bit of classroom instruction on machine guns and had never fired one. He started firing at the diving Japanese aircraft, correcting for lead as a man might swing a hose. Miller was surprised to see an enemy plane blossom into flame. He kept shooting, kept hosing. Another Japanese aircraft dropped, perhaps struck down by his fire. There may have been a third, even a fourth. Doris Miller stayed out on that exposed bridge with the hammering machine gun for about 15 minutes, until flames from the stricken ship's fires were licking up around the bridge and an officer ordered him to safety.

Among the heroic stories that emerged at Pearl Harbor that desperate day, Doris Miller's was the one least welcome to a grudging navy command structure. Not that anyone could question the courage he showed, or deny his accomplishment.

But a mess attendant? A black man? The U.S. Navy, permeated with the racist assumption that blacks were inferior and of little account, was unhappy at having to acknowledge that a "Negro" could act heroically and fight effectively, and on his own initiative. The navy was even more reluctant to honor him publicly. It took a campaign by newspapers and civil rights groups that reached all the way to the White House before Miller was accorded the honor he deserved. Not until it received direct orders from President Franklin D. Roosevelt did the navy act. On May 27, 1942, Admiral Chester Nimitz pinned the Navy Cross on the broad, proud chest of Doris Miller. The citation read: "For distinguished devotion to duty, extraordinary courage and disregard for his own personal safety."

As was the case with many heroes, Miller was later sent stateside for a brief time to rally support for the sale of U.S. war bonds. He was greeted with deep satisfaction in New York's Harlem and in black communities in Chicago and elsewhere. But though he had shown the navy what he—indeed, what any black sailor—might accomplish in combat, he was never given the chance to distinguish himself further in the service of his country. One can only guess at the anger and sense of injustice and betrayal he felt when he was promoted just one grade—to Mess Attendant First Class—and reassigned to his old duty of waiting tables, this time on board the USS *Liscombe Bay*. On November 24, 1943, Doris Miller was among approximately 650 men who perished when the *Liscombe Bay* was torpedoed and sunk by a Japanese submarine in the Gilbert Islands.

The experience of Doris Miller in many ways mirrored more than three centuries of black struggle in the service of America. From skirmishes with Native Americans in the first English colonies to Operation Desert Storm in the Persian Gulf in 1991, African Americans have stood in battle alongside a kaleidoscope of other racial and ethnic varieties of Americans. Black militiamen fought valorously at Bunker Hill in a Revolutionary War that won liberty for the nation, but not for the black slaves among its people. Soldiers of color helped defend American sovereignty in the War of 1812. And during the Civil War thousands of ex-slaves joined free black men in battling bravely to preserve the Union and "earn" their freedom, in a nation where everyone else's freedom was a given. Black "buffalo soldiers" helped subdue the Indians who were resisting American settlement of the Old West and fought side by side with Teddy Roosevelt's celebrated Rough Riders in Cuba during the Spanish-American War. In World War I, 367,000 blacks served both at home and overseas. During the Second World War, African American servicemen like Doris Miller attained distinction in every arena. Black men fought bravely in Korea as the armed forces took tentative steps toward desegregation. And they bore their full share—maybe more—of the fighting and dying in Vietnam.

Black women, too, have served their country with distinction.

One of America's first World War II heroes, seaman Doris Miller is decorated with the Navy Cross for his bravery at Pearl Harbor by Admiral Chester W. Nimitz on May 27, 1942, in award ceremonies held aboard the USS *Enterprise*.

From at least as early as the Civil War they volunteered as army nurses, and through the years have overcome the prejudices they faced both as women and as African Americans to move into all branches of the military. In the Persian Gulf in 1991, black women performed in such capacities as aeromedical evacuation nurses, military police, and aircraft maintenance officers. And with the lifting of the ban on women in many combat jobs in 1993, the roles of black military women will only increase.

In every conflict, African Americans confronted two enemies simultaneously: the enemy of their nation and the enemy within—racism in the armed forces and in American society generally. Pervasive racism confounded the intellect and scorched the souls of black Americans, and it raised the inevitable question: Why fight for such a country? But the black men and women of the armed forces, sometimes disheartened, often fiercely angry, have loyally battled on. They have won some victories. Although white racist attitudes still surface all too often, sometimes among high-ranking commanders, African Americans finally hold positions of respect, trust, and leadership in every branch and at every level of today's all-volunteer services.

The first call to arms took little account of a man's color or status. In the original colonial militias, every able-bodied male between the ages of 17 and 60 was required to help defend the commonweal against Native Americans and Britain's European enemies. But the white men of the colonies soon perceived that arming a slave could be dangerous; even a free black man, practiced in musketry, might become the leader of an insurrection, they reasoned. And so, several colonies in the first half of the 17th century enacted some of the first discriminatory laws in American history, barring all "Negroes" from military service.

But the law created a problem for white colonists. To exempt black men from serving was to bestow on them a perquisite otherwise reserved for clergymen, public officials, and similar august personages in white society. In short order, Virginia and a number of other colonies amended their laws, the first of a series of flip-flops on the question of arming African Americans: Slaves were still to be banned from the militias; free blacks, however, would be required to serve—not as soldiers, but as drummers, fifers, laborers, unarmed guards, and the like. But that didn't work either; white colonists often were simply too few in number to defend themselves. For example, in South Carolina in the early 1700s, the white population was 50,000, compared with the region's 60,000 Cherokee, Creeks, and other Indians. Only by arming their 75,000 slaves could the colonists be assured of victory in battle. So when the Carolinians faced Indian attack in 1703, officials authorized slave owners to distribute weapons to their slaves and went so far as to offer freedom to any slave who, "in actual invasion" should "kill or take one or more of our enemies."

A few years later, however, complaints of economic hardship by plantation interests caused South Carolina to rescind its promise to repay valor with freedom. Beginning in 1719, noteworthy fighters among the slaves would get cash rewards but not liberty. Indian pressures in 1739 called forth another offer to slaves of manumission in exchange for combat; a slave revolt later that same year brought its repeal. Another decade passed, and black men once again had the opportunity to

purchase their own souls at the risk of their bodies when Carolinians were locked in battle with the Cherokee.

So went the white man's laws, whipsawing the slaves between the stirring possibility of winning their freedom and the heartsick-making need to drive the thought from their minds. Even without the offer of freedom, however, black patriots strode forward when the War of Independence broke out in the spring of 1775. But many leaders of the Revolution feared that enlisting slaves in the new Continental Army and thus depriving the South of its labor force would have adverse political consequences. Moreover, for all the myths white people professed to believe about the passivity, lack of courage, and general contentment of the slaves, they could not shake off their deep-rooted fear of arming black men. Thus, in November, General George Washington, himself a wealthy Virginia planter and slave owner, forbade the recruitment of black men, whether slave or free, although those already in service could finish their tours.

Meanwhile, the British were taking precisely the opposite tack. On November 7, 1775, Lord Dunmore, the Royal Governor of Virginia, issued a proclamation promising freedom to all slaves who would bear arms against the colonists. This threw a fright into the Americans, for it required no genius to realize that black men would readily fight for whoever promised an end to their enslavement. That simple fact, and the Continental Army's chronic shortage of troops, gradually brought about a reversal of Washington's original policy. First, free blacks were allowed to enlist; then the northern and Middle Atlantic states quietly included slaves in their quotas. The Lower South resisted bitterly and never did actually arm slaves. But South Carolina eventually enrolled 1,000 of its bondsmen in noncombat service. In all, some 5,000 black army troops served the American cause.

The black enlistees in northern army units soon earned their commanders' trust. An African American soldier named Oliver Cromwell rowed stroke oar in the boat that took George Washington across the Delaware on Christmas night, 1776, and Cromwell was one of 2,400 handpicked men who routed the Hessians at Trenton shortly after. Jack Sisson, a soldier with Rhode Island's mostly black 1st Regiment, and his chief, Lieutenant Colonel William Barton, ran a commando mission one July night in 1777, capturing the major general in command of all British forces in Rhode Island under the very noses of his redcoats. Later that same year, when fortune ran against the rebels at the battle of Brandywine, in Pennsylvania, and a full-scale

Massachusetts governor John Hancock commissioned a silk flag bearing 13 stars and a buck deer under a pine tree (*top*) to honor Boston's all-black Bucks of America, one of two African American units in the Continental Army. The Bucks' silver badge repeated the motif and was inscribed with the wearer's initials.

American retreat was under way, black army teamster Edward Hector refused to abandon his ammunition wagon as ordered. Instead he brought it to safety, stopping now and again to collect weapons cast away by his fleeing comrades. The 125 men—95 of them slaves—of Rhode Island's 1st Regiment wrote further history at the battle of Rhode Island in 1778. Covering a hasty retreat by their countrymen, they withstood three fierce British-Hessian attacks, inflicting casualties of six to one, and thereby enabled six full brigades of Americans to withdraw with all their equipment.

The bravery blacks showed in land battles was echoed in those taking place on the sea. In the early years of the navy, white fears about arming blacks were never strong. The dangers, hardships, and lengthy separations of sea duty discouraged enlistments, and captains gratefully closed their eyes to a recruit's color. Black men were in John Paul Jones's crew on the *Bonhomme Richard* in 1779 when it defeated the more heavily armed British frigate *Serapis*. And from long experience with small boats, gained during seafaring ventures with their masters, black seamen were valued as coastal pilots, particularly on the treacherous waters of Chesapeake Bay.

Despite such history, it took less than a decade after the Revolutionary War for racial discrimination to rule the U.S. military once again. First, the new Constitution instituted black inferiority as a legal principle by counting each black slave as only three-fifths of a person. Then, in 1792, the Congress restricted military service to "each and every free and able-bodied white citizen of the respective states." Only the navy quietly recruited African Americans—to the point where 10 to 20 percent of the fighting navy was black when war again flared up with Great Britain in 1812.

In the battle of New Orleans, the best-known clash of that war, the American side benefited from black patriotism in spite of its racist policies. Louisiana, while under the rule of the French and the Spanish, had trained a large and effective militia of free black citizens. The United States had ordered the militia disbanded upon acquiring Louisiana in 1803, but a decade later the former militiamen shrugged off the shabby treatment they had received and offered their services. And General Andrew Jackson, as pragmatic as he was brilliant, curtly overruled all objections, declaring, "They must either be for us or against us." He promised the volunteers the same pay, rations, uniforms, bounties, and 160-acre grants of land as white soldiers would receive. Two battalions of 300 men each, including black officers for the first time in American history, stood with Jackson when he met the British army outside New Orleans on January 8, 1815. The African Americans ably held their end of the line under massive British attack, then surged forward to help inflict a crushing defeat on the enemy.

Loyalty and heroism, as always,

Black sailors and their white shipmates pull together to row Commodore Perry from his burning flagship to the brig *Niagara* in this detail from William Henry Powell's 1873 painting, *Oliver Hazard Perry at the Battle of Lake Erie*, depicting an important American naval victory in the War of 1812. African Americans composed at least 10 percent of Perry's crew.

had to be their own reward for African American fighting men. The promised federal bounties and land warrants were endlessly delayed; black units were not permitted to march in the city's commemorative parades; and the militia thereafter suffered such neglect from the military authorities that it ceased to exist by 1834. Moreover, the regular U.S. Army still had no place for a black soldier among its 10,000 men.

Shortly after, the navy reacted to complaints from white southerners and fixed its level of black enlistments at no more than five percent of the total. To reach that figure, it dismissed many of its veteran black sailors—a practice that later would be followed again and again in all branches of service. There matters rested until the Civil War—when events and not justice would again dictate the military role white America would permit black Americans to fill.

In 1861 President Abraham Lincoln's secretary of war, Simon Cameron, stated: "This Department has no intention at present to call into the service of the Government any colored soldiers." Whatever Lincoln's personal feelings, he was a politician: He expected the war to be a short one, without any need for black manpower, and he feared defections among the slave-owning border states—Delaware, Maryland, Kentucky, Missouri—that had thus far remained within the Union. To arm black men, he argued, "would turn 50,000 bayonets from the loyal Border states against us."

It required the better part of two years for Lincoln to change his mind, and some Union generals were several steps ahead of him. In May 1861, General Benjamin Butler declared on his own initiative that escaped slaves taking refuge behind Union lines were "contraband of war," and he enlisted them as cooks, carpenters, and engineers. The following summer, in Kansas, General James H. Lane raised the first African American unit to see combat in the Civil War—a 500-man volunteer regiment. In Washington, however, the old falsehoods and fears about black soldiers continued to hold sway—for as long as the government was confident of winning the war. But when a string of defeats and stalemates on the battlefield made it clear to northerners that victory would not be theirs without a long, bloody struggle, President Lincoln groped for some electrifying act that would rekindle the nation's resolve. He decided, in September 1862, to issue his Emancipation Proclamation.

Under the motto *Ferro iis libertas perveniet*—Liberty came to them by the sword—two black Union soldiers are shown advancing toward a Confederate bastion on the Army of the James Medal, also known as the Butler Medal. Members of the African American XXV Corps earned the medal, ordered struck by General Benjamin F. Butler, when they stormed New Market Heights and Chaffins's Farm in Virginia in September 1864.

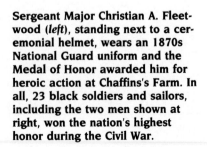

Sergeant Major Christian A. Fleetwood (*left*), standing next to a ceremonial helmet, wears an 1870s National Guard uniform and the Medal of Honor awarded him for heroic action at Chaffins's Farm. In all, 23 black soldiers and sailors, including the two men shown at right, won the nation's highest honor during the Civil War.

First Sergeant Powhatan Beaty

Sergeant James H. Harris

By making the abolition of slavery a Union war aim, Lincoln captured the moral high ground. Now, wherever Union armies conquered, they would bring a freedom sanctioned by law to the slaves. And in the abolitionist spirit of the proclamation, Lincoln proceeded to announce that African Americans would be received into the armed services of the United States.

"Men of Color, to Arms," cried Frederick Douglass. "Liberty won only by white men would lose half its luster." Massachusetts had already begun forming its soon-to-be-celebrated 54th Volunteer Infantry Regiment (*pages* 148-149); a second regiment, the 55th, now followed, and Connecticut, Pennsylvania, Ohio, Illinois, Indiana, and Michigan each raised one or more African American regiments. Where Union armies had penetrated the South, so many freed slaves volunteered that the War Department established a separate Bureau of Colored Troops to oversee their enlistment. Fifty thousand black men were in uniform by December 1863.

The first extensive combat by African American troops took place in May and June 1863, when blacks joined in the assaults against Port Hudson and Milliken's Bend, Confederate strongholds on the Lower Mississippi in Louisiana. At Port Hudson, three hastily organized African American regiments made no fewer than six charges against a well-entrenched enemy. Although the attacks ultimately failed, the 20 percent loss rate suffered by the black regiments showed their will to fight.

The soldiers demonstrated their bravery again when a white commander, General H. E. Paine, lay wounded out on the shell-swept field after the men he was leading had been driven back. A squad of 16 black troops stepped forward. Their spokesman said to the general's adjutant: "We's been thinking Sar, dat dere's got to be a good many killed in this war, 'fore our people can get deir freedom and p'raps it may as well be we as anybody else; so if you please Sar, we'll go after the general." And they did, in groups of four, with stretchers, water, and bandages. The first four men were cut down. The second quartet moved out and were killed instantly. The third group raced for the general. Two were killed. But the other two reached the wounded officer and remained with him, tending his wounds and giving him water until darkness made rescue possible.

The slowly dawning perception of black soldiers' military qualities found widespread public voice. *Harper's Weekly* wrote: "Wherever the Negroes have had a chance they have given evidence of the most exalted gallantry." Yet racial discrimination and injustice remained evident everywhere. Both in garrison and in the field, black troops were strictly segregated from their white counterparts, served under white officers only, and routinely received less training and older-model weapons than white soldiers. Medical facilities for blacks were primitive and doctors were scarce—all of which played a role, gallantry aside, in high casualty rates in black units.

African Americans also bore the added burden of fighting without the protection of tacit rules accepted by both sides regarding prisoners of war. A captured white soldier would be held in a prison camp for the duration and, if wounded, given medical care. But black POWs were treated by rebel forces not as soldiers but as escaped slaves. If wounded, they were likely to be shot; if unharmed, sold into slavery. Time and again, observers told of southerners butchering wounded or cap-

tured black Union soldiers. The worst massacre occurred on April 12, 1864, at Fort Pillow, Tennessee, when Confederate General Nathan Bedford Forrest stood by while his troops, crying "No quarter!" slaughtered more than 100 black prisoners of war.

Neither fear of enemy atrocities nor blatant discrimination by their own command could stem the flow of black volunteers, however, and more and more African American units came into line. Black soldiers fought in most major battles from 1864 onward. In their most celebrated engagement, 38 black regiments were in the thick of the successful fight for the Confederate capital of Richmond, in September 1864. In a desperate battle at a place called Chaffins's Farm, no fewer than 10 black noncommissioned officers won the nation's highest decoration for valor, the newly established Medal of Honor: All had either rescued their colors from the enemy or taken command of assault units when white officers were felled. By war's end, 186,000 African Americans were serving in more than 150 regiments, making up almost 13 percent of the Union army's combat manpower; another 30,000 were in the navy. All told, 37,000 black men died during the four years of fighting.

Following a swift demobilization at the end of the war, four new African American regiments—the 9th and 10th Cavalry and the 24th and 25th Infantry—were organized as part of the Regular Army. These soldiers made up about 10 percent of the army's peacetime strength; but because few white communities in the East or South wanted black units stationed nearby, they were scattered across the western frontier, where for the next 25 years they faced hostility every way they turned. The black troops did their duty by battling the Indians, who respectfully called them buffalo soldiers (*pages* 150-153), while at the same time they were lashed by the bigotry of the white westerners they were risking their lives to protect.

Despite their valiant service, the racism and discriminatory treatment inflicted upon them actually grew worse during this period, particularly among the southern-

Master Sergeant George H. Wanton, displaying citations from two wars, earned his Medal of Honor in the Spanish-American War for repeatedly risking his life to rescue comrades from enemy hands.

In this *Harper's Monthly* Spanish-American War illustration, black medics carry a wounded officer to safety from an artillery battery engaged in heavy fighting.

In 1880 the U.S. Lifesaving Service—a forerunner of the Coast Guard—was suffering from a public black eye: It had just cashiered the white keeper and crew of its Pea Island (North Carolina) station for failing to aid a ship in distress. In a bold move to restore its damaged reputation, the service appointed Richard Etheridge, an African American, to be the station's new keeper and instructed him to choose an all-black crew. Etheridge handpicked his surfmen—the name given to long-time residents of the coast—and put them through such rigorous training that Pea Island Station was soon known in the service as "one of the tautest on the Carolina Coast."

The station's most storied rescue unfolded on October 11, 1896. A hurricane had blown in and the local beaches were awash in churning surf. Etheridge suspended regular beach patrols and stationed a crewman, Theodore Meekins, in the tower. At 7 p.m., through the heavy, blowing rain, Meekins caught the faint streak of a flare. Two miles down the beach the schooner E. S. Newman had run aground, and its crew was signaling for help.

Etheridge saw that extraordinary measures would be needed to reach the ship, which lay helpless a considerable distance from dry land. He tied a line around two of his men, anchored it on shore, and sent the pair wading into the surf. They boarded the Newman, lashed the captain's small daughter between them, then struggled back toward land. Alternating pairs of men repeated this perilous relay nine times to bring everyone safely ashore.

ers they encountered—civilians and soldiers alike. Nor did it abate when war broke out with Spain in April 1898, after the battleship USS *Maine* mysteriously exploded in Havana harbor in Spanish-controlled Cuba, carrying 266 crewmen, including 22 black sailors, to their death.

Without much evidence, an outraged U.S. government blamed the explosion on Spain and declared war. The army's four black regiments were swiftly transported to staging areas in the South for an invasion of Cuba. After their years on the frontier, the seasoned troops of the 9th and 10th Cavalry and the 24th and 25th Infantry were among the army's elite. To a considerable extent, success would rest on their shoulders. But in their Georgia and Florida camps, they were subjected to a racism that knew no bounds. In the land of Jim Crow—that body of laws and unwritten rules that kept southern blacks in a state of subjugation little removed from slavery—the buffalo soldiers faced hatred and abuse without letup on the streets, in eating places, on public conveyances, and even on the army posts themselves. In the worst incident, some drunken Ohio volunteers at Tampa, Florida, amused themselves by using a two-year-old black child as the target of a pretend marksmanship exhibition; the toddler was unharmed, but some of the bullets passed close enough to cut his clothing. Hearing of it, some men in the 24th and 25th Infantry rose in fury, attacking white soldiers and smashing white businesses—until they were overwhelmed and brutally beaten by a regiment of white Georgians.

Two days later, the black troops boarded a ship for Cuba. And there, despite the terrible treatment they had received at the hands of their fellow Americans and supposed comrades in arms, they fought magnificently. In the famed battle on and around San Juan Hill, elements of all four regiments joined Teddy Roosevelt's Rough Riders and other white units in storming Spanish positions.

Six African Americans won the nation's highest award for valor in that brief, bloody war; another 26 were awarded Certificates of Merit. John J. Pershing, a young white officer who would one day command the entire U.S. Army force in Europe during World War I, was a second lieutenant with the 10th on San Juan Hill. Colleagues in white regiments had nicknamed him Black Jack for his service with an African American unit, and he was proud of it. "We officers could have taken our black heroes into our arms," he said. And Teddy Roosevelt announced that no Rough Rider "will ever forget the tie that binds us to the 9th and 10th Cavalry."

Yet Roosevelt did worse than forget,

and rather quickly. Back home and politicking for the governorship of New York, Roosevelt belittled the African American contribution, saying that black noncoms lacked the ability to lead and that black troops had a tendency to "drift to the rear" under the strain of combat. But that gross slander, by a man who knew better, was not even the worst of it. Black units in the South existed in a bitterly racist social milieu, suffered the constant injustice and torment of Jim Crow laws, and even became the target of murderous assaults by gangs of hate-filled whites. Such persistent abuse was bound to cause a reaction; the wonder was that it was so long in coming. On August 23, 1917, a member of the 24th Infantry stationed in Houston, Texas, was arrested by the Houston police, and a rumor spread around the garrison that he had been shot. Between 100 and 150 enraged soldiers ignored an order to remain in their quarters, armed themselves, and headed for town. In the ensuing melee, 16 white civilians and four black soldiers were killed, with many more injured. The army reacted by convicting 110 black men of mutiny; 19 were hanged, and the rest received prison terms of varying severity, many of them life sentences. The harshness of the punishment exceeded anything in U.S. military history, and black Americans were stunned. Episcopal pastor Dr. George F. Miller called it "a military lynching" designed to appease the white South.

But by then the nation was engaged in World War I, and black calls for justice were brushed aside in the general excitement. Once again, despite the chain of past betrayals and disappointments, African Americans saw an opportunity to certify their worth and secure their citizenship. "First your country, then your rights," wrote educator and journalist W. E. B. Du Bois. The Central Committee of Negro College Men proclaimed: "Let us not mince matters; the race is on trial. It needs every one of its red-blooded, sober-minded men. Up brother, our race is calling."

But the opportunity proved fleeting. So many African American men rushed to

Their trim-fitting uniforms suggesting membership in one of the four black Regular Army regiments, a company of African American soldiers of the World War I era assembles for a publicity photograph with a white officer seated in front.

enlist—4,000 within a week—that the four buffalo soldier regiments were suddenly up to wartime strength. Having no more segregated units, the army closed enlistments to black men, while remaining open to an eventual 650,000 white volunteers. No African American volunteers at all were taken by the Marine Corps, and almost none for jobs other than mess steward by the increasingly discriminatory navy.

After snubbing thousands of black men who tried to express their patriotism by volunteering to fight for their country, the army soon found itself facing manpower shortages. Accordingly, it slapped together new segregated units and facilities and drafted almost 370,000 African Americans. Most of these men had been manual laborers in civilian life, and the army employed them as such, in some cases not even bothering to give them the rudiments of military training or issue them uniforms. But others were professionals—doctors, lawyers, teachers—and despite their education and skills, they, too, were mainly assigned to be stevedores, truck and wagon drivers, warehousemen, hod carriers, and ditch-and-latrine diggers.

Black soldiers clamored for combat, and here there was some progress. Although the buffalo soldier regiments, arguably the cream of the entire army, remained scattered around the country, the War Department formed two African American divisions, the 92d and 93d, of four new regiments each and sent them to fight in France. And for the first time, black officers—between 1,200 and 1,300 all told—would be in positions of leadership, at least at the levels of lieutenant and captain.

The 92d Division was hastily trained, poorly led by its white

Warmoth T. Gibbs, who signed up for the first black officers' reserve training camp in 1917, posed for this portrait shortly before his division, the 92d, sailed to France. Buffalo insignia and a campaign medal decorate Gibbs's uniform (top).

Soldiers of the 93d Infantry Division, the only black division in the Pacific theater in World War II, slog through the mud of a South Pacific island in 1944. Because of antiblack prejudice in the U.S. Army high command, the 93d never fought as a division; most of its units were assigned support duties behind the lines.

commanders, and ill regarded at army headquarters—American Expeditionary Force commander Black Jack Pershing, like Teddy Roosevelt before him, seemed to have forgotten the valor of the buffalo soldiers on San Juan Hill. Not surprisingly, the division did not meet with great success in battle. Its sister outfit, the 93d, was parceled out piecemeal to the French, among whom the black soldiers at long last felt welcome. Wrote one officer to his family: "I have never before experienced what it meant really to be free, to taste real liberty—in a phrase, 'to be a man.' " So friendly was the French reception of the African American regiments that Pershing's headquarters saw fit to warn the French about overfraternization and "the vices of the Negro." But the regiments performed illustriously in combat, and the French chose to honor hundreds of officers and men with the esteemed Croix de Guerre or the Legion of Honor, the only American troops to receive either medal.

After the armistice of November 11, 1918, Jim Crow took wing once more. Though the two divisions had suffered 6,000 casualties in defense of democracy, the executive officer of the USS *Virginia* blocked an African American unit from coming aboard for the voyage home and found a white unit to occupy its place. And on board the troop transport *Siboney*, a lone black captain was forced to eat his meals in solitude after 400 white officers had dined. "We return. We return from fighting. We return fighting," said a cruelly disappointed and thoroughly aroused W. E. B. Du Bois.

In spite of Du Bois's ringing words, the two decades after World War I saw little or no easing of antiblack prejudice and discrimination in society as a whole or in the armed forces. The period was one of retrenchment in the military. Manpower was set at low levels, funding was skimpy, and promotions were rare. No chance existed for African American activists to exercise any leverage on what had become once again

The all-black crew of a 40mm Bofors antiaircraft gun watch for German planes in the skies over France in the summer of 1944.

an insular, nearly all-white military establishment.

The situation began to improve a little as World War II approached and more men were taken into the service. Adding his voice to those of Du Bois and other leaders, Judge William H. Hastie, dean of the Howard University Law School, in Washington, D.C., attacked the practice of relegating African Americans in the armed forces to the most menial service jobs. "We will be American soldiers," he stated. "We will be American aviators. We will be American laborers. We will be anything that any other American should be in the whole program of national defense. But we won't be black auxiliaries."

The Selective Service Act passed in September 1940 seemed to address the point by promising that in America's first peacetime draft "there shall be no discrimination against any person on account of race or color." Later that month, black leaders submitted to the War Department a seven-point program calling for the integration of African Americans as officers and men throughout the services, subject only to the limits of their abilities. The administration of Franklin D. Roosevelt responded by promising that black combat units would be established and that African American men would be eligible for officer-candidate school and for pilot and aircrew training. But top officers would still be white only, and there would be no integrated units.

In November 1940, Judge Hastie was appointed a civilian aide to the secretary of war, with the job of coordinating policy on black troops. Then, Colonel Benjamin O. Davis, Sr., was promoted, becoming the army's first African American general. Before long, however, it became clear that in spite of grand pronouncements and a few token actions, the country's wartime leaders preferred business as usual. Judge Hastie would battle futilely for more than two years against racism and discrimination in the armed forces before finally resigning in frustration.

Well over a million black Americans were drafted into the armed forces during the war. Tens of thousands more black men—and women—volunteered. Yet of that vast assemblage, almost 90 percent were assigned to heavy labor of some sort. For justification, the army pointed to its General Classification Test: 80 percent of the black men tested scored in the lowest grades, from which the army drew its laborers. Critics argued that the test measured only educational level, not native intelligence or learning capacity; black men denied education in the South would of course score poorly. To no avail. The army's answer: "There is a consensus that colored units are inferior except for service duties." Thus stereotyped and stigmatized, African American enlisted men were systematically discriminated against in military post exchanges, theaters, buses, mess halls, clubs, even places of worship.

Black officers fared little better. The army made good its commitment to open officer-candidate school to African Americans and commissioned nearly 7,800 men during the war. The Army Air Force likewise trained about 1,000 pilots, who went on

to glory as the Tuskegee Airmen (*pages* 158-159). But officers' billets, messes, and clubs were routinely closed to the African American lieutenants and captains. So angry did African American soldiers become—GIs and officers alike—that riots broke out around the United States and overseas in the summer of 1943. And on a visit to African American troops in England in June 1943, Walter White, secretary of the National Association for the Advancement of Colored People (NAACP), was stunned to learn that when the soldiers talked about the "enemy" they meant their white compatriots, not the Nazis across the Channel.

Despite their justified bitterness, despondency, and blazing anger, African Americans contributed mightily to the Allied victory. And for the first time in any war, a considerable number of black women were allowed into the services. By the summer of 1945, some 120 black officers and almost 4,000 black enlisted women were serving in the Women's Army Corps. Another 479 African American nurses had been commissioned in the Army Nurse Corps. They suffered the same discrimination as black troopers—and perhaps more, as women—but did their jobs all the same.

As might be expected, the contributions by blacks in battle were disputed by some whites. Of three black infantry divisions formed for combat, only one saw heavy fighting, and that one drew sharp criticism from white observers. Reactivated from World War I, the 92d Infantry Division arrived in Italy in the spring of 1944 with a few black officers scattered among its white command structure. After some initial success, the division floundered in late 1944 and early 1945—to the point where it was withdrawn from the front lines.

The problem did not seem to be so much with individuals, considering the division's three Distinguished Service Crosses, 16 Legion of Merit awards, 95 Silver Stars, 753 Bronze Stars, and nearly 1,100 Purple Hearts. Investigators looking at the 92d focused on poor training, poor planning at the top, and poor leadership down the line—the few black officers were demoralized by grinding prejudice, and the white officers were of indifferent quality, resentful at being associated with blacks, and uninterested in the division's success or failure. Altogether, the unfortunate 92d made thoughtful military men wonder about the wisdom of maintaining segregated black units with uncaring, racist white commanders.

There wasn't much time to ponder the question in the wake of what happened immediately after the German army's Christmas 1944 surprise counteroffensive—the Battle of the Bulge. So desperately did the ruptured, back-pedaling American line need replacements that 2,800 African American volunteers were taken from service units, retrained for six weeks as infantrymen, formed into 50 all-black platoons, and slapped into depleted white companies. The black platoons attached to the famed Timberwolf Division proudly called themselves the Black Timberwolves—the fiercest of all the Timberwolves. And they proceeded to prove it, fighting effectively across Germany side by side with white platoons.

Second Lieutenant Frank E. Petersen, Jr., climbs into his Corsair fighter for a mission shortly after his April 1953 arrival in Korea. Petersen, the first African American marine pilot, also served in Vietnam and retired in 1988 a lieutenant general and the Marine Corps's senior aviator.

After the war, African American rights groups would not accept the usual return to the intolerable status quo. They continued to apply all the pressure in their power, until on July 26, 1948, President Harry S Truman issued Executive Order 9981, which stated: "It is the declared policy of the President that there shall be equality of treatment and opportunity for all persons in the armed services without regard to race, color, religion or national origin." Two years later, only the newly independent air force seemed to be seriously desegregating. Then, on June 25, 1950, the Korean War overtook events within the U.S. military, and the eruption of a desperate battle forced rapid change. Among the first units hurled against the Communist North Korean invaders of South Korea was the old 24th Infantry, still all black and now attached to the Eighth Army's 25th Division. The 24th fought about as well as other ill-prepared outfits drawn from sedentary garrison duty in Japan. And it had its share of heroes, including the first two African Americans to win the Medal of Honor in the 20th century: Private William Thompson, who died while single-handedly holding off overwhelming enemy numbers, and Sergeant Cornelius H. Charlton, who gave his life leading three charges to capture a North Korean position.

But white officers leveled strong accusations against the 24th as a whole, claiming that it performed badly before the enemy. Being a black regiment, it endured the harshest sort of criticism, along with a spate of court-martials so swift and severe that the NAACP mounted an investigation by attorney Thurgood Marshall, who later became the first African American member of the Supreme Court. Marshall uncovered such blatant injustice at the trials that 22 of 39 convictions for "misconduct before the enemy" were reduced or reversed. The root of the 24th's problem, Marshall announced, was the pervasive segregation that destroyed a black soldier's morale and sense of purpose, the very values that sustain men in combat.

To Far Eastern commander General Matthew B. Ridgway, long opposed to segregation on moral grounds, the solution appeared obvious: Desegregate. With the Pentagon's concurrence, Ridgway deactivated the all-black 24th and folded its men into previously all-white formations. He also used replacements and transfers to bring his units to a level of 10 to 15 percent black. The results spoke for themselves. African American soldiers responded so well to no longer being segregated into second-class status that their performance improved dramatically. Soon training commands and other army organizations followed suit. The army in Europe began genuine integration in the spring of 1952. Once moving, it progressed so swiftly that the service was widely integrated

Jesse Brown, the first black man to earn the navy's "wings of gold," mans his F4U-4 Corsair on the carrier USS *Leyte* during the Korean conflict. Brown was killed on December 4, 1950, while on a mission to help free a trapped marine division. Posthumously awarded the Distinguished Flying Cross and other medals, in 1973 he was also honored by having a ship named after him—the USS *Jesse L. Brown*.

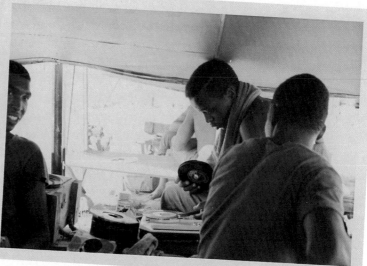

by the time the Korean War ended the following year. The navy and the marines also got down to business in 1952, but they had a long way to go.

Integration did not automatically produce equal treatment or opportunity, however, nor did it end white racism. A generation later the strains of the long, terrible Vietnam War tore great rents in the still-fragile fabric of black-white military relations. To begin with, a cluster of social circumstances combined to place black servicemen in Vietnam at greater risk of being wounded or killed than their white counterparts. In the first years of Vietnam, many African Americans, like most of their countrymen, supported the war. More than that, young black men, faced with relentless racism and discrimination in their quest for jobs in civilian life, tended to regard the armed forces as more integrated than any other segment of American society, the place where they had the best chance to advance on their merits. Thus, blacks volunteered for the armed forces at a significantly higher rate than did whites, and their reenlistment rate was much higher as well.

Proud to serve and eager to prove their mettle as bold, confident young fighting men, African Americans also volunteered in disproportionately high numbers for elite combat units, often making up more than 25 percent of marine line companies and army airborne outfits. And they showed what they were made of in noble fashion. When the fighting in Vietnam escalated dramatically in the late 1960s, black troops again and again exhibited outstanding combat effectiveness and selfless courage. Lieutenant Colonel (later to be General) Charles C. Rogers, though wounded three times, rallied his men in countercharge after countercharge to defeat three human-wave assaults on his artillery position. Sergeant Donald R. Long hurled himself on an enemy grenade to protect the eight men riding in his armored personnel carrier. And Marine Private First Class Oscar P. Austin left his safe position to bring back a wounded buddy lying exposed to heavy enemy fire, shielded the man from a grenade blast with his body, and then, with painful wounds of his own, interposed himself between his fellow marine and an enemy rifleman, knowingly giving his life to save his comrade. All three were awarded the Medal of Honor, and before the end of U.S. involvement in the war, 17 other African Americans would win the nation's highest decoration. In addition to their high rates of enlistment, reen-

In a photograph (*above, left*) taken by a fellow Blood, as African American troops in Vietnam called one another, Marine Lance Corporal Al Brogdon leads a search-and-destroy mission south of Danang in 1967. Brogdon was killed in action later that year. Bloods (*above*) enjoy a day's relaxation at a platoon patrol base, where Lance Corporal Ernest E. Washington prepares to play a record.

listment, and membership in elite combat units, African Americans were also being drafted in disproportionately high numbers. By 1966 they made up almost 16 percent of all draftees, a rate attributable to a relative lack of college exemptions among blacks. This meant that black troops were often at the forefront of the fighting and suffered terrible casualty rates.

Ironically, black Americans had struggled throughout most of U.S. history for the right to fight for their country. But by the time of Vietnam, when the fighting qualities of African Americans were no longer in question, racism seemed to have taken another tack: Put blacks out on the line, while keeping whites in the safe, rear-area jobs. In 1967, twenty percent of army fatalities were black, leading to a charge that blacks were being used as cannon fodder. Eventually, over the entire Vietnam period, the casualty rates evened out—deaths of black servicemen made up 12.5 percent of all deaths, a rate that more or less matched the 11.6 percent proportion of African Americans in the U.S. forces in Vietnam. But the surge of deaths among black soldiers in the late 1960s was deeply disturbing to African American leaders.

Black advocacy groups pointed an accusing finger at military classification tests. These tests, they said, were racially and educationally biased, ensuring that the average black recruit would wind up being trained for and assigned to either a combat unit, where his life would be at hazard, or to a low-skilled, dead-end service position, where he would perform menial labor and receive no training useful in the civilian world. The sort of high-tech training that would win promotions in the service and well-paying jobs in civilian life was going primarily to whites. And for all the talk about black officers, only 116 nonwhites were attending the service academies in 1969, and less than three percent of the combined officers' corps of all the armed forces were black. Most of these languished in junior ranks; among 380 battalion commanders in Vietnam in 1967, only two were African Americans.

Many of these findings became public at a time when the civil rights movement was battling more and more with prejudice and injustice at home. In the minds of many black leaders, the only proper place for a young African American to be fighting was back home in racist America, not in an unholy war on some distant field. Starting in 1966 and continuing until his assassination in 1968, Dr. Martin Luther King, Jr., spoke out with growing anger against U.S. participation in the Vietnam War. Dr. King's message, coupled with a rising sense of self among young African Americans and continuing inequities in the services, brought a reversal in attitudes among black servicemen. Blacks who were making careers in the military began to be regarded as Uncle Toms, and in consequence reenlistment rates plummeted. At the same time, African Americans gave voice to a torrent of pent-up grievances and charges of racism in the services.

Black servicemen complained of an insensitivity to black cultural identity in the white-dominated command structure. Post exchanges generally carried no black periodicals, no music that appealed to black tastes, no favored foods or products. Moreover, many white soldiers persisted in demonstrating hatred and contempt for black people. A thing that particularly angered blacks was the proliferation of Confederate flags, bumper stickers, and auto tags. And it wounded and infuriated African

Americans when white sailors at a shore post in Vietnam donned improvised Ku Klux Klan robes to make merry over the assassination of Martin Luther King.

When African American troops lashed out in reaction to such insults and outrages, they were the ones punished. Indeed, black servicemen charged that they were routinely disciplined for things white troops got away with. Thus, African American soldiers were scourged not only by the open hostility of many of their fellow enlisted men but also by bigotry and injustice at command levels. In the Vietnam era, an astounding 45 percent of all black enlisted men, a number far higher than in any previous war, received less than honorable discharges upon completion of service.

In July 1969, a platoon sergeant of the army's 506th Infantry Regiment leads his men through a sweltering tropical rain forest in the A Shau Valley of Vietnam.

Matters came to a head in 1970 and 1971, when a series of race riots, sit-down strikes, and other disruptions swept through the armed forces. Military authorities, acting in an atmosphere of alarm and tension, launched investigations that revealed that African Americans were justified in their rage. "There is discrimination and racism in this command," confessed the Air Training Command, "and it is ugly."

Clearly, racism had to end, or the military might well unravel. As a first step, the Pentagon announced that fitness reports for both officers and noncoms would include ratings on their racial attitudes and commitment to equal opportunity. Further, all officer-promotion boards henceforth would have minority representation. A 15 percent objective for black enrollment in officer-candidate schools was established, and the 1972 roster at Annapolis included 150 blacks among 905 midshipmen. Commanders everywhere were instructed to be aggressive in dealing with de facto segregation and racial discrimination wherever they might be found. Suddenly, Afro haircuts were okay, PXs stocked up on black products, and even a Black Power salute became acceptable, so long as it signified a greeting between brothers.

By now the divisive, bloodletting American role in the Vietnam War had wound down. The U.S. government announced that the draft would be discontinued and the military would convert to an all-volunteer force. African Americans waited to see how strong and continuing would be its commitment to equality.

The armed forces that fought in Grenada, Panama, and the Persian Gulf and responded to the humanitarian crisis in Somalia have been composed, to the last man and woman, of people who chose to serve. The all-volunteer military became a reality in 1973, and for African Americans it offered fairness and opportunity heretofore largely denied. The response has been both dramatic and troubling.

So much have the armed forces improved that they cast an unflattering light on the status of opportunities for African Americans in civilian life. Many bright young

black people who would prefer a civilian career find that the military now far out-strips the private sector in living up to the ideals expressed in the Constitution and the Bill of Rights. For many the military has—by default—become the career of choice. More than 400,000 black servicemen and women were on active duty in 1992, making up 30 percent of the army, 20 percent of the marines, and 13 percent of the navy. Strongly affirming the openness of the military to minorities, an African American officer, General Colin Powell (*page* 177), sat at the apex of all U.S. armed forces as chairman of the Joint Chiefs of Staff, and another 100 black officers wore at least one star. Black officers skippered navy aircraft carriers and nuclear submarines and directed air force commands and marine divisions. There was depth as well: almost 19,000 black commissioned officers, along with 94,000 of the noncoms who are the core of every military establishment. And as of late 1989, black women made up 13 percent of the armed forces' female officers' corps. Among them were two brigadier generals, Clara Adams-Ender and the now-retired Sherian Cadoria (*pages* 172-173).

Up and down the line, blacks and whites lived in the same barracks, ate at the same tables at the same messes, and received equal treatment at PXs, barbershops, theaters, bowling alleys, and swimming pools. The once-segregated clubs were no more, and the atmosphere was amicable. "Today one is more likely to hear racial jokes in a faculty club than in an officers' club," wrote one observer. "And in an officers' club one will surely see more blacks."

No one pretends that all issues have been resolved. Though their percentages in combat units have declined sharply, African Americans still are more likely than whites to wind up in support units and less likely to be found in such super-tech fields as signal intelligence and electronic warfare. Charges continue to be leveled of unfair punishment for infractions, laggardly advancement, and a persistent imbalance in the number of black officers. But in general the new partnership is growing and flourishing. Doris Miller would be glad to know that.

Watching for Iraqi jets, an African American marine guides a buddy as he targets a possible intruder with a Stinger surface-to-air missile launcher in February 1991 during Operation Desert Storm.

OPERATING UNDER COVER IN THE REVOLUTIONARY WAR

It was 1781, and the Revolutionary War was in its sixth year. Benedict Arnold, a former American general, had already turned traitor and was leading British army troops on raids in Virginia. For assistance, Arnold depended on a helpful black man named James Armistead, a slave from a nearby farm who had volunteered to guide the redcoats along the local roads. But what Arnold did not know was that Armistead was an undercover American agent. Like a number of other patriotic blacks of the time, including a South Carolina slave named Antigua (*document, near right*), Armistead had offered to serve as a spy for the colonies. With his master's permission, he became an agent of the Marquis de Lafayette, the French nobleman who had come to General George Washington's aid in 1777.

Armistead's role proved crucial in containing the British raids. As Arnold's servant, he was often present when plans were being made for the attacks, and as a black man and a slave, he was all but invisible to the white officers, who spoke freely around him. Armistead sent Lafayette reports on British activity almost daily. Using his information, the patriots once staged a raid on the British camp that nearly bagged Benedict Arnold himself.

When Arnold was sent north, Armistead signed on with Lord Cornwallis, commander of the British forces in the South, who was then based on the Virginia coast at Portsmouth. Serving in Cornwallis's tent, he again was able to overhear the staff officers laying out strategies, which he secretly passed to Lafayette.

In July 1781, a fleet of ships dropped anchor near Cornwallis's camp, and the next month the British commander and his force set sail to an unknown destination. Armistead relayed the news to Lafayette, who passed it on to Washington, explaining that the intelligence came from "a correspondent of mine, servant to Lord Cornwallis."

Lafayette's scouts found the British army at Yorktown, a small tobacco port on a river that empties into the Chesapeake Bay. Cornwallis was digging in and fortifying the town, Armistead reported. In response, Washington ordered a fleet of ships, which the French government had provided in 1781, to blockade the bay, and dispatched troops to surround the British camp. Meanwhile, Cornwallis sent his trusted servant Armistead to spy on Lafayette.

Cornwallis was trapped by the French fleet and, in what would be the last major battle of the Revolution, surrendered. When he presented himself at Lafayette's headquarters, he was shocked to find his servant James there, obviously on good terms with the French military leader. He is said to have shaken his head in surprise that he had been deceived by an African American spy.

Armistead secured a written testimonial of his exploits from Lafayette, which he used in 1786 to persuade the Virginia legislature to free him and, later, award him a pension. After the war, he went by the name James Lafayette, in honor of the marquis.

This 1783 South Carolina law praises the spy called Antigua, a slave about whom little is known, for obtaining information "from within the enemy's lines, frequently at the risk of his life." The act frees Antigua's wife and child; presumably he remained enslaved.

Topped by a likeness of James Armistead Lafayette, this souvenir copy of the certificate in which the Marquis de Lafayette attested to the former slave's daring service as a spy during the Revolutionary War was probably created in 1824, the year the two men last met.

THE HIGH PRICE OF GLORY

Sergeant William H. Carney (*above*) displays the flag he carried during the battle at Fort Wagner. Badly wounded in his legs, arms, and chest, Carney later declared that "the old flag never touched the ground." His Medal of Honor, inscribed "for gallantry at Fort Wagner, S.C.," is shown at right.

Boston buzzed with excitement in May 1863, when the thousand black volunteers of the Massachusetts 54th Infantry Regiment marched off to do battle in the Civil War. In occupied parts of the Confederacy, former southern slaves and free black men were already fighting for the Union. But the men of the 54th, led by white commissioned officers, represented something new—the first regiment composed mainly of free black volunteers from the northern states. Massachusetts governor John Andrew, an abolitionist, had gotten permission for this "noble experiment," as he called it, shortly after the Emancipation Proclamation became law on January 1, 1863. The nation waited to see the results.

The Confederacy was well known for its ruthless contempt for black soldiers. Wounded black prisoners of war were shot dead, and the healthy ones sold into slavery. And just days before the Massachusetts 54th marched out of Boston, the Confederate Congress issued a proclamation announcing that white officers captured while leading black troops would be executed.

Even the federal government did not throw its full support behind the new black unit. It offered the men of the 54th little more than half the pay of white soldiers. Massachusetts was willing to make up the difference, but the men refused anything less than the full amount from the leaders in Washington, D.C. In addition, white skeptics, including military personnel, questioned whether black men would stand up under enemy fire.

The answer came six weeks

later, when the 54th led the charge against Fort Wagner, a Confederate stronghold at the mouth of the Charleston, South Carolina, harbor. Although the attack failed, the black soldiers of the 54th proved their mettle. Advancing through the darkness along a narrow strip of beach, they were raked by ferocious rifle and cannon fire from the fort. They pressed on and scaled the parapets in desperate hand-to-hand fighting. White regiments arrived to bolster the Union force, but the men were too few and the enemy too fierce; the troops were forced to retire.

Almost 300 of the 54th's men were killed or wounded in the assault. But the regiment had won the respect due a true fighting unit. Four of its enlisted men were decorated for bravery. One, Sergeant William Carney (*left*), became the first African American to win the highest U.S. military award, the Medal of Honor.

Not until June 1864 did Congress grant the men full pay, including back wages. But the 54th's heroism had opened the door to black enlistment. By the war's end, at least 186,000 men of African descent had served under the Union flag.

The heroes of the Massachusetts 54th, led by Colonel Robert Gould Shaw (*foreground*), are immortalized in this bas-relief, created as part of an 1897 Boston monument by the well-known sculptor Augustus Saint-Gaudens.

THE BUFFALO SOLDIERS: SENTINELS OF THE FRONTIER

Within a year after the Civil War ended, the vast Union army had disbanded, its hundreds of thousands of veterans sent back home. Left in its place was a peacetime army of about 54,000 men that was about to become engaged in the Indian wars of the western frontier. Fully a fifth of that thin line of western soldiers were African Americans, taken into the army as regulars for the first time in the nation's history.

Of the 35 permanent army regiments that evolved by 1869, four were all-black units—the 9th and 10th Cavalry and the 24th and 25th Infantry. They were stationed on the frontier, and would remain mostly segregated from society for the better part of a century. These African American units would play a major role in developing the West. But their most important job for 25 years after the Civil War was to protect Americans from outlaws, Mexican revolutionaries, and, especially, Indians, who were fighting for their homelands. The black troops came to be called buffalo soldiers by their Native American foes, a name of honor believed to have been inspired by the resemblance between their fighting spirit and that of the buffalo, revered by the Plains Indians for its strength and stamina.

Of the total number of men who enlisted in the four buffalo soldier regiments—about 12,500 between 1866 and 1898—most reported for duty with little education and almost no experience. Nevertheless, within a few years the black regiments boasted some of the ablest soldiers on the Plains. Because they had the army's lowest desertion rates and highest reenlistment rates, the regiments soon were manned almost completely by veterans, experienced in

A machine-gun company of the 24th Infantry Regiment passes in review on its way to Mexico to chase down the perpetrators of an attack on Columbus, New Mexico, in 1916 (*below*). The canteen and cap at left were 25th Infantry standard issue in the late 19th century.

the terrain and the fierce fighting style of the Indians.

The 24th and 25th Infantry ranged across the West. Their duties, if not glamorous, were demanding and important. They constructed military posts; opened roads, strung telegraph lines, and laid railroads; tracked horse thieves and cattle rustlers; fended off Indian attacks; and guarded strategic points.

The 9th Cavalry, established near New Orleans, headed for west Texas, a region fraught with conflict between American settlers, Comanche and Kiowa Indians, and Mexicans. During the 9th's service there, Sergeant Emanuel Stance of F Troop received the Medal of Honor—the first of 18 that would be awarded to buffalo soldiers for bravery between 1869 and 1890—while leading a mission to find two whites who had been kidnapped during an Indian raid. The 9th also confronted Apache bands led by such indomitable chiefs as Victoria, Nana, Cochise, and Geronimo. The regiment was later transferred north, where it performed scout duty in Sioux country during the winter of 1890-91, when the Indian wars came to an end.

The 10th Cavalry was best known for its frequent confrontations with Cheyenne, Comanche, Kiowa, and Apache warriors. Organized at Fort Leavenworth, Kansas, and stationed in Kansas and Indian Territory, the 10th reported to its post in September 1867. It ran head-on into the Cheyenne when a 34-man scouting party was attacked by a force of 70 to 80 warriors; after six hours of battle, the soldiers escaped, only to be chased on horseback for 15 miles before reaching safety. In the same month, 60 Cheyenne attacked a small party of the 10th; the battle lasted two days, with only two civilian laborers killed and one soldier wounded. Among the 10th's later achievements was the rescue of about 50 scouts who had suffered heavy casualties and run out of rations while under siege by some 700 Indians on an island in the Republican River. The 10th also participated in the final capture of the great Apache chief Geronimo.

One of those serving in the 10th was Lieutenant Henry Ossian Flipper, who had endured cruel racism at West Point to become the first African American graduate of the military academy, in 1877. In 1878 Flipper was assigned to the 10th at Fort Sill, in Indian Territory—the first black officer to serve in a buffalo soldier regiment. But in 1881, the young officer was court-martialed on a trumped-up charge, lodged by white racist fellow officers, that he had misused government funds. "The trap was cunningly laid," Flipper wrote of his ordeal, "and I was sacrificed." Flipper

The Machine Gun Troop of the 10th Cavalry assembles for inspection at Fort Myer, Virginia, near Washington, D.C., in 1932.

went on to have a distinguished career as a civil engineer; he died in 1940. In 1976 his case was reopened, the charges declared false, and he was awarded a posthumous honorable discharge.

Indeed, Prejudice and discrimination proved as daunting an enemy to the buffalo soldiers as the most brilliant Indian war chief. They routinely received third-rate equipment, horses rejected by white cavalry units, and terrible rations. White officers often refused to work with them, and the very people who depended on them for protection frequently treated them worse than they did the outlaws and Indians. Despite the hardships, however, the record of the buffalo soldier regiments shines with distinction. After the Indian wars, they formed the hard-fighting core of the American forces in Cuba during the Spanish-American War and, accord-ing to some sources, led the charge up San Juan Hill.

These crack units were relegated to stateside non-combat duty in World War I, but they did get into World War II. That war saw an end to fighting on horseback, and the 9th and 10th Cavalry were deactivated in 1944, their manpower for the most part distributed among service units. The 25th Infantry, placed in the new all-black 93d Division, was scattered when that division was broken up in 1944. The 24th Infantry carried the proud history of the buffalo soldiers into the Korean conflict, as did the 9th and 10th Cavalry, which were reactivated as tank battalions; but all trace of the buffalo soldiers' organizational lineage passed into oblivion when the army was desegregated in the early 1950s.

This 10th Cavalry regimental flag—in army terminology a "national standard"—was used by the buffalo soldiers unit from 1898 to 1902.

152

Jones Morgan. "It was like a scout camp," said 110-year-old Jones Morgan (*below*), speaking in 1992 of his stint as a buffalo soldier in the cavalry. Morgan, a minor, ran away from home twice to enlist in the army. The first time, the 15-year-old spent six months in training with "a gun made out of sticks" before his family found him and took him back home. But he soon lit out again, and this time had contact with Indians and saw action in Cuba before his second and last removal from the service.

"Ready and forward" reads the motto of the buffalo soldiers, which was adopted in 1902.

"The Indians wasn't fighting much against us," he recalled of his days in garrison with the buffalo soldiers out West. "The Indians was grown," while he and his equally underage buddies who had run away to enlist together "wasn't grown. We got along well," he said of the Indians. "I'd tell them my belly hurt and they'd make the medicine"—cedar tea and other natural remedies.

In Cuba, as a very young cavalryman, Morgan helped tend the mounts of Teddy Roosevelt and the Rough Riders. He was treated with the same respect accorded white soldiers in the battle: "You had to work together," he said. Morgan became a hotel cook and a railroad worker after leaving the military.

John Morton-Finney. A Kentucky-born lover of learning—he had earned 11 academic degrees by 1989, his 100th year—John Morton-Finney (*above*) enlisted in the 24th Infantry in 1911, at age 22. He had his eyes on the future. "I saved my money so I could go to school when I left the army," he said in 1993. "Black and white, they paid us $15 a month."

Morton-Finney arrived at his first post, in the Philippines, on January 1, 1912. "It was a time of peace," he recalled, so his most vivid memories of the experience were not of combat but of figuring out his unit's location during secret maneuvers by recognizing scenes he had learned about in his study of Philippine history.

Morton-Finney rose to corporal and then to sergeant, but he ran into a stone wall of racial discrimination when he aspired to earn a commission as an officer. "After that, I said, 'There isn't anything for me in the army,' and I got out," he recalled. In 1914, with $300 in his pocket, he "made a beeline straight for Howard University." He would go on to become a teacher and lawyer, along the way acquiring fluency in six foreign languages—including French, which he picked up in 1918-19 after being drafted back into the army during World War I and serving in France. Honored at Harvard University in 1990 for his lifetime of scholarship, Morton-Finney referred in a later interview to his enslaved forebears to explain his passion for education: "I always kept in mind how they were denied, by law and by custom, the right to read or write."

153

This photo, taken from the Fort Brown side of Garrison Road, looks down Cowen Alley, where spent shells were found on the night of the shooting. The alley was named for the Cowen house (*foreground*), from which two persons claimed to have seen the soldiers fire. But not one clue was ever found that incriminated them.

AN UGLY CASE OF PEACETIME RACISM

In the summer of 1906, the white residents of Brownsville, Texas, were outraged to find that a battalion of black soldiers from the 25th Infantry had been stationed at Fort Brown, a local army post. The resulting tensions led within weeks to a mysterious shooting incident and the discharge of almost every enlisted man in the battalion's three companies.

It began sometime near midnight on August 13, when a sentry at Fort Brown heard shots being fired from Garrison Road, a lane separating the barracks from the town. A trumpeter sounded the call to arms, and the soldiers formed up for a roll call. All 167 men were accounted for—165 were present and two were away on 24-hour passes. The battalion officers, who were white, assumed the fort had been attacked by a mob; on the other side of Garrison Road, townsfolk thought they had been attacked by the soldiers.

Whoever fired the rounds disappeared, leaving behind a white man who had been fatally shot and a wounded police officer; a handful of spent cartridges, left by the raiders, was found in a nearby alley. Examination revealed that the shells could have been fired only by the army's new Springfield rifle.

Government investigators focusing on the soldiers failed to find the culprits and accused the black battalion of a "conspiracy of silence." President Theodore Roosevelt then dismissed all 167 soldiers "without honor," barring them from further military service. Among those drummed out was Sergeant Mingo Sanders, who eight years earlier had shared his company's hardtack with Roosevelt's Rough Riders in the Spanish-American War.

At a Senate hearing held in 1908 at the urging of Ohio senator Joseph Benson Foraker, questions about the investigation were raised. For instance, several of the shell casings found after the shooting had been fired from a rifle that was in a locked storeroom at the time of the incident. Nothing, however, came of the hearing. A year later, again in response to Foraker, an army court of inquiry heard the case; their verdict deemed 14 men eligible to reenlist but left the status of the remaining 153 unchanged.

Decades passed. Then Augustus Hawkins, a black congressman from California, read a 1970 book, *The Brownsville Raid*, by John D. Weaver, that argued for the men's innocence. Hawkins made an impassioned speech before the House of Representatives, sparking a Defense Department review of the case. On September 28, 1972, the secretary of the army cleared all the men, citing "gross injustice." Only two former members of the battalion were still living: Edward Warfield, one of the 14 men allowed to reenlist, and Dorsie Willis, who had been shining shoes for 59 years. "That dishonorable discharge kept me from improving my station," said Willis. "Only God knows what it did to the others."

This 1907 cartoon mocks Senator Joseph Foraker for his defense of the black soldiers. At one point, investigators tried to implicate members of Company B's baseball team simply because their picture (*right*) happened to be available.

COMRADES TO THE FRENCH

In the predawn hours of May 14, 1918, Privates Henry Johnson and Needham Roberts of the black 369th Infantry Regiment were manning a forward observation post near Allied lines in north-eastern France. Suddenly Johnson heard a cutting sound coming from a nearby barbed-wire barrier. He quickly sent up a flare to alert the rest of the regi-ment and shouted for the corpo-ral in charge of the guard detail. Before the 369th could scramble into action, however, a raiding party of about 20 German sol-diers came into view. The Ger-mans launched a grenade attack, and the black soldiers found themselves alone at the center of a desperate fight. Roberts, badly wounded, was nearly tak-en prisoner by two Germans. He was saved by Johnson, who, though crippled by a broken leg, killed one of the attackers; the other fled. The two Americans continued to fight off the enemy until the raiders finally retreated.

The skirmish was one of many proud moments for the more than 2,000 men of the 369th, who called themselves the Black Rattlers. (The Ger-mans, perhaps acknowl-edging the soldiers' feroci-ty, called them Hellfight-ers.) It also won Johnson (*right*) and Roberts the Croix de Guerre, France's highest military award.

Private Henry Johnson proudly wears the Croix de Guerre (*far right*), awarded for heroism in battle. He and Private Need-ham Roberts, both from the 369th Infantry Regiment, were the first Americans to win the French military decoration.

James Reese Europe, the 369th's bandleader, conducts an open-air jazz concert in Auteuil, France. Army reg-ulations stipulated 28-member bands, but Europe, a well-known musician, negotiated for a 48-piece group.

Flag-waving crowds lining the streets of Harlem welcome home the 369th Infantry during its 1919 victory parade. In peacetime, the unit had been part of the New York 15th National Guard; its Harlem armory was a cigar store and the dance hall upstairs.

Soon after their homecoming, members of the 369th enjoy a stateside chicken dinner in celebration of their return.

A year earlier, nothing had seemed more unlikely. The American military routinely assigned its segregated black troops to serve in support positions rather than in combat. But as it became clear in the spring of 1917 that the United States would be drawn into World War I, black leaders protesting the military's discriminatory policy made some headway. Along with several other black units, the 369th was sent overseas to fight. But they would not be serving alongside white Americans. Instead, General John J. Pershing, commander of the American Expeditionary Force, ordered the regiment to strengthen French forces stationed some 75 miles northeast of Paris. The French received their new comrades with open arms, supplying them with equipment and uniforms. The 369th repaid their hosts in part with concerts by the regimental band, which is often credited with bringing jazz to France.

The band toured Europe early in 1918, rejoining the regiment around April, in time to take part in the first of four campaigns the 369th would fight that year. It was in the fall, however, in the Meuse-Argonne campaign, that the unit saw some of its heaviest combat. During the period from September 26 to October 1, the 369th suffered 785 casualties, about one-third of its strength. By war's end that winter, the regiment had served 191 days in combat—more than any other American unit—and won an as-tounding 170 medals, all awarded by the French.

For the soldiers of the 369th, peace brought with it a sharp reminder of the racial tensions they would face in the States: One troopship refused to transport them home. The men did return to America on February 12, 1919, and a few days later they marched with other soldiers down New York's Fifth Avenue (*background*). The 369th was then permitted to break off to parade through Harlem, where they received a heroes' welcome.

FIGHTING TO FLY: THE TUSKEGEE AIRMEN

It was the best Coca-Cola of his life. In the heat of the North African desert, on July 2, 1943, Lieutenant Charles B. Hall, a fighter pilot from Brazil, Indiana, was celebrating with his buddies. The men belonged to the Army Air Corps's first all-black flying unit, the 99th Fighter Squadron, and Hall had just scored the outfit's first kill, shooting down a German fighter plane over Sicily. Someone fetched "the closely guarded squadron prize," recalled a fellow pilot, and "eyes and mouths watered as C.B. took the chilled bottle of Coca-Cola and guzzled it down to the last drop."

For the pilots of the 99th, getting into the war at all had been quite a feat. In 1917, during World War I, Georgia-born combat pilot

Eugene Jacques Bullard had flown with the French because his own country had no use for a black airman, and by the eve of World War II, U.S. policy had changed little. So few African Americans could overcome racial prejudice to get flight training that only 102 black civilians held pilot's licenses before the war. The army, aside from its official stand that blacks were mentally and physically inferior to whites, knew it could not muster enough trained pilots to form a complete unit. "We fought two wars," recalled squadron member Louis R. Purnell, echoing a familiar lament, "one with the enemy and the other back home in the U.S.A."

In 1939 Congress passed the Civilian Pilot Training Act,

which—under pressure from concerned individuals, the nation's African American press, and organizations such as the National Urban League and the NAACP—included young black men, affording them their first federally funded chance to earn their wings. But the Army Air Corps snubbed Congress's initiative and continued to turn blacks away from service for another two years—until a Howard University student sued the War Department in January 1941. The army relented immediately, announcing plans to build a military pilot training unit for black Americans at the Tuskegee Institute in Alabama.

On July 19, the first 13 cadets began training at the new Tuskegee Army Air Base. Meanwhile,

Charles Anderson, a pilot and trainer, escorts First Lady Eleanor Roosevelt on a 30-minute flight around Tuskegee Air Base in the late 1930s.

Captain Erwin B. Lawrence, commander of the 99th Figher Squadron in April 1944, was killed during an attack on a German airfield—one of 66 Tuskegee Airmen to perish in World War II.

almost 300 black GIs had been sent to Chanute Field in Illinois to learn aircraft maintenance, armaments, and communications. The future unit—the 99th Pursuit Squadron, later called the 99th Fighter Squadron—would be all black from the ground up. "I don't think any other air force group stuck together as a team like we did," said Master Sergeant Fred Archer, an armaments specialist.

Tuskegee began graduating its fighter pilots the following March—three months after Pearl Harbor—but the army kept the unit in Alabama as subsequent classes of cadet pilots went through the same training. With no combat experience, recalled Purnell, "it looked as though the black squadron was in danger of becoming a white elephant."

At last, in April 1943, a jubilant 99th shipped out to North Africa for theater indoctrination—military parlance for instruction about their mission. The next year, they merged with the 100th, 301st, and 302d fighter squadrons to form the all-black 332d Fighter Group, known popularly as the Tuskegee Airmen. From a new base in Italy, the pilots escorted Allied bombers through treacherous European airspace, repelling German interceptors in hair-raising dogfights—and destroyed ground targets with machine-gun fire and rockets. The 332d, unlike other escort units, gave door-to-door protection in their distinctive red-tailed fighter planes. Instead of hanging back out of flak range during a bombing run and rejoining the bombers on their way out, the Tuskegee Airmen stayed with the bombers throughout the attack. So "brave a choice," said one bomber pilot, made them "the best of shepherds."

By the end of the war, the 332d had flown 1,578 missions, destroyed or damaged more than 950 vehicles on the ground and 400 enemy aircraft—charting one air-combat record of 13 kills in a single day—and had even sunk a German destroyer. Winning some 900 medals, the four squadrons also received a Distinguished Unit Citation praising them for "outstanding performance of duty." Perhaps most impressive, they set a record that was unmatched by any other unit with as many missions: Of all the bombers they escorted, they never lost one to an enemy fighter.

BATTLING THE ELEMENTS ON THE ALCAN HIGHWAY

"NO PICNIC," warned the army's 1942 advertisement recruiting civilian workers to help forge the first overland route to Alaska. "Men hired for this job will be required to work and live under the most extreme conditions imaginable." Thousands willingly signed on, but for the 3,695 soldiers in the all-black 93d, 95th, and 97th regiments of the U.S. Army Corps of Engineers, Uncle Sam offered no choice. Shipped north in the spring of 1942, these men made up about a third of the military force that, together with a large contingent of civilians, bulldozed and bridged 1,500 miles of rugged terrain—including five mountain ranges and 100 rivers—to construct the Alaska-Canada Military Highway. Snaking between British Columbia's Dawson Creek and Delta Junction, near Fairbanks, the Alcan—now called the Alaska—Highway was completed in only eight months and 12 days, allowing trucks to bring supplies and personnel to America's northernmost territory, which lay under the threat of an imminent Japanese invasion.

The African American soldiers were to work south from Alaska and meet up at the border with all-white regiments heading north from Canada. Although conditions were grueling for everyone, the black regiments suffered the most. To appease an army general who believed African American troops would mix with Indians and Eskimos to create a "race of mongrels," officials assigned the black units to the remotest areas of the route, where there were no facilities, limited human contact, and little fresh food. In addition, the black soldiers often had to work with worn-out equipment and did not get enough even of that. Despite the hardships, the soldiers' morale was high; they saw the conditions as a challenge and itched to show their stuff in a competition with white troops.

In the first months, as spring stretched into summer and the sun shone around the clock, the men worked in shifts 24 hours a day, seven days a week. The temperature rose to 90 degrees, transforming the frozen ground into muck and forcing the men to adopt an arduous road-building method called corduroying—setting logs crosswise to the direction of the road, up to five layers deep.

The miseries of summer were compounded by mosquitoes incubating in the soggy ground. They emerged by the millions, forcing the soldiers to cover their heads with netting. "Every time you'd lift the net to take a bite of food, dozens of mosquitoes would fly in and bite you on the face," recalled Clifton Monk, a staff sergeant in the 97th. At the other extreme, the winter of 1942-43 brought the coldest weather ever recorded in Alaska, at times more than 70 degrees below zero. While the white troops, nearer civilization, lived in heated barracks, the African American soldiers had to make do with tents.

When the southbound 97th arrived at the Canadian border in September 1943, they were all alone. "We were supposed to meet the 18th coming up from the south," said Walter E. Mason, an officer with the 97th. "When they didn't show up, we kept on going." On October 25, Corporal Refines Sims, Jr., bulldozing some 20 miles deep into Canada, met an identical machine piloted by a private in the all-white 18th Regiment. Slowly approaching each other, the two touched blades in a ceremonial gesture.

The job done, the army cited the 93d, 95th, and 97th for meritorious conduct. And while other black soldiers, who had not had a chance to prove their mettle, were being relegated to "housekeeping" duty in the States, these hardy men were assigned combat roles in campaigns around the globe.

Members of the Army's all-black 95th Engineers pause in their work on the Alcan Highway to warm themselves over a fire. The soldiers had no access to indoor heating.

160

Men of the 95th construct a log bridge across the rushing Sikanni Chief River in July 1942. Given only a week to build the bridge, they finished in half the time, producing a structure so sturdy that it long outlasted the war.

Black engineers lay a corduroy road-bed of logs over a mushy stretch of peat bog and decaying vegetation called muskeg (*above*). At left, GIs pull back the netting that protects them from Alaska's voracious mosquitoes just long enough for a photographer to get a shot of their faces.

CRACKING THE NAVY'S COLOR LINE

On a spring day in 1944, twenty-seven-year-old George Cooper strode into Chicago's main railroad terminal, neatly turned out in his new uniform: dress blues with the naval officer's insignia on his cap. Cooper's appearance produced a surprised hush in the terminal as passengers and ticket agents turned to stare. "Everywhere I'd go, everything would stop," he later recalled. Cooper was black, and no one had ever seen a black naval officer. In the 146-year history of the U.S. Navy there never had been one. Cooper and 12 other young men—the Golden 13, as they came to be called—had just put an end to that racist record.

Before World War II, the navy, then the most racially restrictive branch of service, had either refused to take in black volunteers or limited them to menial jobs such as mess steward. Even after the Japanese attack on Pearl Harbor in 1941, the navy clung to its policy of discouraging black enlistments and barring black sailors from any sea duty except as messmen.

Pressure from the White House and black rights activists soon forced open some doors. African Americans began streaming into the navy as volunteers or draftees, and sea-duty opportunities for black sailors increased. Then, in 1943, President Roosevelt ordered an unwilling navy to include black candidates in a new training program for officers.

"The brown envelope was sealed and had my orders in it, but I didn't know what they were for at the time," said Jesse Arbor, stationed in Boston in January 1944. Like 15 other black sailors, he had been summoned to the naval training station at Great Lakes, Illinois. To their surprise, the men learned that they were to receive officer training. None of the 16 knew why they had been singled out, nor did they ever discover why three of their number were quietly dropped soon after the training began. The navy has since lost its official records relating to the program.

But each of the 13 survivors had shown a talent for leadership, all but one possessed a college degree or more, and several were outstanding athletes, which the navy equated with leadership ability. "We came to the conclusion that we were involved in an experiment, and we determined that we were not going to fail," recalled Samuel Barnes. "We knew that we were the foot in the door for many other black sailors."

At Great Lakes, the future officers were drilled in navigation, seamanship, gunnery, and naval regulations and law. "Everybody," said John Reagan, "worked together, stuck together, and supported each other." George Cooper remembered "sitting in the

During the 1982 reunion of the Golden 13 on the navy destroyer USS *Kidd*, an African American officer shows his predecessor Frank Sublett, Jr., the latest technology.

head after lights out, just drilling each other back and forth until it hurt." Their efforts paid off: They scored higher than any indoctrination class ever. In March 1944 the navy, omitting the traditional graduation and commissioning ceremony, swore in 12 of the men as ensigns and the 13th as a warrant officer in the U.S. Naval Reserve.

Most of the new officers were given low-priority, noncombat assignments; few received sea duty, and none ever commanded a vessel. Only Dennis Nelson pursued a navy career after the war, eventually retiring with the rank of lieutenant commander. The others went on to successful careers in engineering, law, business, education, sports, and social work.

The navy, prodded by Nelson to atone for the ceremony it had denied the men 33 years earlier, held a reunion for the Golden 13 in 1977. All but one of the 10 surviving members met in Monterey, California, for the first of what would become regular get-togethers, gathering with dozens of younger black officers who had followed in their footsteps. "We saw wall-to-wall black officers—admirals on down," rejoiced Reagan. "It was the most amazing thing for me to see so many of these bright, young, beautiful, clean people—all ranks, all types of assignments." During a toast, one of the younger men acknowledged the debt all sailors owed to the Golden 13: "If it hadn't been for you guys, we wouldn't be here."

The Golden 13 in 1944 (*left to right, from bottom*): James E. Hair, Samuel Barnes, William S. White, Dennis Nelson II; Phillip G. Barnes, George C. Cooper, Reginald E. Goodwin; Graham E. Martin, Charles B. Lear, Frank E. Sublett, Jr.; John W. Reagan, Jesse W. Arbor, Dalton L. Baugh.

James Hair, missing from the reunions until 1982 because of a name mix-up, receives a warm hug from Samuel Barnes on the *Kidd*, as Graham Martin (*left*) and Dalton Baugh wait their turn.

BLACK SERVICEWOMEN: BEYOND RACE AND SEX

Susie King Taylor, shown in a photo from her book, *Reminiscences of My Life in Camp*, wrote the only firsthand account of black Civil War nurses.

Hoping to be called to military service during the First World War, black nurses attend a "hospital garments" class at a New Orleans chapter of the American Red Cross. The war ended before the army would let them serve.

On November 15, 1866, a rugged six-foot-tall African American from Trinidad, Colorado, walked into a U.S. Army field office and signed up for the 38th Infantry—a regiment that would soon be combined with a unit of the all-black buffalo soldiers (*pages* 150-153). Enlisting under the name Williams Cathy, the soldier performed all the duties of an infantryman for the next two years—but then fell ill and had to be hospitalized. Only then did doctors discover that Williams Cathy was actually Cathy Williams, a black woman whose desire to serve in the army was so great that she disguised herself as a man to achieve it.

Like a handful of white women who, as early as the American Revolution, passed themselves off as men to serve and fight, Private Cathy relied on subterfuge and quick wits to become a soldier. But black women have had to fight doubly hard—overcoming barriers against both their race and their sex—for the right to serve in the American military. And when the barriers finally came down, they did so because of the efforts of thousands of African American nurses who, from the Civil War onward, proved themselves not only capable but often indispensable.

Women who traveled with army units during the Civil War attended to essentials like nursing, laundry, and cooking. One such aide was Susie King Taylor (*left*), a former slave who lent help to the 33d Regiment of U.S. Colored Troops. Taylor was liberated by the Union army at age 14, in 1862, and soon afterward was nursing sick and wounded troops and assisting surgeons. Although she spent four years with the regiment, she was never

In December 1942, African American servicewomen demonstrate their truck-repairing skills learned during training at Fort Des Moines, Iowa.

In late 1918, just weeks after the war ended, Stewart and 17 other black nurses made history when the army finally called them to active duty, making them the first black women to officially enter the U.S. armed services. Half were sent to Camp Sherman, Ohio, to nurse ailing soldiers in a desegregated hospital. The hospital service itself, Stewart said, "was the only side of the Army that was integrated. We proved that it was possible for blacks and whites to work together. We paved the way."

Not until World War II, however, did wider opportunities open up for black women in military service. In 1942 Congress established the Women's Army Auxiliary Corps—"Auxiliary" was dropped from the name a year later—and the War Department pledged that 10 percent of the volunteers accepted would be African American, though they would serve in segregated units.

formally enrolled as a nurse, nor was she paid for her work.

The next time the country took up arms—in 1898, in the Spanish-American War—the surgeon general of the army specifically sought the services of black nurses to care for hordes of soldiers who were falling prey to typhoid and yellow fever in Cuba and the Philippines. Believing that many African Americans were immune to such illnesses, the military hired black nurses to care for sick troops coming home from the tropics.

As a result of the essential services provided by all nurses—black and white alike—during the conflict, Congress in 1901 established the Army Nurse Corps, which admitted women into the army on a permanent basis for the first time. The invitation to enroll, however, was for white women only.

Sixteen years later, Aileen Cole Stewart was attending nursing school at Freedmen's Hospital in Washington, D.C., when the United States entered the First World War. "The Red Cross recruited us before we graduated in 1917, and we were eager to go," she recalled in 1989 at age 94. But the army refused to enlist the hundreds of black nurses who were standing by in the Red Cross—despite the desperate need—because no segregated living quarters were available and integrated quarters were unthinkable to the army brass.

Black women of the 6888th Central Postal Battalion work alongside French civilians to help move a huge backlog of mail in Europe after World War II.

The army planned to limit Wacs—as they came to be known—to cooking, driving, and clerical jobs. But severe manpower shortages opened many other assignments to women; African American Wacs were able to take on jobs as laboratory and dental technicians, photographers, aircraft-maintenance workers, and parachute packers.

But just as African American nurses were confined almost exclusively to four Negro hospitals in the States, their sisters in the Wacs were to be assigned only to posts where black men were serving in large numbers, or near cities with large black populations. Overseas, they could be stationed only where a commander had filed a request for black women. This limited their postings to about 30 installations in the United States and just one in Europe.

As African American rights groups pressed for greater opportunities for black servicewomen, the military set up the 6888th Central Postal Battalion in 1945 to help Europe's postal systems recover from the devastation of World War II. Made up of some 800 black women from the army, the air force, and an organization called the Army Service Forces, the 6888th served in Britain and France.

That year—nearly three decades after the army first admitted black women—the navy finally allowed African Americans into the Waves, its branch for women. Although black women had served in the Army Air Force during the war, they were not admitted to the newly independent U.S. Air Force until June 1948, about a year after its creation. The women went directly into racially integrated units, howev-

Marcelite Harris, the first black female general in the U.S. Air Force, served for 25 years in West Germany, Thailand, Japan, and the United States before receiving her star in 1985.

Newly commissioned lieutenant Ida Wells (*left*) and Ensign Frances Wills were among the first blacks the navy admitted into its women's auxiliary corps— the Waves—in 1945.

An African American U.S. Marine staff sergeant takes care of children in a Saigon orphanage in 1970 during the Vietnam War.

er, as the air force was the first and fastest of the services to desegregate following President Harry S Truman's executive order mandating equal opportunity in the armed services. Black women were first admitted to the marines, into an all-black unit, in September 1949.

Truman's equal-opportunity order meant that black women could now serve in any post in the United States or overseas—greatly expanding their range of possible work assignments and chances to earn promotions.

Still another barrier—against all servicewomen—fell during the 1970s, when the draft was eliminated and the army opened all but about 10 percent of its many career fields to women. Since then, African American women have joined all branches of the all-volunteer military in great numbers—and have risen to ever-higher ranks.

In September 1979, army colonel Hazel Winifred Johnson became the nation's first African American woman to attain the rank of general. Clara Adams-

Ender, the army's fourth black female general, followed a military nursing path, as had General Johnson, serving in posts both overseas and at home. As supervisor of a worldwide staff of 40,000, Adams-Ender said in 1991, "I'm proud of the fact that today's Army represents the best and the brightest soldiers—morally, academically, and physically—that we've ever had in the history of the United States."

Brigadier General Marcelite Harris—the first black woman general in the air force and the recipient of a Bronze Star, a Vietnam Service Medal, and many other decorations—took a less traditional career path. In her early days in the air force, she said, "women couldn't fly, so the next best thing was to repair the planes men flew." Turned down twice for an aircraft-maintenance job, Harris persisted and eventually became the first woman aircraft maintenance officer and, later, the first commander of a maintenance squadron in the Strategic Air Command. She paid tribute to the women who went before her for doing "a tremendous job of opening doors and proving capabilities," and counseled those who would follow to "do some soul-searching to determine how you can contribute to society. Personal achievement will come with it."

U.S. Army lieutenant Phoebe Jeter, shown here with a downed Iraqi Scud missile, earned a commendation for destroying at least two Scuds during the Persian Gulf War of 1991.

BESIEGING WEST POINT'S FORTRESS OF PREJUDICE

According to its own tradition, the U.S. Military Academy, at West Point, New York, has instilled in its cadets the values of duty, honor, and country. But while long on patriotism, West Point has been, for most of its history, grievously short on racial justice. From its establishment in 1802 through the end of World War II, a mere 27 African Americans were admitted to the academy; seven graduated. All were either ignored or abused by their white classmates. Only since the late 1960s has West Point managed to exorcise the institutional racism that so fiercely guarded its gates.

The trickle of African Americans admitted to West Point began after the Civil War. The first black cadet, a South Carolina carpenter's son named James Webster Smith, entered in 1870. He soon found that race hatred was rampant at the elite institution.

Cadet Smith's white classmates refused to speak to him, none would share a room with him, and all tried to avoid him in the dining hall. So completely was he ostracized that the upperclassmen would not even subject him to the ritual of freshman hazing.

Smith described his ordeal in letters to a benefactor, who was so outraged that he took one letter to a newspaper. The resulting public outcry forced an inquiry, but it came to nothing. Smith was accused of exaggerating and of trying to gain "social equality" rather than a military education. Court-martialed twice in his first year for minor scuffles with white cadets, he was ordered expelled, but the secretary of war intervened. Smith remained for three

more years, but finally was dismissed in 1874 for purportedly failing his exams.

During Smith's tenure, three more young black men entered West Point but left prematurely. It was a former slave from Georgia named Henry Ossian Flipper who became the academy's first African American graduate. After surviving his four years of isolation, Cadet Flipper was commissioned a second lieutenant in 1877, but he, too, fell prey to racism and was ultimately forced out of the army (*pages* 151-152).

Racist attitudes were not confined to the cadets, as was demonstrated by the case of Johnson Chestnut Whittaker, who entered the academy in 1876. Whittaker was found mutilated, unconscious, and tied to his bunk so securely that he had to be cut loose. Against all reason, the academy superintendent decided Whittaker had inflicted the wounds on himself to avoid an upcoming exam and court-martialed him. Again, the secretary of war set aside the verdict, but Whittaker, too, was eventually dismissed for academic failure.

Charles Young (*right*), who graduated in 1889, was the last 19th-century black cadet, and the last to win a commission as an officer from the academy for 47 years. Not until 1936 did another African American graduate—Benjamin O. Davis, Jr., son of the man who in a

This autographed picture of a healthy-looking Colonel Charles Young belied his serious medical condition. Seeking to demonstrate his fitness for service in the First World War, Young created a stir by riding horseback 500 miles from Ohio to Washington, D.C.

Unlike their predecessors, African American West Pointers now engage in maximum interaction with their fellows—as in hand-to-hand combat training (*left*). Below, two recent black graduates exchange congratulations at commissioning ceremonies.

few years would become the army's first black general. Like others before him, Davis was subjected to what white cadets called the silent conspiracy. Yet he persevered, graduated, and went on to distinguish himself as the first black general in the air force.

African American cadets kept coming, a few at a time, even though their treatment by white classmates did not improve much until after 1968, when the academy established its Equal Admissions Opportunity Program. The number of black cadets entering West Point rose immediately, to 77 in 1969; in 1991, West Point graduated its 1,000th African American. But proof of greater racial tolerance came in 1987, when General Fred A. Gorden became the first black commandant of cadets at West Point.

A TRAILBLAZER FOR BLACK CADETS

Charles Young, son of former slaves, became West Point's first African American graduate to succeed in military service. Surviving the trial by ostracism and harassment that was the lot of every black cadet until recent decades, Young was commissioned in 1889 and, in an outstanding 34-year career, rose to the rank of colonel.

His army service took him to the western frontier, the Philippines, Haiti, and Liberia. But he became a center of controversy in 1917 as the United States prepared to enter World War I. Then a lieutenant colonel, Young was recommended by his superiors for promotion, but a medical checkup revealed that he suffered from high blood pressure and a serious kidney disorder. He was involuntarily retired, a move that angered his many supporters, who, unaware of his condition, accused the army of going to any extreme to avoid putting a black man in line for a brigadier general's star and command of white troops. Though promoted to colonel, Young was forced to sit out World War I.

At the war's end, Colonel Young returned to active service, and in 1919 was posted again as a military adviser to Liberia. There, in January 1922, he finally succumbed to his kidney ailment. Young was buried with full military honors at Arlington National Cemetery on June 1, 1923.

A BLACK PILOT'S HIGH-FLYING CAREER

In the early 1930s, when Daniel "Chappie" James, Jr., was a teenager in Pensacola, Florida, he would gaze at airplanes streaking overhead from the nearby naval air station and dream of becoming a pilot himself, undaunted by the whites-only policy of the military air arms.

Born in 1920 to parents who taught their children pride and perseverance, James was a precocious youth who worked odd jobs at a local airfield in exchange for flying lessons. After finishing high school in 1937, he enrolled in Tuskegee Institute, one of the country's top black colleges. A year later, as the threat of world war loomed, the federal government started a new pilot training program for civilians—including blacks. Tuskegee was chosen as one of the sites for the program, and James grabbed the chance to fulfill his boyhood dream.

He excelled as a trainee—"He had more guts than anyone I had ever seen," a trainer remembered. When America entered World War II in 1941, he tried to join Tuskegee's new Army Air Corps Aviation Cadet Program (*pages* 158-159), but the first available vacancy would not come up until January 1943. Once he got in, James impressed his instructors with his intelligence and his skills.

Graduating first in his cadet class, James earned a commission as a second lieutenant in the Army Air Corps. But instead of an assignment to one of the black fighter squadrons seeing action in North Africa, he was trained as a medium-bomber pilot at bases in Michigan and Indiana.

There, for the duration of the

An ailing Chappie James joins Sammy Davis, Jr., on stage at the Air Force Academy field house in November 1977. The general, who formed his own band during his last command, in Colorado Springs, resigned the following February and died a few weeks later.

"The band got quiet, there were whispered conversations, and I could see the heads turn in my direction." But his superlative flying, warm manner, and leadership abilities eventually won him respect and friendship. Later he was transferred to war-torn Korea, where he earned the Distinguished Flying Cross—one of his many medals—and a promotion to captain for leading a major combat mission.

James continued to take on greater command responsibilities while rising through the ranks; he attained his colonelcy in 1964. In 1967 he co-led the Bolo MIG strike in Vietnam, the greatest American air victory of that war. "Yea, though I fly through the valley of death, I shall fear no

evil," James would say to his pilots with typical fighter-jock swagger, "for I am the 'meanest muthah' in the valley."

Later that same year, he won a medal from the Freedom Foundation, a patriotic organization, for an essay in which he declared that individuals determined their own destiny and that America's strength lay in its unity. At a time when the country roiled in conflict over civil rights and Vietnam, James's views served as a bridge between factions—and drew favorable notice from the White House and Defense Department. His promotion to general in 1970 coincided with an assignment to the Office of Public Affairs at the Pentagon.

James received his third star in 1974 and, only a year later, became the first African American to reach the level of four-star general, the highest rank in the peacetime armed forces. "If my making an advancement can serve as some kind of spark to some young Black or other minority," James noted at the time, "it will be worth all the years, all the blood and sweat it took in getting here." James died of a heart attack on February 25, 1978.

war, James's fight was against the prejudice and discrimination he and his black comrades experienced. After Germany and Japan surrendered, most of his buddies left the shrinking postwar military in the face of minimal opportunities for black officers. But not Chappie James. He told his friends, "I am staying in and I expect to make general."

In 1949 James and one other black officer were sent to Clark Air Force Base in the Philippines. "I never will forget the first night I walked into the Officers' Club," James reflected.

During the Vietnam War, Colonel Daniel "Chappie" James, Jr. (front), and First Lieutenant Bob C. Evans prepare for takeoff in their F-4 Phantom fighter craft.

Women's Army Corps School, Fort McClellan, July 1960

Holy Ghost Elementary School, 1951-52

Visit to Egypt, 1965

BRIGADIER GENERAL SHERIAN CADORIA

"I was brought up believing that if you're going to go into something, excel at it," says Sherian Cadoria. "Go after it and give it everything you've got." Acting on her belief, Cadoria embarked on a successful military career in the 1960s, when opportunities for women in the armed services were limited to administrative and nursing duties and the road for black advancement through the ranks was an obstacle course. When she retired from the U.S. Army in 1990, at age 50, Cadoria had become a brigadier general, was the highest-ranking black woman in the armed services, and was one of only four female generals in the army.

Sherian Cadoria came to hard work early in life. Born in 1940, she grew up in Marksville, Louisiana, where as a toddler she helped her mother, Bernice, and her sister and brother pick cotton. Cadoria's father had fallen ill and been hospitalized when she was an infant; her mother raised the family alone. "My mother is a very strong lady," Cadoria says. "She taught us to be trustworthy, and she taught us the importance of education."

After high school, Cadoria enrolled in Louisiana's Southern University. During her junior year, in the summer of 1960, she was recruited for a four-week WAC training program at Fort

McClellan, Alabama. "It was so difficult," Cadoria says, but she found that she enjoyed the discipline of military life, and when she graduated from college the next year, she joined up.

Although Cadoria says she experienced more discrimination "from being female in a man's world than from being black," racism was a formidable adversary, especially in the Deep South. At Fort McClellan, where she was stationed again in 1962 and early 1963, Ku Klux Klan members—sometimes dressed in robes and hoods—would periodically stand at the gates of the base to protest integrated military training and to intimidate

172

White House social aide to President Ford, 1975-76

General Robert Elton and Bernice Cadoria pin on BG rank, 1985

Receiving NAACP Roy Wilkins Meritorious Service Award, 1989

Brigadier General Sherian Cadoria

the soldiers. And once, when Cadoria ventured into town alone, a local restaurateur refused to give her a hamburger, even from the back door; incensed that she had had the nerve to ask, he gave her five minutes to get back across the street.

Such incidents were hard to swallow, but Cadoria knew "my family and my people were depending on me." Prayers, hard work, and a leadership style that was both demanding and compassionate served her well during a 29-year career filled with firsts. She was the first woman to command a male battalion, the first black woman director of manpower and personnel for the Joint Chiefs of Staff, and the first black woman to attend the U.S. Army Command and General Staff College and the U.S. Army War College. She was also the first woman to achieve the rank of general by following a traditionally male route—through the military police—rather than by rising through the nursing corps.

Cadoria's accomplishments meant a great deal to her family. When she broke the news to her mother about being made brigadier general, Bernice Cadoria exclaimed, "We're going to be a general!" That was her daughter's proudest moment.

"ABOVE AND BEYOND THE CALL OF DUTY"

When Specialist Five Lawrence Joel of the 173d Airborne Brigade woke up on the morning of November 8, 1965, he assumed the day would be "fairly routine." But Operation Hump, a search-and-destroy mission being conducted by his unit near Bienhoa, South Vietnam, would put the 37-year-old native of Winston-Salem, North Carolina, in the history books as the first of only two black medics to receive the nation's highest military award, the Medal of Honor. "For gallantry and intrepidity at the risk of his life above and beyond the call of duty," read the citation on the medal that President Lyndon Johnson presented to Joel at the White House on March 9, 1967.

Soon after landing by helicopter that November morning, the 36 men in Joel's platoon, advancing through dense jungle growth in four squads, walked within close range of a well-concealed battalion-size force of Vietcong. Opening fire with machine guns and automatic rifles, the enemy killed or wounded many of the Americans, including virtually every soldier in the first squad. Joel took a bullet in his right leg. Bandaging his wound, injecting himself

with morphine, and shouting to his wounded buddies to hang on, Joel used a makeshift crutch to move from man to man. Even though he was hit again, in his other leg, Joel managed to treat 13 seriously wounded paratroopers, saving one from certain death by placing a plastic bag over his sucking chest wound.

When another platoon arrived and its medic was disabled by enemy fire, Joel went to help the wounded in the new unit. Unable to walk, he dragged himself from man to man, administering aid and attending to the men until the enemy finally withdrew nearly 24 hours later.

Joel spent three months recuperating in Saigon and Tokyo hospitals before returning to the United States. Despite the honors he won, he insisted, "I don't consider myself a hero. I just consider myself a soldier doing his job."

Joel died in 1984 of complications from diabetes, but his name lives on. At Fort Campbell, Kentucky, where he had twice been stationed, a granite monument was erected to memorialize his courageous acts, and a street was named after him. In 1989 Winston-Salem named a new coliseum after him, and the Walter Reed Army Medical Center in Washington, D.C., dedicated its main auditorium to his memory two years later.

Less than a year after Joel was decorated on the White House lawn, another African American soldier, Private First Class Clarence Eugene Sasser of Chenango, Texas, would exhibit the same remarkable courage while "doing his job" in the Ding Tuong Province of Vietnam—and become the second black medic to earn the Medal of Honor.

A part-time student at the University of Houston, Sasser was only 18 years old when the army drafted him in 1967 and sent him to serve in Vietnam. On January 10, 1968, his company was making a helicopter-borne assault when enemy rifle, machine-gun, and rocket fire ripped into its landing zone from three sides. In only a matter of minutes, more

A Vietnam medic's kit held a variety of supplies, including scalpel blades, a tourniquet, an airway, bandages, tape, cotton, ointments, inhalant, scissors, and a hemostat.

than 30 soldiers lay wounded.

Sasser braved a storm of fire to cross an exposed rice field, wearing a 35-pound backpack of medical supplies. He had just pulled one wounded man to safe cover when exploding rocket fragments tore into his left shoulder; refusing to stop for help, he continued to dodge enemy fire, treating the wounded and searching for other victims. Hit twice in the legs and

weak from loss of blood, Sasser nonetheless crawled more than a hundred yards through mud to aid another wounded soldier and then inched his way an additional 200 or more yards to tend to yet another group before all were evacuated. As he put it later, "I really deep down felt that if I could help somebody get back up and fight, then we might all get out of here alive."

On March 9, 1967, after receiving the Congressional Medal of Honor for his heroism in Vietnam, Specialist Lawrence Joel stands with President Lyndon B. Johnson on the White House lawn for postceremony photographs.

A carefree Colin Powell (*second from right*) posed with neighborhood friends as a teenager. A few years later saw him a serious young man, trim and correct in his army ROTC uniform.

A SOLDIER AT THE SUMMIT

In 1963 Colin Luther Powell was in a position shared by many other African Americans. He was a U.S. serviceman, sworn to put his life on the line in defense of the country's democratic ideals and national interests—in Powell's case as an adviser to a South Vietnamese infantry battalion fighting Communist insurgents in Southeast Asia. Yet half a world away in America, his family was enduring the barbs of unfettered racism. "My wife and infant son were living in Birmingham, Alabama," he said, "during those days when not only blacks were marching, but Bull Connor and his dog were marching as well."

Soon young Captain Powell, back in the States and settling into an assignment at Fort Benning, Georgia, would feel those barbs himself. Yet Powell saw a difference between his treatment in the army and life outside that setting. "I was helped in the early part of my career," he said, "when I lived in the South and I could do things on an Army post that you darn well better not think about doing off an Army post. . . . Was that respect for human rights and making sure that everybody wearing a uniform had the opportunity to succeed? I think it was."

Powell's military career started almost by accident. He was born in Harlem, raised in the Bronx, and went to college because, he said, "my parents expected it."

His mother and father, both Jamaican immigrants, worked in the garment trade, and wanted something better for him and his sister. At the City College of New York, he floundered for a year, then found the Pershing Rifles, an elite unit within the army's Reserve Officer Training Corps (ROTC). He enjoyed his military-science courses, drill field exercises, and summer training camps, excelling from the start and rising eventually to the highest ROTC rank, cadet colonel. When he graduated in 1958 with a bachelor's degree in geology, he also received a commission as an army second lieutenant.

Intent on an army career, Powell went through the demanding airborne and ranger schools. Over the years he earned promotions in assignments at home and overseas. In 1968, on a second tour of duty in Vietnam, he won the Bronze Star for bravery in combat and the Soldier's Medal for going back into a burning helicopter to rescue injured men.

In 1971 Powell received a master's degree in business administration from George Washington University, in Washington, D.C. The following year he won a prestigious White House Fellowship, which gave him valuable exposure in Washington's corridors of power. Powell was in and out of Washington over the next 17 years in a series of appointments that would eventually carry him to the top military office in the land.

While at Fort Leavenworth, Kansas, in 1982, he noticed that only the names of two alleys near the post cemetery existed to commemorate the black buffalo soldiers (*pages* 150-153) who had once served there. He started a project to honor them with a statue, and at its dedication he paid them tribute. "Look at this statue," he said of the sculpted figure of a black cavalryman. "Imagine him in his coat of blue, on his horse, a soldier of the nation, eagles on his buttons, crossed sabers on his canteen . . . every bit the soldier that his white brother was. He showed that the theory of inequality must be wrong."

In 1987, after Powell had distinguished himself in several Pentagon assignments, President Ronald Reagan appointed him national security adviser, the first black American ever to hold that post. Two years later President George Bush named him to the nation's highest military job, chairman of the Joint Chiefs of Staff. Powell, at 52, became the youngest man to serve in this post, as well as the first African American.

The appointment capped a career marked by profound changes in the world political situation. His first duty assignment, at the height of the Cold War in 1958, was as a young second lieutenant in command of a platoon of GIs in West Germany, guarding a key sector on the frontier of Western democracy opposite the tanks, guns, and divisions of the Red Army and its Warsaw Pact allies. Thirty years later, as JCS chairman, he saw the Warsaw Pact dissolved, European communism discarded, the Soviet Empire broken up. The Cold War was over, and his side had won.

The general often expressed his pride in America's armed forces, their accomplishments and, perhaps most of all, their spirit. Of those who fought in the Persian Gulf War, he said: "They were family. It didn't make any difference what color they were, where they came from, whether they were rich or poor. They were all Americans 8,000 miles away from home."

Powell has spoken freely of the effect of his race on his career: "I suspect it worked both against me and for me. I think, in some cases, people may have had lower expectations of me because I was black and because of their own prejudices. And in other cases, people, whether I performed up to standards or not, were going to put me down because I was black." Either way, he added, he was determined that his race would be "somebody else's problem, not mine."

Still, Powell never neglected to pay homage to those who had paved the way for him and other African Americans. Speaking to a gathering of the Tuskegee Airmen (*pages* 158-159), pioneering black fighter pilots of World War II, he said, "I never forget for a day, or for an hour, or for a minute, that I climbed to my position on the backs of the courageous African American men and women who went before me."

Twenty-three years after service as a major with the 23d Infantry Division in Vietnam (*below*), Joint Chiefs of Staff chairman Powell conducts a briefing during the Persian Gulf War in 1991.

BLACK SOLDIERS IN BLACK AFRICA

By the end of 1992, the East African country of Somalia was devastated by famine and torn apart by armed warlords fighting for control of the nation. With an estimated 3,000 Somalis dying daily, the United States and other countries sent aid, and the U.S. military deployed nearly 25,000 soldiers to help secure air- and seaports and food centers, and to protect relief-organization workers.

Of the U.S. troops sent to Somalia in December 1992, one-fifth were African Americans. Their training kept them focused on the job at hand, but that didn't prevent many from having powerful feelings—good and bad—about this mission on the continent of their ancestors. Many black American soldiers said they were offended by what they saw as Somali racism and shocked by the violence of Somali society. At the same time, some also felt a deeper connection. One officer, who attended a show put on by Somali dancers, was struck by the bond he felt with the Africans: "I'm in a fraternity, and some of the steps they were doing were some of our fraternity steps. It really touched me. And I looked to my left and there was a Botswanan officer, and to my right was a Nigerian officer. I looked forward and saw Somalis performing onstage. It gave me a great sense of pride. This is like a Mecca for me as far as my heritage is concerned."

An American soldier searches a local man for weapons at a roadblock in Mogadishu, the capital of Somalia.

A newly arrived soldier clutches her gear in this late-1992 photograph. Female soldiers in Somalia acted as mechanics, truckdrivers, and police.

A U.S. Marine hands food to local children over the barbed-wire fence that surrounds his base at Baidoa—a town located 150 miles inland from Mogadishu. A distribution center for food and medicine, Baidoa was among the first towns from which soldiers routed aggressive Somali warlords.

Away from home during the holidays, a soldier in Somalia gazes wistfully at a small stack of gifts piled under a makeshift Christmas tree. Despite some homesickness, most of the black soldiers agreed with Lance Corporal Maurice Poe, a 22-year-old marine from Atlanta, who said, "I couldn't be doing anything better."

ADVOCATES FOR CHANGE

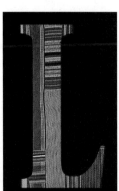

A *phalanx* of soldiers from the 101st Airborne Division escort the first African American students to desegregate formerly all-white Central High School in Little Rock, Arkansas, in 1957.

ate in the summer of 1955, fourteen-year-old Emmett Till and his cousin Curtis Jones left their homes on Chicago's South Side to spend a two-week vacation with Till's great-uncle Mose Wright, a sharecropper and preacher who lived in a shack outside the small town of Money, Mississippi. Emmett Till never made it back. On August 24, the black eighth-grader supposedly whistled at a local white woman named Carolyn Bryant, and then said, "Bye, baby." Five days later he was found dead in the Tallahatchie River, his body weighted down by a cotton-gin fan. He had been beaten, then shot to death.

Till was the only child of 33-year-old Mamie Till Bradley, and when his body, distorted beyond recognition, came back to Chicago, she deliberately held an open-casket funeral. Mamie Bradley wanted to show the world what it felt like to have a family member "returned to you in a pine box, so horribly battered and waterlogged that someone needs to tell you this sickening sight is your son—lynched." Thousands of people filed past the boy's body, and a picture of his swollen face was featured in *Jet* magazine, sparking nationwide outrage. Black political activist Amzie Moore of Cleveland, Mississippi, later said Till's murder marked "the beginning of the Civil Rights Movement in Mississippi in the twentieth century."

From a legal standpoint, the evidence seemed strong against two suspected ringleaders in the lynching, Carolyn Bryant's husband, Roy, and his half-brother J. W. Milam. The men were identified by Mose Wright, one of the first black men ever to rise in a Mississippi courtroom and name white men as criminals. "Thar he," Wright said as he pointed first at Milam and then at Bryant, whom he had seen ordering young Till out of bed that August night. Wright, fearing for his life, later fled Mississippi, leaving behind his dog and his car. Another black witness, 19-year-old Willie Reed, testified that he saw the defendants driving a pickup truck with Till in the back. Reed, whose family also sent him out of state for his own safety, told the court he later heard Till being beaten in a nearby barn. He said the punches and slaps were punctuated by Till screaming "Mama," and "Lord have mercy, Lord have mercy."

Despite such testimony, the five defense lawyers faced no great tactical challenge in the case. They simply asked the jury of 12 white men from Tallahatchie County to find their fellow white Mississippians innocent; one lawyer urged them to show "that every last Anglo Saxon one of you has the courage to free these men." The jury took just one hour and seven minutes to return a verdict of not guilty, and even then they had dawdled, following the advice of a sheriff who, they said later, had told them to take their time and drink sodas so it would "look good." The whites who filled the front seats in the courtroom applauded, gathered around the defendants, and lit cigars. Meanwhile, black spectators, segregated in the standing-room area at the back of the courtroom, quickly left the building.

As far as the local whites were concerned, the controversial case had been put to rest. Black leaders who had come from outside the state to observe the trial, including Michigan congressman Charles C. Diggs, Jr., were denounced by a white community leader as troublemakers. A deputy sheriff told one reporter that, by contrast, the local blacks were unconcerned by the verdict. "Ours is out picking cotton and tending to their own business," he said. They may have been going about their work, but the black men and women in Tallahatchie County were anything but unconcerned. The message of the white racist South had once again been hammered home: If your skin is black, your life is worth nothing.

Emmett Till's murder was one of several such incidents during the 1950s that were publicized across the nation, a sad reminder that, 90 years after the end of legalized slavery, the lives and destinies of black Americans were still largely controlled by whites. The war against slavery had simply given way to a new struggle—a long, drawn-out fight on many fronts against political, social, and economic inequalities rooted in the same racist ideas once used to rationalize more than two centuries of slaveholding. Civil rights activists, both black and white, had worked hard since the end of the Civil War to break down the American system of racial oppression, but their efforts had yielded only a few tangible results by 1955. Over the next decade that would begin to change. The century-old civil rights movement would win some of its greatest victories, revolutionizing voting rights, opening up legal access to education and public accommodations, and arguing for equal protection under the law from bias and from racially motivated violence like that which took the lives of Emmett Till and thousands of others.

Throughout the euphoric years of emancipation and Reconstruction, racism remained a powerful force in the United States. In the North and West, blacks lost out to whites in the fight for jobs and were relegated to society's economic and social margins. And with the removal of federal troops from the South in 1877, race relations in the former Confederacy quickly reverted to socially and legally imposed racial divides that mimicked the old divisions of slavery.

No longer under federal supervision, the southern states enacted laws that made it nearly impossible for blacks to vote, leaving political power exclusively in white hands. One common provision was the poll tax, a flat fee charged for the privilege of voting that effectively barred sharecroppers and other poor folks from the voter rolls. After Mississippi adopted its poll tax in 1890, a white congressman from

In the segregated South, no aspect of life was too trivial for local whites to brand with their race obsession, as is evidenced by this "white customers only" soft-drink vending machine (*above*).

Pointing an accusing finger from the witness stand, Mississippi sharecropper Mose Wright (*left*) identifies the two white men who killed his 14-year-old great-nephew Emmett Till in August 1955. Wright later said he could feel "the blood boil in hundreds of white people" in the courtroom as he incriminated the murderers.

that state estimated—approvingly—that the tax had disenfranchised 90 percent of eligible black voters. Some southern states also adopted a so-called understanding clause that required registrants who could not read to interpret a section of the state constitution after it was read aloud to them. Not surprisingly, few white registrars felt black applicants had passed the test. Most whites who went to register did not have to take any test, because of new, so-called grandfather clauses exempting those who had voted—or who had ancestors who had voted—before 1867.

Social customs that separated the races in every aspect of daily life also began to be codified into law. Such statutes came to be known as Jim Crow laws, after a common stereotype of black people based on a buffoonish minstrel-show character by that name. The first such laws governed railroad passenger trains, where the customs against race mixing often broke down. In 1890, a New Orleans newspaper wrote that the racial situation on trains had become unacceptable. "A man that would be horrified at the idea of his wife or daughter seated by the side of a burly negro in the parlor of a hotel or at a restaurant cannot see her occupy a crowded seat in a car next to a negro without the same feeling of disgust." Segregationist laws passed to "correct" the situation provoked a number of black legal challenges.

In one of several such efforts, some prominent black residents of New Orleans arranged a test case. On June 7, 1892, thirty-four-year-old Homer Adolph Plessy took a seat in the white first-class car of an East Louisiana Railway train headed from New Orleans to Covington, Louisiana. Plessy had one black great-grandparent, which classified him as black under Louisiana law. Railroad officials, who had been informed of this fact, told him to move into the "colored" first-class car. When Plessy refused, he was arrested and later convicted by a Louisiana court.

As he and his backers had planned, Plessy then appealed to the United States Supreme Court under the Reconstruction-era 13th and 14th Amendments, which had outlawed slavery and guaranteed equal treatment regardless of race. But the legal challenge backfired. In May 1896, the high court ruled that the railroad was obligated to give Plessy a first-class seat—but did not have to seat him with white passengers. Laws were "powerless to eradicate racial instincts," the Court found, and separate-but-equal facilities for the two races were wholly constitutional.

The lone dissent was filed by a white Kentucky native, Justice John M. Harlan. Harlan argued that the law compelling racial segregation on railroad cars violated the 13th Amendment's ban on slavery, since, in his view, the amendment also outlawed "any burdens or disabilities that constitute badges of slavery or servitude." He also worried about the case's broader implications. If the legal system could be used to separate certain Americans traveling on a railroad, Harlan wrote, "why may it not so regulate the use of the streets of its cities and towns as to compel white citizens to keep on one side of a street and black citizens to keep on the other?" He concluded that "the destinies of the two races in this country are indissolubly linked

together and the interests of both require that the common government of all shall not permit the seeds of race hate to be planted under the sanction of law."

Harlan had accurately foretold the consequences of putting federal authority behind Jim Crow laws. The high court's stamp of approval helped the practice of race separation expand to every aspect of southern life. In the years that followed, parks, playgrounds, ticket windows, hospitals, swimming pools, and other facilities would be built for segregated use as a matter of course, subjecting black men and women in the South to constant, daily indignities. Two years after the *Plessy* decision, the Court also upheld poll taxes, literacy tests, understanding clauses, and grandfather clauses because they were not explicitly based on race.

In this poisoned atmosphere of legal oppression, white violence against blacks became commonplace. In the nation's cities, tensions periodically led to white race riots that often destroyed black property and resulted in injuries and death in the black population. Execution-style murders called lynchings—a form of frontier justice in the 19th-century West—spread through the South. The victims were usually black men, and often their only "crime" was being too successful or too outspoken. Sometimes, as in the case of Emmett Till, the victim had supposedly been disrespectful to white women. Till was also from out of town, and lynch mobs were likely to single out black strangers, who lacked white supporters in the local community.

Especially high numbers of black Americans were lynched in the 1890s, accord-

Sharecroppers Joseph Riley and Virgil, Robert, and Thomas Jones—four out of thousands of black lynching victims—hang from a Russellville, Kentucky, tree (*left*) in August 1908. Their "crime"— expressing sympathy for a black man who killed his white employer in self-defense. A note attached to one body cautioned other blacks to "let white people alone or you will go the same way."

ing to reports compiled by the Tuskegee Institute in Alabama. At least 161 died in 1892 and 134 in 1894. But as the Till case suggests, the terrorism continued as a fact of American life for decades. The last recorded mob lynching in the United States took place in 1964. According to Tuskegee, that victim was the 4,742d person known to die in a lynching on American soil since 1882.

For African Americans, the last years of the 19th century marked a low point in organized black resistance. Many turned to the black church for community leadership. Some purely secular black political organizations also sprang up, primarily in the North. In New York in 1898, T. Thomas Fortune formed the Afro-American Council (AAC), which has been called the first American civil rights organization. Like other northern civil rights groups in the decades to come, the AAC took on southern racial injustice as a key target. After a white race riot in Wilmington, North Carolina, in the council's first year, the group held an emergency meeting. "We have at last come to the point in our race history," said black journalist Ida B. Wells-Barnett, who headed the organization's Anti-Lynching Bureau, "where we must do something for ourselves and do it now." Yet the Afro-American Council disbanded within a few years. Its only real contribution was as a training ground for Wells-Barnett and other activists, including Harvard-educated professor and author William Edward Burghardt Du Bois.

Neither W. E. B. Du Bois nor Wells-Barnett was the black community's best-known spokesperson at the time, however. That honor went to Booker T. Washington, a former slave who argued that black Americans should give up their immediate demands for social equality and focus instead on economic development. For years, such arguments won him support in both the white and the black community, and he dominated the black political landscape. But Du Bois was one of many African Americans who did not agree with Washington. In his 1903 book *The Souls of Black Folk*, Du Bois wrote that black Americans should not accept second-tier status in an American caste system. "The problem of the 20th Century," he observed, "is the problem of the color line; the relation of the darker to the lighter races of men in Asia and Africa, in America and the islands of the sea." Two years later, Du Bois met with Wells-Barnett and other black intellectuals at Niagara Falls to address the question of the "color line." Rejecting Washington's gradualist approach, the Niagara group demanded the vote for all black men (women of any race could not vote) and emphasized the need for equal educational opportunities. "We want the constitution of the country enforced," wrote Du Bois, and "we want our children educated."

The Niagara movement, like the Afro-American Council before it, soon disbanded. But a few years later many of its key members participated in the formation of the interracial National Association for the Advancement of Colored People, or NAACP. The group that would become the NAACP organized in response to white race riots in 1908 that took place not in the South but in Springfield, Illinois, where Abraham Lincoln was buried. Over the course of two days, black homes and businesses were burned, 46 black residents were killed, and more than 2,000 black men and women fled the city. Two who died were lynched less than half a mile from Lincoln's grave.

Reports of the atrocities galvanized several white activists, including social worker Mary White Ovington and Oswald Garrison Villard, grandson of abolitionist William Lloyd Garrison. They joined with two black ministers, Bishop Alexander Walters and the Reverend William Henry Brooks, to form what was originally called the National Negro Committee. At meetings held on May 31 and June 1, 1909, in New York City, the group was formally inaugurated, proclaiming its goal to be the end of American racial prejudice. Among those who attended, and who later rose to key positions in the organization, were W. E. B. Du Bois and Ida B. Wells-Barnett.

The alliance, which took the name NAACP the next year, fought to stop newspapers from practicing the double standard of highlighting every crime committed by a black, while underreporting white crimes or never mentioning the racial identity of white criminals. It gave legal help to a black Kansas City couple whose new house in a white neighborhood was bombed. And it also joined a successful fight to outlaw grandfather clauses in both Oklahoma and Maryland.

Despite these successes, the NAACP in its first decade did not win overwhelming support in the black community, which generally perceived it as a group of upper-class whites and blacks. Rural as well as urban blacks across the country were listening instead to the compelling message of a confident young Jamaican named Marcus Garvey (*pages 202-205*). Garvey, who came to the United States in 1916, belittled the white-led NAACP and other black efforts to work with whites. The NAACP, in Garvey's view, intended for black people "to become white by amalgamation." He advised black people instead to honor their own African history and culture, to take pride in their black identity, and to work for self-determination through his Universal Negro Improvement Association, or UNIA.

Even as Garvey continued to draw a large following, the NAACP began to find its feet with a coordinated program to combat lynching. The campaign attracted many prominent blacks, including author James Weldon Johnson, a leading figure in the artistic and literary Harlem Renaissance of the teens and twenties. In July 1917, in his role as NAACP field secretary, Johnson organized a "Negro silent protest parade" that drew an estimated 10,000 black people to New York City's Fifth Avenue. They marched to the funeral-like pounding of muffled drums as Boy Scouts handed out cards that read, "Give me a chance to live," "Your hands are full of blood," and "Mother, do lynchers go to heaven?"

Du Bois urged the NAACP to investigate each lynching that it could, and it conveyed the details to public officials and newspapers. During one five-day period in Georgia in 1918, for example, eight black people were lynched, including a pregnant woman who had cried out against the mob for lynching her husband. She and her unborn child died together. "She was slowly burned to death," Mary Ovington reported to the NAACP board, "and as she burned the infant fell to the ground and was trampled under a white man's heel."

The NAACP had little success with the antilynching campaign, however, and the organization's board began to fret that it was spending too much time and money on that one objective, instead of promoting examples of good race relations. But James Weldon Johnson insisted that the fight go on. Johnson, who became the NAACP's first black executive secretary in 1920, lobbied hard for a federal antilynching bill,

A somber banner announcing the latest reported lynching flies from the New York City headquarters of the NAACP in this photograph from the early 1900s. The device was one of many that the organization used to bring home the everyday horror of racial violence.

first proposed in 1918, that would have made lynch mobs subject to federal prosecution for murder and provided legal penalties for local law officials who cooperated with a lynch mob. Though he pursued the antilynching campaign until his retirement in 1930, his efforts were in vain. Johnson later warned in his 1933 autobiography that such legislative indifference had its price. Lynching and other forms of racism had led many African Americans, he wrote, to "the cultivation of a hard, keen, relentless hatred of everything white."

The NAACP went back to Capitol Hill with a second antilynching campaign, led by Walter White, Johnson's successor. This time, the bill under consideration held penalties for local law officers who did not prevent lynchings. The bill failed in 1934. Still, the NAACP's public-education campaign bore some fruit. Lynchings became less common in the late 1930s as the tide of white public opinion turned against the practice.

By that time, the NAACP had begun an equally uphill battle against racially segregated education. Spearheading the effort was a skillful, dedicated black attorney named Charles Hamilton Houston. The son of a lawyer, Houston had served as an army officer in World War I and had witnessed unfair treatment of black soldiers in court-martial proceedings. Along with other black officers, he experienced constant criticism of his abilities, and even had his life threatened. Houston later recalled it was those incidents that persuaded him to go to law school. "I would study law," he said, "and use my time fighting for men who could not strike back."

After graduating from Harvard Law School in 1922 and receiving a legal doctorate in 1923, Houston joined his father's firm in Washington, D.C., supplementing his income by teaching at Howard University's law school. At the time, the school operated only as a night school, with an inadequate library, an inexperienced faculty, and low admission standards for applicants. Houston was frustrated by conditions there, but found that matters were not much better in other black law schools. Most black American lawyers, for example, had had little classroom exposure to constitutional law—a field essential to the civil rights cases that he saw as a way of reshaping American society. In 1929, Houston was temporarily appointed to run Howard Law School, and he leaped at the chance to upgrade the facility.

Houston made Howard Law a full-time day school, established stronger academic requirements for admission, recruited top students, and fired some of the

faculty. He met with immediate resistance and was criticized in newspaper editorials for pushing poor black students out of the school. But in two years the law school had gained full accreditation from the American Bar Association—and Houston had begun developing young lawyers who would become experts on constitutional law.

"In all our classes," recalled Edward Lovett, one of Houston's students, "whether it was equity or contracts or pleadings, stress was placed on learning what our rights were under the Constitution and statutes—our rights as worded and regardless of how they had been interpreted to that time. Charlie's view was that we had to get the courts to change." Houston's students often quoted him as telling them that "a lawyer's either a social engineer or he's a parasite on society."

Houston took his own advice. By 1933 he was working on civil rights cases for the NAACP, and in 1935 he took a leave of absence from Howard to become the organization's chief legal counsel. Inspired by an earlier NAACP memo on ways to fight school segregation, Houston developed a long-range strategy to challenge the laws against race mixing, laws that had been accepted as constitutional since the *Plessy v. Ferguson* decision in 1896. Houston planned to chip away at the separate-but-equal doctrine one piece at a time.

Working with a former student, Thurgood Marshall, who had joined him at the NAACP, Houston fought to desegregate the University of Maryland Law School, which routinely rejected black applicants. In Baltimore city court in 1935, the lawyers successfully showed there was no state-run, separate-but-equal law school for black Marylanders; indeed, there was no separate black law school at all. In a similar case, Houston and Marshall represented Lloyd Lionel Gaines, a black student who had been refused admission by the all-white University of Missouri Law School. Gaines lost in local and state courts, which enabled Houston to appeal the case to the United States Supreme Court. In his 1938 argument before the Court, Houston asserted that the Missouri system violated the Constitution because it did not provide black citizens an equal opportunity to learn the laws of the state. The Court agreed, requiring Missouri to give Gaines "facilities for legal education substantially equal to" those "afforded for persons of the white race."

The ruling did not overturn *Plessy v. Ferguson*, but in practice it was a damaging blow, giving states the choice of creating and funding parallel black institutions or admitting black students to formerly white schools. Houston's grand strategy had begun to pay off—as had his plan of training young lawyers to follow in his path. In 1940, when Houston left his job as head of the NAACP's Legal Defense Fund to

go back to private practice, Thurgood Marshall was ready to take his place.

That same year, as segregation continued to reign at home, the nation girded for a war against Nazi racism abroad. Many African Americans worried about the status of blacks in the American military, which had changed very little from the racist institution that had so galled young Charles Houston. The chance to be a soldier meant a chance to hold a job—as well as to get a shot at Nazi white supremacists. But in the prewar army of 1940, there were 230,000 enlisted men, fewer than 5,000 of them black. In the South many draft boards refused to induct black men.

As the nation readied for war, Walter White of the NAACP joined with A. Philip Randolph, the nation's most prominent black labor leader, to ask President Franklin Roosevelt for a draft that would allow recruits of both races to join any unit, be trained for any job, be promoted to officers, and serve as doctors. Roosevelt opened the door to black enlistment, but he refused to desegregate the ranks. Black recruits found themselves in Jim Crow units, often working as kitchen help or laborers.

Segregation was equally entrenched in the defense industry. To press the government to demand racial equity in the hiring of defense-plant workers, A. Philip Randolph proposed a march on Washington for July 1, 1941. "Negro America must bring its power and pressure to bear upon the agencies and representatives of the Federal Government," he said. "We loyal Negro American citizens demand the right to work and fight for our country."

The idea of 100,000 black people marching through the capital as America prepared for war alarmed the White House. Roosevelt summoned Randolph to the Oval Office and told him that the march could jeopardize American race relations and give the appearance of a divided nation to potential enemies overseas. But Randolph refused to budge. Six days before the march was to take place, Roosevelt blinked. He issued an executive order that made it illegal to discriminate in hiring for jobs at defense plants. Randolph called off the march.

Randolph was a hero in black America. And two years after the war, in 1947, he attacked another objective: desegregating the military itself. Congress was planning to order a new, peacetime draft of soldiers, and Randolph met with Harry Truman, who had become president on Roosevelt's death in 1945, to tell him that black Americans would no longer fight for the United States "until all forms of bias and discrimination are abolished." Randolph testified before the Senate that black citizens would prefer jail to "military slavery," and said he would counsel black soldiers to "refuse to fight as slaves for a democracy they cannot possess and enjoy."

Some senators leveled charges of treason. But Harlem's black congressman, Adam Clayton Powell, told his colleagues on Capitol Hill that Randolph was accurately reflecting the mood of black America. "If the finger of treason can be pointed at anyone," Powell wrote to them, "it must be pointed at those of you who are traitors to our Constitution and to our Bill of Rights. There are not enough jails in America to hold the colored people who will refuse to bear arms in a Jim Crow army."

Randolph's cause was also helped by internal Democratic party politics. For some time, the Democratic party had struck an uneasy balance between a conservative, southern white wing and a more liberal group that claimed to represent the

NAACP attorneys Thurgood Marshall (*far left*) and Charles Houston (*near left*) prepare a case against the University of Maryland Law School for its race-based exclusion of their client Donald Gaines Murray (*center*). Their 1935 victory in the case was the first of many that led to the end of legal segregation in public schools.

party's national interests. As the 1948 Democratic convention approached, Truman found the latter group attacking him for not standing up to the southern segregationists. Just after the convention, he signed Executive Order 9981 guaranteeing equal opportunities in the military for citizens of all races. Within a few years, this led to real military desegregation.

For the forces of segregation, an even bigger blow to the status quo was on its way. During the war, the NAACP had temporarily suspended its pursuit of school desegregation in favor of other issues such as fair treatment in court. But in 1946, the organization returned to the education battle. Thurgood Marshall and the NAACP Legal Defense Fund lawyers resumed their long-term strategy, setting the precedents that would one day topple school segregation throughout the land.

In that year, Marshall's team represented Heman Sweatt, a black mailman who had been accepted at the University of Texas Law School but assigned to a separate black "law school" in three basement rooms. The lawyers also took the case of a 68-year-old professor named George W. McLaurin, who had been admitted to a doctoral program in education at the University of Oklahoma but found himself sitting at a desk that was designated as "Reserved for Colored." A table in the cafeteria and library were similarly designated for him alone. The Legal Defense Fund lawyers argued that when universities segregated black students inside otherwise-white professional schools, the students were denied an equal education—an argument that was supported by the Truman administration's Justice Department. The Supreme Court agreed. On June 5, 1950, it ruled that any state that maintained segregated educational institutions had to provide fully equal schools. Sweatt was admitted to the law school and McLaurin was integrated into the student body.

Just before the ruling was handed down, Charles Houston died of heart failure at the age of 54. NAACP lawyer James Nabrit later recalled that on his hospital bed, Houston had agreed that the time had come to take on *Plessy v. Ferguson* directly. The Legal Defense Fund decided to attack the separate-but-equal doctrine with multiple cases. Marshall wanted to show the Court that in different states, under different administrators and teachers, racial segregation always led to inferior education for black students and was therefore inherently unconstitutional.

Black Americans like these Wacs, en route to Europe in 1945, served their country by the hundreds of thousands during World War II, all the while assigned to strictly segregated units. Three years after the war ended, labor leader A. Philip Randolph successfully urged President Truman to issue an order providing equal opportunity in the military for all races. The order led within a few years to desegregation of the military.

The first example the NAACP lawyers found was in Clarendon County, South Carolina, which spent an average of $179 a year on each white student but only $43 on each black student. To bolster the NAACP case, Marshall asked Dr. Kenneth Clark, a black New York psychologist, to measure the psychological impact of segregation on Clarendon County's black children. Testing 16 African American students between the ages of six and nine, Dr. Clark discovered that 10 preferred a white doll to a black doll; 11 of the children said that the black doll was "bad." The results suggested to Clark a direct relationship between the children's segregated education and their poor concept of themselves and their race.

Marshall's lawyers found a second case in Topeka, Kansas, where seven-year-old Linda Brown was not allowed to attend a modern elementary school just blocks away from her house because it was reserved for white children. To get to the black elementary school, she had to walk across the tracks at a railroad switching station and wait for a school bus. When state courts saw nothing illegal in the situation, the NAACP took *Brown v. the Board of Education of Topeka, Kansas,* to the Supreme Court.

The third case was brought forward by Spottswood Robinson, a lawyer working as a special representative for the NAACP in Virginia. Students at all-black Moton High School, in Prince Edward County, Virginia, had organized a protest strike against overcrowding and other poor conditions, but in 1952, a federal court upheld the county's segregated schools as consistent with southern customs. Robinson and the Legal Defense Fund lawyers appealed to the Supreme Court. The NAACP also brought two other school desegregation cases to the Court. Confronted with so many similar disputes, the Supreme Court decided to hear all five cases on the same day, combining them under the name of the Brown case, which was seen by the Court as the least inflammatory to white opinion because it was outside the South.

On December 9, 1952, the cases were argued before a packed courtroom. The fireworks began with the South Carolina case, in which Thurgood Marshall, in his 16th appearance before the Court, faced 79-year-old John W. Davis, a legal legend who had argued before the Supreme Court more than 250 times. Making light of Clark's "doll evidence" as inconclusive and unprecedented, Davis noted that leading black scholars, including W. E. B. Du Bois, were not convinced that having black children attend all-black schools was a problem. Davis also argued that Congress had not intended to make racial segregation illegal when it passed the 14th Amendment in 1865, since it had allowed segregated schools in Washington, D.C. Marshall responded that the only justification for segregated education would be if Davis could prove that black children were "different from everybody else."

The arguments lasted three days; the Court's deliberations took months. Then, instead of ruling on the highly sensitive issue, the Court took the unusual step of posing further questions to each side. In the middle of this process, Chief Justice Fred M. Vinson, who Court insiders had believed would not overturn segregation, died; he was replaced by former California governor Earl Warren. A year after the first arguments began, the Court heard the desegregation cases once again.

On May 17, 1954, the Supreme Court delivered its opinion. The final vote, Chief Justice Warren announced, had been nine to zero. The Court agreed, he said, that segregated education had a detrimental effect on black children's development "even though the physical facilities and other tangible factors may be equal." He continued, "In the field of public education the doctrine of 'separate but equal' has no place. Separate educational facilities are inherently unequal."

But the battle to desegregate public schools was to continue for years, as many southern states or counties chose to disregard the ruling. Again and again, the NAACP and other plaintiffs had to appeal to the courts for specific, timely remedies in particular school systems. As the fight raged on, the desegregation battleground grew to encompass public accommodations—a term that includes restaurants, hotels, buses, and other businesses that serve the general public, all of which had been racially segregated in the South since the era of *Plessy v. Ferguson*. An accommodations showdown had been in the making for years over the bus system of Montgomery, Alabama. In 1949 Jo Ann Robinson, an English teacher at all-black Alabama State College, had been humiliated on a Montgomery bus when she was ordered to walk to the rear by the driver; she got up and ran off the bus. Robinson went to the black Women's Political Council (WPC) of Montgomery, but the WPC was unable to force a change in the bus policy. The *Brown* decision breathed new life into the struggle. Soon after Marshall's victory was announced, Robinson and the WPC conferred with Edgar Daniel Nixon, a local activist who had been the town's NAACP chapter president, about challenging the bus company again. Months went by as they waited for just the right incident to rally around.

Finally, on December 1, 1955, they got their chance. Rosa Parks, an active NAACP member who worked as a tailor's assistant at a downtown department store, got on a bus, paid her dime, and took a seat in the middle section. When a group of whites got on at the next stop, one white man was left standing, and the driver ordered the black people seated in the middle section to stand at the rear. Three black passengers went to the back of the bus, but 43-year-old Parks did not move.

She was arrested and jailed, but was quickly bailed out by Nixon. Parks's attorney Fred Gray alerted Jo Ann Robinson, and she and the WPC got to work mimeographing and circulating some 35,000 fliers that called for a one-day bus boycott on the Monday that Parks was to be tried. On the Sunday before the boycott, local black preachers spread the word from the pulpit. There was widespread doubt, among both whites and blacks, that the boycott would succeed, since most black Montgomery residents had to use the buses to get to work. But that Monday morning the buses were eerily empty; only a handful of black passengers were to be seen. By contrast, the city's black taxicabs, which charged only 10 cents, the price of a bus ride, were crammed with people.

As expected, Rosa Parks was found guilty that day and fined $10, plus court costs of $4. But the success of the boycott created a new energy among black people in Montgomery. That night, huge crowds attended a mass meeting at the Holt Street Baptist Church and enthusiastically affirmed that the boycott should continue. The newly chosen president of the boycott committee, a 26-year-old minister named Martin Luther King, Jr. (*pages* 214-215), electrified the gathering with an impassioned speech. "There comes a time," King said, "that people get tired. We are here this

Almost two decades before his 1954 victory in *Brown v. the Board of Education*, NAACP lawyer Thurgood Marshall visited South Boston, Virginia, to report to his organization on the separate—and far from equal—schools there. White students attended the modern three-story brick facility above, while black students were assigned to the dilapidated one-story building at right.

evening to say to those who have mistreated us so long that we are tired—tired of being segregated and humiliated, tired of being kicked about by the brutal feet of oppression. When the history books are written in future generations the historians will pause and say, 'There lived a great people—a black people—who injected new meaning and dignity into the veins of civilization.' "

By the standards of a later day, the initial demands of the boycotters were very modest. They simply wanted the same segregated system that prevailed in other Alabama cities, in which blacks filled up bus seats from the rear forward and whites filled up from the front, with no one forced to vacate a seat once taken. The boycott committee also called for more courteous treatment from bus drivers and for the hiring of black drivers. Even so, the boycott encountered strong resistance. The local White Citizens' Council doubled its membership. Police began enforcing a minimum-cab-fare rule to make taxis less affordable and arrested private drivers who overloaded their cars. The situation became still more tense on January 30, 1956, when a bomb exploded at King's home, causing damage but no injuries. The attack was only one of several violent incidents, some involving snipers.

The harder the bus company and its supporters pushed, however, the harder the boycotters pushed back. The boycott committee now demanded true desegregation, rather than the polite compromise it had proposed earlier. To bring the issue before the courts, Fred Gray filed suit on behalf of five black women who had been harassed or ordered to move to the back of the bus in the period before the boycott. Before that challenge was resolved, the bus company's supporters struck again. In March, 25 ministers, including King, were indicted for conspiracy to boycott under an obscure Alabama law; only King was convicted. Far from stopping the protests, the violence and the jailings reinforced them by attracting the spotlight of national publicity. The press, which had covered the Emmett Till lynching the preceding summer, treated the boycott as another racial cause célèbre.

Six months after the boycott began, in June 1956, a special federal district court panel voted that the bus segregation policy was unconstitutional, in part because of the precedent set by the Brown case. The bus company appealed, but the United States Supreme Court let the ruling stand. Black passengers did not get back on the buses, however, until the Court's written order reached Montgomery on December 20, 1956. The bus boycott had lasted 382 days.

With that victory to savor, King, fellow minister Ralph Abernathy, and other like-minded black clergymen created the Southern Christian

Leadership Conference (SCLC) on January 11, 1957. Using black churches as a base for organizing, the SCLC planned to continue the spirit of the Montgomery bus boycott and challenge segregation with similar tactics throughout the South.

The Montgomery struggle, with its victory, had been inspired by the *Brown* decision, but the key issue of that case—school desegregation—continued to smolder. In 1957, three years after the verdict, racial mixing in the schools became a hot election topic in Arkansas, where Governor Orval Faubus faced a challenge from segregationist candidate James Johnson. Faubus responded by opposing plans to integrate schools in the state's capital of Little Rock that September. The proposed integration was on a very small scale: Nine students from the city's black school system were selected to attend Central High School. But at Faubus's orders, the teenagers were turned back by the Arkansas National Guard on the first day of class (*pages* 208-209). President Dwight Eisenhower finally sent in elements of the 101st Airborne Division to escort the "Little Rock Nine" from class to class all year.

National press coverage of the Little Rock Nine helped fuel increasing activism by black high-school and college students, as did encouraging new stories about developments in Africa itself. Confronted by growing independence movements, the European powers were relinquishing many of their former colonies on that continent. In 1960 alone, 11 new African nations would emerge, all led by black men and populated by a predominantly black citizenry.

Change was in the air, and in early 1960 a tidal swell of civil rights activism, primarily by young protestors, began to move across the South. It began in February with a sit-in at a whites-only lunch counter in Greensboro, North Carolina. Sit-in protests had been taking place sporadically—and successfully—for years (*pages* 212-213), as black patrons who were refused service by a business simply stayed in their seats, living evidence of discrimination. But in Greensboro, when four North Carolina Agricultural and Technical College freshmen refused to leave a segregated F. W. Woolworth lunch counter, they opened the floodgates. Within months, thousands of protestors, black and white, had participated in demonstrations throughout five southern states, desegregating many businesses, including the original Woolworth lunch counter. Some young activists, many of whom had been NAACP Youth members, soon created an organization of their own. In April, students from several schools met at Shaw University in Raleigh, North Carolina, to form the Student Non-Violent Coordinating Committee, or SNCC.

Still other young protestors were drawn to the so-called Freedom Rides aboard interstate buses, in which black and white volunteers defied southern custom by riding together. This kind of protest had first been tried in 1947, when the United States Supreme Court outlawed segregation on interstate buses. A pacifist Christian group called the Fellowship of Reconciliation, along with one of its organizational offshoots, the Congress of Racial Equality (CORE), had tested that ruling with a single interracial bus trip in the Upper South. Its young volunteers of both races were arrested, and some of them were convicted and sentenced to work on chain gangs; no further rides were attempted. But now the time seemed ripe to try again.

Balancing a box of turnip greens on her head, a Montgomery, Alabama, woman walks rather than taking the city's segregated buses. About 50,000 black residents honored the 1955-56 boycott, which brought the Rev. Martin Luther King, Jr., to national prominence.

A jubilant Coretta Scott King kisses her husband, Martin, soon after he was convicted in early 1956 for violating an Alabama law against boycotts. The young minister's conviction guaranteed the Montgomery bus protest would make front-page news nationwide.

On May 4, 1961, thirteen Freedom Riders on two commercial buses left Washington, D.C., bound for New Orleans. Outside Anniston, Alabama, one bus was stoned and later firebombed. An hour later, the second bus came through. When the bus stopped, its riders were badly beaten; one man, as a result of the beating, later suffered a stroke that left him paralyzed. But the riders pressed on, only to meet angry white mobs in Birmingham and Montgomery. A few weeks after Anniston, in another violent incident, a representative of United States Attorney General Robert Kennedy was beaten unconscious while accompanying a Freedom Ride. Despite the danger, the young volunteers, black and white, kept coming. Like the riders in 1947, they were also subject to arrest for violating local segregationist laws at bus terminals. This time, however, the laws would not stand. In September 1961, the Interstate Commerce Commission ruled that the terminals must accept bus riders on an integrated basis.

The forces of segregation were clearly losing ground. Some civil rights leaders— including A. Philip Randolph—argued that the time had come to shift to issues of economic justice. Randolph recalled his notion of a vast march on Washington, the mere threat of which had desegregated wartime defense plants. Now he called for a new March on Washington for "jobs and freedom." On August 28, 1963, the march drew more than a quarter of a million people to the capital (*pages 220-223*).

Although many activists spoke, the day would be forever marked by the impassioned "I Have a Dream" speech delivered by Martin Luther King, Jr., on the steps of the Lincoln Memorial. In one vivid sentence after another, King painted his dream of an America without racial prejudice, in which people would be judged "not by the color of their skin, but by the content of their character." His words captured the sweep of history as well as the shining idealism of the civil rights movement as it then existed. The success of the March on Washington as a peaceful, multiracial gathering strengthened demands for the federal government to take a greater role in ending Jim Crow laws and practices and job discrimination nationwide. Eleven months later, over the vehement objections of conservative southern senators, Congress passed the Civil Rights Act, ending racial bias in most public accommodations.

Although the massive demonstration that helped bring about passage of the Civil Rights Act had been for economic and social justice—"jobs and freedom"— activists had also been taking aim at political power, beginning with the very foundation of democracy: the ordinary citizen's right to vote. Especially in the South, legal, physical, and economic intimidation still kept many black Americans from registering to vote. In some parts of Alabama and Mississippi, not one black person was listed on the election rolls. To help change that, SNCC began sending voter-education volunteers into the most rural and white-controlled areas of the South in

1961. Their efforts were brave, and the positive response of some black residents was heroic. White segregationists, some of them local officials, were quick to beat, jail, and even kill black men and women whom they saw as threatening their political and economic power.

In 1963, SNCC workers in Mississippi held a mock election, which they called the Freedom Vote, a kind of rehearsal exercise meant to show black people they could register and vote without reprisals. Ninety three thousand black men and women from Mississippi participated. Bob Moses, SNCC's Mississippi coordinator, decided to launch an effort to actually register black voters in the summer of 1964, a project that became known as Freedom Summer. He recruited more than 800 students for the campaign, most of them white and from middle-class families outside the South.

Of the first group of students who ventured into Mississippi, one vanished within 24 hours. Andrew Goodman had accompanied veteran fieldworkers James Chaney and Mickey Schwerner to Longdale, Mississippi, where an earlier attempt by black residents to register voters had resulted in the torching of a church. All three disappeared. The next wave of volunteers kept their pledge to go into Mississippi, but they did so knowing that their lives were at stake. Indeed, six weeks into Freedom Summer the bodies of Chaney, Goodman, and Schwerner were found dead, buried in Philadelphia, Mississippi, under a dam. Chaney, the black member of the team, had been savagely beaten and then shot; the other two had simply been

shot. The FBI later arrested 21 men, including the local sheriff and his deputies.

Against this fearful backdrop, an estimated 1,200 southern African Americans nevertheless registered to vote during Freedom Summer. SNCC also established free health clinics and about 50 informal schools for black residents. Its efforts led as well to the formation of the Mississippi Freedom Democratic party, an alternative to the state's all-white Democratic party (*pages* 226-229).

The racial realities of southern life meant that voting rights were still to be won, however. In January 1965, the national press drew attention to Selma, Alabama, where Martin Luther King, Jr., and other civil rights workers had tried to register a significant number of black voters. News photographs showed Selma's sheriff, Jim Clark, beating black people trying to register to vote. "If blacks could vote," said King, "there would be no Jim Clarks." On February 18, just five miles outside Selma, police again attacked people leaving a voting rights meeting. When a young man named Jimmie Lee Jackson tried to defend his mother, a trooper shot him; Jackson later died of the wound. King and the SCLC, as well as other groups, planned an interracial

Freedom Rider David Dennis (*above, center*) keeps a wary eye on the Mississippi National Guardsmen escorting him, seatmate Julia Aaron, and 25 others as they ride an interstate bus in 1961. Local police arrested the riders in Jackson when they refused to leave a whites-only waiting room.

march of protest along the 54 miles from Selma to the Alabama state capitol in Montgomery. The marchers set out on March 7, but were halted by policemen on horseback, armed with tear gas and clubs, who charged into the crowd of demonstrators. The day was described nationwide as Bloody Sunday.

Undeterred by the violence against them, the marchers planned to resume their symbolic journey on March 25. After a federal court ruled that the march could not be banned by state officials, President Lyndon B. Johnson federalized the Alabama National Guard and ordered them to protect the protestors. For Johnson, the events in Selma provided the final argument for a federal bill aimed specifically at ensuring voting rights. Five months later he signed the Voting Rights Act into law, ending the literacy tests, understanding clauses, and other strategies that had for so long kept black Americans from exercising their constitutional right at the polls. In the next two months, the number of black registered voters in Selma alone rose from less than 10 percent of those old enough to vote to more than 60 percent.

Just as the movement achieved its greatest legislative victories in Washington, however, the northern inner cities crowded with black families began to explode in riots. As the events of Freedom Summer rippled across the Deep South in 1964, violence erupted in New York, New Jersey, Chicago, and Philadelphia. In 1965, the year the Voting Rights Act was passed, a five-day riot, lasting from August 11 to 16, gripped the Watts section of Los Angeles. The conflagration was sparked by a seemingly minor incident. After police stopped and arrested a drunken driver—a young black man—a crowd gathered. The driver's mother, encouraged by the jeers of spectators, began arguing with the officers. The police called for reinforcements and drew their weapons. The crowd began throwing stones and glass bottles, and the violence spread, eventually resulting in 34 deaths and an estimated $40 million in property damage. It was estimated that 5,000 black people participated in the Watts riots, facing off against 14,000 National Guardsmen.

The trouble in the big cities was daunting to civil rights activists, who had historically focused on clear-cut, easily identifiable oppression in the South. In 1965 and 1966, Martin Luther King, Jr., and the SCLC tried to export some of their civil rights strategy to Chicago, a city with hundreds of thousands of black residents, many of them born in Mississippi. The effort was an embarrassing failure. Outside the South, racial discrimination in jobs, housing, and other aspects of daily life was not codified into Jim Crow laws that could be challenged in court or protested on the streets. "There were no obtainable, immediate results for the northern, ghettoized black whose housing is getting worse; who is unable to find work, whose schools are deteriorating; who sees constantly more rats and roaches and garbage in the streets," SCLC organizer Bayard Rustin once said, adding, "He needed Malcolm, who brought him an internal victory." Rustin was talking about perhaps the best-known spokesman for blacks in the northern slums: Malcolm X.

Born Malcolm Little in Nebraska in 1925 to a preacher and his wife, he had an excellent record before he dropped out of school after the eighth grade; he was later convicted on a burglary charge in Massachusetts in 1946. While in prison, he became

a member of the Nation of Islam, a black-led religious group based in Chicago. Like others in the group, Little dropped his "slave" last name and substituted the letter "X." In 1954 he came to New York, preaching the word of the Nation of Islam. On Harlem's street corners, Malcolm X became a forceful advocate for his faith, and a strong critic of American race relations.

Malcolm X was not active in the civil rights movement and was often critical of its leaders. In his view, the March on Washington was orchestrated by white leaders to channel black discontent along harmless lines. He also saw nonviolent protest as a kind of self-victimization. "If they make the Ku Klux Klan nonviolent, I'll be non-violent. If they make the White Citizens' Council nonviolent, I'll be nonviolent," he told a group of black Mississippi high-school students on New Year's Day, 1965. "If the leaders of the nonviolent movement can go into the white community and teach nonviolence, good. I'd go along with that. But as long as I see them teaching non-violence only in the Black community, then we can't go along with that."

Civil rights legislation was another futile attempt at equality, in Malcolm X's opinion, one that would bring little change in the lives of black Americans. Instead, he hammered away with incisive analysis of America as a country with a racist heritage that had crippled black people. His willingness to say that African Americans had a right to fight back against segregationist violence, and his insistence on black-run organizations, had a powerful effect on his listeners.

Malcolm X was to die on February 21, 1965, assassinated at a public meeting in Harlem, but during the last year of his life he went through a period of profound personal and philosophical development (*pages* 230-231). After his death, his vision of black strength and self-reliance continued to have a powerful influence on a number of young African American leaders, including SNCC chairman Stokely Car-

As civil rights protests swept the South, so did a violent white backlash. In the hastily snapped photograph below, two black women who happened to be shopping in Montgomery a few days after a 1960 sit-in are beaten by white vigilantes—including one swinging a baseball bat.

Two civil rights volunteers help a black Mississippi couple fill out voter-registration forms during 1964's Freedom Summer. The form included a question asking the applicant to interpret a portion of the state's constitution.

michael. In 1966 Carmichael participated in a march held to protest an armed attack on civil rights pioneer James Meredith, the first black student to attend the University of Mississippi. As the demonstrators walked through the state, Martin Luther King, Jr., called for an end to violence and spoke of Christian principles. But when King left to fulfill another commitment on the night of June 16, Carmichael appealed to the assembled gathering with a distinctly different cry: Black Power. The following night, King heard the slogan for himself, as Willie Ricks, another SNCC member, led the crowd in a chant. "What do you want?" he asked. "Black Power!" they roared. "What do you want?" "Black Power!"

The shift in language was an ideological leap, from appeals for integration and equality to a condemnation of whites and a focus on black people as powerful, fully capable of taking charge of their own destiny. SCLC activist Andrew Young later recalled that King, who made no public comment on the matter, thought the slogan was a mistake. " 'If you go around claiming power, the whole society turns on you and crushes you,' " Young reported King as saying. " 'If you really have power, you don't need a slogan.' " Yet the words "black power" had struck a deeply responsive chord.

Black Power became a popular refrain among young activists, and the white mainstream press was inevitably drawn to the threat of black insurrection that it implied. King's SCLC and Roy Wilkins of the NAACP were portrayed as older, integrationist leaders who were losing touch with younger, more militant separatists. The National Urban League, a long-established black community-service organization, got the same treatment. It released a statement: "The National Urban League does not intend to invent slogans, however appealing that may be to the press." But the leaders of CORE—the group that had organized the interracial Freedom Rides—said at their 1966 convention that Black Power represented a "unified Black Voice reflecting racial pride in the tradition of a heterogeneous society." Overnight, scores of local and national African American groups sprang up to express the new black identity with bravado and with community-organizing projects meant to give a voice to people and neighborhoods ignored for too long. One of the more influential, and certainly the best known, was the Black Panther party (*pages* 232-235). Based in Oakland, California, the Black Panthers quickly became a lightning rod for government harassment as well as for black nationalist enthusiasm.

The popularity of Black Power during the late 1960s was matched by another slogan, Black Is Beautiful. In different tones, both phrases conveyed an emerging

sense of pride and self-empowerment among a long-oppressed and psychologically repressed minority. Black men and women affirmed their race with natural Afro hairstyles, African names, clothes, and foods, a renewed interest in Black English as a language in its own right, and books, movies, and music on similar themes. Hair straighteners, skin bleaches, and the like were condemned as representing white values and notions of beauty. Black Americans reaffirmed their interest in the emerging nations of Africa, expressing solidarity, forming some international political ties, and traveling to the motherland.

Such inner affirmation could not end the economic and social discrimination of the ghetto, however, and in 1966 and 1967 riots continued to rumble through the nation's black urban neighborhoods. Parts of Chicago, Cleveland, Newark, and Detroit were briefly transformed into centers of violence, death, and destruction, with nearly all of the lasting physical damage confined to black neighborhoods. In April 1968, when Martin Luther King, Jr., was gunned down in Memphis, Tennessee, 125 cities across the nation, including Washington, D.C., were ripped apart by riots. It was a strange expression of grief over the death of an advocate of nonviolence, but a true measure of the urban rage of the times.

The years between the *Brown* decision in 1954 and the Voting Rights Act of 1965, a period when there was a sense of growing cohesion between black and white Americans over the problem of race, were now consumed by the fires of anger and argument. Riots and bitter rhetoric spread fear among many white Americans as support for the civil rights movement took second place to concerns over public safety and crackdowns on crime. Black political activism outside the South brought racial issues uncomfortably close to home for some whites, who had previously regarded the matter as a televised morality play happening somewhere else. Amid growing debate over the conflict in Vietnam, the social order cracked still further during the 1968 presidential election, in which Robert Kennedy, one of the Democratic party's stronger civil rights advocates and its probable nominee, was killed on June 5, just two months after King's assassination. The Democrats' standard-bearer that fall was Hubert Humphrey; Humphrey was defeated by Richard Nixon, who had appealed to the fears of some whites with an emphasis on law and order. Third-party candidate and white supremacist George Wallace drew 9.9 million votes.

The shared commitment to repair the damage of past inequities degenerated into polarizing debates over affirmative action, busing to improve education for

Angela Davis learned her first lessons about racism growing up in the Dynamite Hill district of Birmingham, Alabama—so named for the frequent bombings of black homes. As a teenager, she reacted by organizing interracial study groups and demonstrating for civil rights. Davis went on to graduate study and a professorship in philosophy at the University of California at Los Angeles, where she actively participated in SNCC, the Black Panthers, and the Communist party—an affiliation that at one point led to her temporary dismissal. She also organized rallies for the Soledad Brothers, three black prisoners charged with murder on little evidence. On August 7, 1970, the 17-year-old brother of one of the men took a judge hostage at gunpoint; the kidnapper, the judge, and two others died. Police traced the guns to Davis, who was listed among the FBI's Ten Most Wanted until her arrest two months later. After an international movement to "Free Angela Davis" rocketed her to prominence, Davis was acquitted on all charges. She went on to found the National Alliance Against Racist and Political Repression. In the 1980s and 1990s, Davis continued to speak out against social injustice as an activist, author, and teacher. "My life," she has said, "belongs to the struggle."

black children, and the efficacy of government programs meant to help blacks—and poor people in general—share in America's prosperity. Many colleges, corporations, and government agencies took steps to increase black participation in the institutions of American life, but demographic and social trends pushed hard the other way. Urban unrest had led large numbers of whites to leave the nation's inner cities, accelerating a historic pattern of residential racial segregation. Many middle-class blacks, now able to move into previously segregated suburbs, also left the ghettos.

Although the average incomes of African Americans have risen since the 1940s, black Americans have made few gains relative to whites since the early 1970s. Blacks have also become polarized economically. Although many African Americans enjoy a middle-class income and lifestyle, for at least 20 years about a third of all black Americans have remained below the official poverty line. In the cities, many black Americans have endured crushing poverty for generations. The 1992 Los Angeles riots that erupted after four white police officers were acquitted in the beating of black motorist Rodney King, despite the evidence provided by a videotape of the incident, were attributed by community residents to the lack of jobs and opportunity.

The struggle for equal educational opportunity that had resulted in the *Brown* decision was meant, in part, to remedy such economic woes, but the victory in the schools remains incomplete. African Americans born in the late 1950s and 1960s now have roughly the same amount of education, measured in years, as whites born in the same period. But underfunded city public schools and racially segregated housing patterns suggest that for many black children education remains unequal.

On the political front, while the campaign for voting rights has had some effect, it too has a long way to go. During the 1970s, 1980s, and 1990s, predominantly black districts elected a growing number of black mayors and other black officeholders. Some black politicians have also won office in districts that are largely white. After the presidential election year of 1992, black politicians held nearly 8,000 elected positions at the federal, state, and local levels. Yet blacks remain underrepresented in American politics, making up only two percent of all elected officials in a nation with a 12 percent black population.

Although the numbers show real progress in dealing with racial oppression in American society and demonstrate the lasting effects of many civil rights victories, they also confirm that much has yet to be done. A passage written by Du Bois in 1908 still aptly describes the issue of race relations in the United States as the 20th century draws to a close: "The forward movement of a social group is not the compact march of an army, where the distance covered is practically the same for all, but is rather the straggling of a crowd, where some of whom hasten, some linger, some turn back, some reach far-off goals before others even start, and yet the crowd moves on."

In a scene broadcast around the world during the 1968 Mexico City Summer Olympics, Tommie Smith (*center*) and John Carlos (*right*)—gold and bronze medal winners in the 200-meter track event—give the Black Power salute. Silver medalist Peter Norman (*left*) of Australia later told the press he supported the protest. Smith and Carlos were allowed to keep their medals but were suspended from the United States team and barred from further competition because of the incident.

201

MARCUS GARVEY'S POWERFUL VISION

In March 1916, a 28-year-old black Jamaican named Marcus Garvey paid his first visit to Harlem. The young activist hoped to recruit members for the Universal Negro Improvement Association (UNIA), an organization he had founded to promote black nationalism and self-reliance. But Garvey, virtually unknown in the United States, could not raise much interest in his cause. To learn more about his audience, he embarked on a yearlong tour of black American communities in 38 states throughout the rural South, the West, and the North. When he returned to Harlem in June 1917, his eloquence on matters close to the hearts of his audience inspired many African Americans and West Indian immigrants to join the UNIA. In the next few years, it would become the largest black American movement yet, with a total membership worldwide of hundreds of thousands.

Garvey was born in rural Jamaica in 1887, a descendant of that country's maroons, fugitive slaves from the island's plantations who had established their own permanent, independent communities. He got his first taste of political action at the age of 18 when, as a printer in Kingston, he participated in a major strike. In 1910, restless to see the world, he began working his way around the globe, witnessing for himself the mistreatment of black people everywhere. Then one day in London in 1914 he picked up a copy of Booker T. Washington's autobiography, *Up from Slavery*. Garvey was so struck by the book's advocacy of black economic development that then and there, he later wrote, "my doom—if I may so call it—of being a race leader dawned on me." Within weeks, he returned to Jamaica and founded the UNIA.

When Garvey established the UNIA in the United States a few

Staff members assemble outside the offices of the *Negro World*, a journal founded by Marcus Garvey—shown at right in a 1921 portrait— with the motto A Newspaper Devoted Solely to the Interest of the Negro Race.

years later, he also shifted the organization's world headquarters there. The UNIA's international voice became that of the *Negro World*, a weekly newspaper that Garvey founded in New York in 1918. At the height of its 15-year run, the paper's circulation was estimated at between 60,000 and 200,000. As he explained in the *World*, Garvey believed that all black people should return to Africa to unite with black Africans in throwing off white colonial rule and building a black nation. In such a separatist state, he wrote, "every black man, whether he was born in Africa or in the Western world, will have the opportunity to develop on his own lines."

Like Booker T. Washington, Garvey also pushed hard for businesses owned and operated by blacks. And he derided groups like the NAACP, in which black leaders made an effort to work with members of other races. Only black men and women could join the UNIA. "We are organized," he wrote, "not to hate other men, but to lift ourselves, and to demand respect of all humanity."

As one manifestation of this racial uplift, in 1919 Garvey established the Black Star Line, a commercial steamship line meant to trade between Africa, the West Indies, and the United States. The line, which served black businesses, was intended to be captained and crewed by black sailors, although in practice it employed at least one white captain. That same year Garvey also founded the Negro Factories Corporation, which, over time, managed UNIA laundries, restaurants, tailoring and millinery establishments, a printing press, and a factory that manufactured black dolls.

Riding this wave of success, Garvey organized the first of a number of UNIA international conventions in 1920. Held at Madison Square Garden in New York City, the meeting attracted 25,000 people from all over the world and lasted the entire month of August. Splendidly uniformed Garveyites marched by the thousands in parades, and Garvey knighted some followers

In a scene from the 1920 UNIA convention, ceremonial guards and high-ranking delegates form an opulent court around Marcus Garvey, seated on a throne.

and gave others titles of nobility.

A few moderate black leaders mocked Garvey for all the pomp and ceremony, but such extravaganzas were a powerful testament to black pride. No one, wrote a contemporary black observer, could "see one of Garvey's ostentatious parades, hear Garvey's magnetic voice, read his *Negro World*, watch the sweep of his ideas and then say there was nothing to it."

The 1920 convention drafted and approved the Declaration of the Rights of the Negro Peoples of the World, which stated that Africa belonged to the black race and demanded, among other things, the teaching of black history in public schools, the use of a capital "N" in "Negro," and the end of lynching. Convention delegates also honored a new flag of red, black, and green—red for blood lost in the pursuit of liberty, black to honor the color of their skin, and green to evoke Africa's vegetation. The colors still represent black pride, although sometimes gold, symbolizing mineral wealth, is substituted for one of the three colors.

Garvey held another convention the following year, but his success was not to last. The dogmatic Jamaican had no shortage of political opponents, both white and black. NAACP leader W. E. B. Du Bois once called him "either a lunatic or a traitor." In January 1922, Garvey and three Black Star Line officials were arrested and indicted for using the mails to defraud investors. Essentially, the charge was representing the shipping line as a good investment even after it was clear that it was not profitable and would likely fail. As the investigation proceeded, eight black high-ranking NAACP members wrote a letter urging the prosecution on. NAACP activists coined the slogan Garvey Must Go.

During the trial, the charges against Garvey came down to the

In a portrait by the eminent black photographer James Van Der Zee, members of an American family (*left*) pose in full Garveyite regalia in 1924, a year before Garvey was imprisoned on charges of mail fraud. Garvey's second wife, Amy Jacques Garvey (*below*), directed the UNIA and published a collection of her husband's writings while he was in jail.

mailing of a single envelope containing a misleading prospectus—and even at that, the postmarked envelope introduced as evidence was empty. Nevertheless, when the prosecutor asked the jury, "Will you let the tiger loose?" the answer was no. His fellow defendants were acquitted, but Garvey himself was found guilty and sentenced to five years in federal prison. Though deeply depressed, the Jamaican had the last word. Referring to the prosecutor's remarks, he claimed that his enemies would find that "there are millions of cubs loose all over the world."

When Garvey entered an Atlanta penitentiary in 1925, the UNIA splintered, despite the efforts of his second wife, Amy Jacques Garvey, to hold it together. Still, many Garveyites united to campaign for his release. In 1927 he was pardoned by President Calvin Coolidge and immediately deported to Jamaica. Although he continued as head of what remained of the UNIA, he never fully regained his following. In 1940 he died in London of a stroke.

"When I am dead wrap the mantle of the Red, Black and Green around me," Garvey once wrote. "Look for me in the whirlwind or the storm, look for me all around you, for, with God's grace, I shall come and bring with me countless millions of black slaves who have died in America and the West Indies and the millions in Africa to aid you in the fight for Liberty, Freedom and Life."

The *Shady Side* (*far left*), a Black Star Line ship used for Hudson River excursions, floats at anchor in 1925. Those who bought a share in the doomed Garvey line received certificates of investment like the one shown here.

SCOTTSBORO BOYS

It was March 25, 1931, and the slow-moving freight train that wound its way from Chattanooga through parts of Alabama and Mississippi on its way to Memphis carried more than the usual grain or cattle in its cars: Nine young black men, two white women, and a number of white men had jumped aboard. Like many destitute Americans during the Depression, they were riding the rails looking for work.

Some of the drifters moved from the chilly open cars into an enclosed gondola, and somewhere between Chattanooga and Stevenson, Alabama, a fight broke out. The white men demanded that the black riders leave the car, and in the ensuing struggle, the blacks put all of them except one off the train. The bloodied white men went to the stationmaster, who notified the sheriff at a stop down the line. Plans were made to arrest all the blacks and transport them to Scottsboro, Alabama, the county seat.

When deputies searched the train they turned up the nine black riders, who ranged in age from 13 to 20; they also found a white youth and the two young women, Ruby Bates and Victoria Price. As the black men were being handcuffed and loaded onto a school bus for transport to the Scottsboro jail, Bates told the sheriff that she and Price had been raped by the blacks.

Word of the rape charge—which carried a sure death sentence for a black offender—spread quickly, and soon an angry mob gathered outside the jail, demanding that the men be handed over for lynching. "The

The Scottsboro Boys with their attorney in 1933: Haywood Patterson (*seated*); Olen Montgomery, Clarence Norris, Willie Roberson, Andrew Wright, Ozie Powell, Eugene Williams, Charley Weems, and Roy Wright (*left to right*).

crowd was howling like dogs," one of the black youths, Clarence Norris, recalled. "All I could think was that I was going to die for something I had not done." The National Guard was called out to clear the streets.

Trials for the Scottsboro Boys, as they became known, were set to begin April 6. The court appointed the defendants a lawyer—described by an acquaintance as an "extremely unreliable, senile individual"—but back in Chattanooga, where four of the accused had lived, a coalition of black preachers raised a total of $50.08 to retain Stephen Roddy, a white lawyer who drank up most of the money he earned. His first—and only—interview with his clients before the trial began lasted less than half an hour.

"I didn't know what a lawyer was supposed to be but I knew this one was no good for us," Norris remembered. "He had liquor on his breath and he was as scared as we were."

Evidence against the young men was presented in four separate trials that lasted a total of three days. Some of the defendants swore they had never seen Bates and Price on the train, while others, in a feeble attempt to save themselves, proclaimed their own innocence while testifying that others of the nine had

During retrials in 1933, lawyers for the defense produced a replica of the train in which the rapes allegedly took place. Witnesses testified that the men rode in separate cars from their accusers, Victoria Price and Ruby Bates. Bates admitted on the stand (*above*) that she had lied about the rapes.

raped the women. The jury found each man—with the exception of Roy Wright, a 13-year-old whose trial ended with a hung jury—guilty, and the judge sentenced them to death; they would be electrocuted on July 10. (Roy Wright was later retried and given life imprisonment.) There were cheers "all over town," Norris said, and "dancing in the streets."

Publicity kept the case alive, however. While the Scottsboro Boys waited on death row, they were interviewed by reporters from around the country. Thousands of demonstrators marched in Harlem and in other cities demanding that the youths be freed.

Although the NAACP was aware of the case, it had remained distant during the proceedings. It had no branch in the area, and as far as the organization knew, the nine men had obtained adequate counsel. After the verdicts, however, the NAACP and the Communist Party-USA vied to take on the case. Both realized its value in calling attention to the treatment of southern blacks, and the CP-USA wanted to attract blacks to the party. Its International Labor Defense (ILD) sent teams of lawyers to interview the young men in jail and launched a worldwide protest; the CP-USA eventually wrested the case from the NAACP.

The ILD won the Scottsboro

Boys a stay of execution and appealed the case to the United States Supreme Court. In November 1932, in the landmark ruling *Powell v. Alabama*, the Court ordered that the case be retried on the grounds that the state had failed to provide the men with adequate counsel. For the upcoming trials, the ILD retained New Yorker Samuel S. Leibowitz, considered to be one of the best criminal lawyers in the country.

The new trials began in March 1933, and to the surprise of many, Ruby Bates was a witness for the defense. Of her previous testimony that she had been raped, she explained, "I said it, but Victoria told me to." But Bates had been approached by the ILD and had traveled to New York to confer with its staff, before returning to testify. The jury—apparently thinking that she had been "contaminated" on her trip north—discounted her new story, and two of the eight defendants were again convicted.

Trials for the remaining six young men, who waited in jail, were postponed while the ILD appealed the two convictions. Two years later, the U.S. Supreme Court reversed the convictions on the grounds that blacks had been improperly excluded from the trial jury.

The next round of trials—in

which one black farmer sat on the jury—began in 1935, and by 1937 the outcomes had changed for some of the youths. All charges were dropped against four of the men; the rape charges against one man were dropped, but he received 25 years for assaulting a deputy sheriff; one man was given 75 years for rape, another 99 years, and the third a life sentence. But one by one the defendants were paroled, and in 1950, Andrew Wright, the last Scottsboro Boy still in prison, was released. "I'm not mad because the girl lied about me," he said of Victoria Price, whose deceit had cost him 19 years behind bars. "I feel sorry for her because I don't guess she sleeps much at night."

STUDENTS ON THE FRONT LINES

Beginning in the 1930s, the NAACP and other organizations waged legal war on the segregated classrooms of America, slowly breaking down race barriers at every level from the primary grades to professional school. But if Thurgood Marshall and other attorneys were the generals on this battlefield, students were the infantry. The young plaintiffs in each case persisted in the fight for months or even years. Then, after each court victory, courageous young black people followed through, attending formerly all-white schools despite harassment and occasional violence. Here and on the following pages, four stories of desegregation—some famous and some little known—suggest the trials these student pioneers endured.

Ada Fisher, daughter of an Oklahoma minister, was the first black admitted to the state's law school.

Ada Lois Sipuel Fisher

"On January 19, 1946, I applied for admission to the University of Oklahoma Law School," Ada Fisher told a New York audience in October 1948. "The president of the university, his advisers and the dean of admissions admitted that I was qualified in every respect except one: I am a Negro."

As a graduate of Oklahoma's segregated public schools and a segregated college, Fisher had not intended to wage a civil rights battle. But the law school was only for whites. To become a lawyer, Fisher had to desegregate it.

Represented by the NAACP, Fisher took her case to the Supreme Court. On January 12, 1948, the Court ruled that "equal education facilities" must be made available to black students. The university responded by throwing together a black law school in two weeks. The "school" had three faculty members and a token student, a waiter who soon left under pressure from black leaders.

Fisher argued in court that the new school did not offer equal education. The university, now facing legal challenges from black applicants to its graduate schools, backed down, permitting the enrollment of blacks at the graduate level. On June 18, Fisher enrolled in the University of Oklahoma Law School—where she was assigned a roped-off area in each classroom and in the cafeteria. Despite these humiliations, she got her degree and went on to practice law in Oklahoma, later becoming a professor at Langston University. In a telling irony, Fisher was named in 1992 to the Board of Regents of the University of Oklahoma—the school that once refused to admit her.

The Little Rock Nine

In September 1957, nine teenagers were to be the first black students at Central High School in Little Rock, Arkansas. But Governor Orval Faubus, mindful of an upcoming election, called out the National Guard to stop them. Not until federal troops arrived could the "Little Rock Nine" (*opposite*) even enter the building.

The students had been in school for less than three hours when administrators concerned about an unruly mob outside sent them home again by car from an underground garage. Junior Melba Pattillo recalled that the danger was so great that a policeman told her driver, "If you hit somebody, you keep rolling."

Even once the students were attending class regularly, they were constantly harassed. One day at lunch, Minnijean Brown poured chili on a white boy who kept calling her names. Brown was suspended; several weeks later, she was expelled after exchanging insults with a white girl.

During their ordeal, the students got considerable help and advice from Daisy Bates, president of the Arkansas Conference

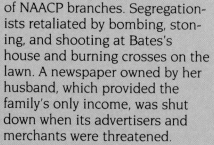

On the first day of class at Central High in 1957, eight of the Little Rock Nine went to school together (*left*); they were turned back at the door by Arkansas National Guardsmen. Elizabeth Eckford did not get the message to travel with the others and tried to enter alone at another end of the building. A jeering white mob (*below*) was on the point of attack when a white woman hastily escorted her to safety.

of NAACP branches. Segregationists retaliated by bombing, stoning, and shooting at Bates's house and burning crosses on the lawn. A newspaper owned by her husband, which provided the family's only income, was shut down when its advertisers and merchants were threatened.

But that May, Bates watched proudly as senior Ernest Green graduated. When his name was called, there was silence instead of the customary applause. "I figured they didn't have to," Green said. "After I got that diploma, that was it. I had accomplished what I had come there for."

Green, who later served in the Carter administration as an assistant secretary of labor, was the only one of the nine to graduate from Central, which closed the next fall to avoid integration. The Supreme Court ruled the closure unconstitutional, however, and in 1959 the school reopened—this time, as an integrated institution.

Accompanied by Daisy Bates, who stands at left with Jefferson Thomas at her feet, the Little Rock Nine enjoy a June 1958 trip to New York. Clockwise from upper left, the other eight are Thelma Mothershed, Gloria Ray, Ernest Green, Carlotta Wells, Terrance Roberts, Minnijean Brown, Melba Pattillo, and Elizabeth Eckford.

Television journalist Charlayne Hunter-Gault, shown in a 1992 snapshot below, was an intrepid college student 31 years earlier, when she was escorted to classes at the University of Georgia in Athens (*right*), one of two students to integrate the state institution.

Charlayne Hunter

Familiar to television audiences today as an aggressive, insightful journalist, Charlayne Hunter-Gault (*above*) was an unknown 18-year-old named Charlayne Hunter when she and Hamilton Holmes became the first African American students to attend the University of Georgia in January 1961. Hunter-Gault has often recalled the experience in interviews and writings. "There was conflict and there was pain. There was crisis and there was ignorance," she once said. "But I emerged as a whole person and the university came out the better for it."

The first day of the new term, Hunter attended class and was interviewed in her dormitory by a reporter. A crowd formed outside, but at first took no action. As Hunter tried to rest in her room that night, however, the mob got noisier and then became violent. A brick and a glass bottle were thrown through her window.

"At this time," she later wrote, "I did not know that all the students had been told by the riot planners to turn off the lights in their rooms when it got dark. With the rest of the building in darkness, the three brightly lit windows of my apartment must have made an inviting target."

The violence forced Hunter and Holmes off-campus, but, refusing to be intimidated, they courageously returned the next week. Because she had already taken some college courses, Hunter was able to cut short her stay at the university and graduate in just two years, in 1963. The press coverage of this part of her life influenced her to become a journalist, first at the *New Yorker*, and then at the *New York Times* and on television. Twenty-five years after graduating, in 1988, Charlayne Hunter-Gault was invited back to the University of Georgia to address the graduating class, becoming the first black commencement speaker in the school's history.

On September 30, 1962, federal marshals (*left*) guard the administration building at the University of Mississippi against rioters looking for James Meredith, the school's first black student. So much tear gas was released during the night that the next day Meredith had to breathe through a handkerchief (*below*) as he registered and went to class.

James Meredith

After serving nine years in the U.S. Air Force, 27-year-old James Meredith returned to his home state of Mississippi in 1960 and applied to the University of Mississippi. "Ole Miss" was the all-white university of what may have been the most stubbornly segregationist state in the country. Meredith, as he pointed out in his note to the registrar, was black. Not surprisingly, the school sent him an abrupt rejection.

With the backing of the NAACP, Meredith sued, and in September 1962—with classes at Ole Miss scheduled to start October 1—the Supreme Court ruled in his favor. President John F. Kennedy directed the secretary of defense to enforce the decision. On September 26, Meredith made out his will. "The price of progress is indeed high," he wrote, "but the price of holding it back is much higher."

By September 30, tensions on the Ole Miss campus had reached the riot stage. An armed mob stormed the administration building (*above*) with guns, incendiary bombs, and rocks. Several hundred federal marshals fought back with tear gas and night sticks. By dawn a French reporter and a local man were dead. But that day, James Meredith registered and attended his first class.

In the months that followed, Meredith, accompanied to class by Justice Department officers, endured a daily barrage of catcalls and insults. His parents in rural Mississippi had their home shot up by nightriders. But Meredith persisted. Having completed most of his college work during the years he battled for admission, he spent one year at Ole Miss before graduating with a degree in political science. At his graduation, James Meredith wore a segregationist political button under his gown—pinned on upside down.

A MIDWESTERN PROTEST

Until the mid-1960s, most news reports portrayed the civil rights movement as a strictly southern affair, largely confined to Mississippi and Alabama. But protests against racial discrimination were never a monopoly of the Deep South. In Chicago in 1942, for example, the Congress of Racial Equality (CORE) used a "sit-in" technique to desegregate two restaurants; a group of white and black CORE volunteers took seats in each establishment and requested service. When they were denied food, the activists stayed put, returning day after day, until the policies barring black customers changed. In the late 1950s, not long after the Montgomery bus boycott and the Little Rock confrontation, similar protests took place in several midwestern cities.

The first in this new round of sit-ins began on July 19, 1958, when 10 young black men and women walked into Dockum Drugs (*above*) in Wichita, Kansas, and headed for the lunch counter. Like other drugstores and five-and-dime stores in the predominantly white city, Dockum restricted its African American customers to carry-out meals from the counter; black men and women were not allowed to sit down and be served by the white help.

That Saturday morning, however, the 10 young African Americans each took a seat and quietly waited for service. After a while, a waitress told them, "I can't serve you here." Wichita University freshman Ronald Walters, president of the local NAACP Youth Council, responded for the group. They expected to be served, he said, and would not leave until that happened.

The protestors sat in place until the store closed for the day, and they came back to sit again—at first twice a week and then more often. Some whites were sympathetic—a number of white students from Wichita University even joined the protest—but others spat on the demonstrators and taunted them. One day, a white motorcycle gang walked in and threatened to rough up the sit-in participants. The police were called, but claimed that they saw no disturbance and left. Walters then put in a call to friends in the black community, who responded in force. With the arrival of carloads of black residents—some armed with clubs and knives—the white rowdies were forced to flee.

Finally, as the sit-in entered its fourth week, a representative of the drugstore chain's management came by. "Serve them. I'm losing too much money," he told the manager. An official change in store policy soon followed. Heartened by its success, the youth group targeted a second drugstore lunch counter, and soon others in Wichita fell in line as well.

Word of the victory spread to NAACP Youth Councils elsewhere, and that September, NAACP Youth members in Oklahoma City began desegregating lunch counters the same way. For the next year or two, sporadic sit-ins occurred in relative obscurity, until a February 1960 protest in Greensboro, North Carolina. This time the story was in the South, and the national press reported it. The publicity sparked a wave of sit-ins (*right*) that desegregated lunch counters and other public facilities in 14 southern states.

A SERIES OF SIT-INS

Sit-ins like the one described at left remained isolated incidents until national coverage of a 1960 protest in Greensboro (*right*) popularized the method. The protestors' ability to remain calm in the face of harassment gained them grudging admiration even from segregationists. "Here were the colored students, in coats, white shirts, ties," wrote one southern editor. Outside, he wrote, was a "gang of white boys come to heckle, a ragtail rabble, slack-jawed, black-jacketed, grinning fit to kill." The segregationist editor conceded that the contrast between the groups "gives one pause."

Ignored by a store employee, Joseph McNeil, Franklin McCain, Billy Smith, and Clarence Henderson wait for service at Woolworth's whites-only lunch counter (*above*) on day two of the Greensboro, North Carolina, sit-in in February 1960. The sit-in lasted six months.

Smeared with ketchup, mustard, and sugar by segregationist opponents, three demonstrators ignore their harassers during a 1963 lunch counter sit-in in Jackson, Mississippi.

Above, students picket the F. W. Woolworth annual meeting in New York in May 1960, supporting fellow protestors who were staging sit-ins at segregated Woolworth's counters across the South.

PREACHING CIVIL RIGHTS TO A NATION

Martin Luther King, Jr., was born in Atlanta, Georgia, on January 15, 1929, the first son of Alberta Williams King and the Reverend Martin Luther King, Sr., pastor of the Ebenezer Baptist Church. For the rest of his life, the traditions of the black church would pervade not only his philosophy but also his career and his politics.

Martin knew early on that his father wanted him to be a preacher, but he himself was uncertain. In 1944 he graduated with a superb academic record from a local segregated high school and entered Morehouse College that fall at the age of 15. At Morehouse, the teenage Martin at last felt a calling to the ministry, and after college, he went on to Crozer Theological Seminary in Pennsylvania.

There King encountered, and at first rejected, the ideas of Mahatma Gandhi, whose nonviolent tactics had helped liberate India from the British. After earning a divinity degree, King pursued a doctorate in philosophy at Boston University. In Boston, he met and married Coretta Scott.

Coretta was pregnant with the first of their four children when the Kings moved in 1955 to Montgomery, Alabama, where Martin became pastor of the Dexter Avenue Baptist Church. That December, local activists recruited the 26-year-old to lead a boycott of the city's segregated bus system (*pages 192-193*). The protest converted King to a belief in the power of nonviolence and led him and other black ministers to found the Southern Christian Leadership Conference (SCLC), which had its first permanent headquarters in Atlanta. Although King continued to serve his congregation, his activities on behalf of the SCLC grew too demanding. In late 1959 he resigned his position in Montgomery and moved to Atlanta with his family, becoming a full-time SCLC activist.

During the early 1960s, King's rising prominence also brought him to the attention of the FBI, which had long been suspicious of the civil rights movement. The agency began a deliberate cam-

In a 1936 snapshot (*left*), seven-year-old Martin Luther King, Jr., known in the family as M.L., stands tall beside his younger brother, Alfred Daniel, or A.D. The third King child, their older sister, Christine, is not pictured.

Above, police officers unfamiliar with King's appearance arrest him for loitering after he was prevented from entering a Montgomery courthouse on September 3, 1958. Embarrassed officials refused to jail him.

King (*below, right*) leads a rally on March 25, 1965, marking the end of the 54-mile Selma-to-Montgomery march for voting rights, which had been halted by violence two and a half weeks earlier before resuming under federal protection. "How long will it take?" was the refrain of his speech. "Not long!" chanted the crowd.

paign of surveillance, and eventually harassment, aimed at King.

In the spring of 1963, King and the SCLC targeted Birmingham, Alabama, one of the South's most conservative cities, for a desegregation protest. When demonstrations in April had little effect, the SCLC deployed thousands of teenagers and children in a series of marches. On May 2, the first day, hundreds of youngsters were arrested. Then the police response escalated. For the next five days, the young marchers were met by attack dogs and the blast of fire hoses. In the resulting glare of publicity,

Birmingham business leaders yielded to many SCLC demands.

The fragile peace lasted four months. In mid-September—just two weeks after King's inspired speech at the March on Washington (*pages 220-223*)—four young black girls died in a church bombing. King mourned with their families: "At times, life is hard," he said, "as hard as crucible steel."

In December 1964, King received the Nobel Peace Prize. His efforts over the next few months, culminating in the Selma-to-Montgomery voting rights march, helped lead to the 1965 Voting Rights Act. But the tide was turning against King. Urban riots had become a yearly crisis, and disillusioned young activists were rejecting non-violence as a tactic.

In 1967, King broke with other civil rights leaders when he criticized the American role in Vietnam. During this time, he also came to realize the extent of the FBI's wiretapping and other operations against him. The realization seemed to fill him with foreboding, and he often spoke of his own death. In a speech given in Memphis, Tennessee, on April 3, 1968, he said: "Longevity has its place. But I'm not concerned about that right now. I just want to do God's will. And He's allowed me to go up to the mountain, and I've seen the promised land. I may not get there with you. But I want you to know tonight, that we, as a people, will get to the promised land." A day later, Martin Luther King, Jr., lay dead of an assassin's bullet at the age of 39.

Although King was influenced by the non-violent philosophy of Mahatma Gandhi, whose portrait gazed down on the King dinner table (*above*), his ideas grew out of the black church. At left, King preaches in 1960 at Atlanta's Ebenezer Baptist Church, which also served as headquarters for the Southern Christian Leadership Conference.

A FREEDOM RIDER'S RISKY ODYSSEY

As her bus pulled away from the Tennessee State campus in Nashville in May 1961, twenty-one-year-old Lucretia Collins had much to reflect on. "I kept thinking about the people in my family who would not understand this and who would perhaps be hurt if anything happened to me," she said later in an interview. But Collins had no doubts about her decision: Just weeks short of graduation, she was leaving school to join an interracial Freedom Ride.

Days earlier, 13 black and white volunteers had taken part in 1961's first Freedom Ride, riding together in the South on two interstate buses. They had been attacked in Anniston, Alabama, and halted by mob violence in Birmingham. Now Collins was one among several volunteers who planned to resume the Freedom Ride in Birmingham, carrying the protest forward by riding to Nashville. Before they could begin, however, Birmingham police threw all 17 of the riders in jail, supposedly as protection against mob violence. After a day and a half, Collins and six other prisoners were shoved into cars and dropped off at the Tennessee state line. As dawn broke, they were 93 miles from home base in Nashville. Luckily, the riders found a friendly black family with a telephone and called for help.

The call soon brought a protest coordinator from Nashville, who drove the Freedom Riders back to Birmingham to join more volunteers. Then came a new ordeal. "We tried to catch every bus that left," Collins recalled, but the bus drivers refused to let them aboard. Night fell, and passed. Finally, Collins said, "We began to sing. I don't think that song—'We Shall Overcome'—ever had so much meaning as it did that morning." The next bus driver, who was headed for Montgomery, Alabama, let them on board.

When the Freedom Riders got to Montgomery, they held a briefing for reporters who had followed the bus from Birmingham. Almost at once a hostile white crowd moved in, beat-

Jim Zwerg (*above, right*) feels for a lost tooth shortly after he and fellow Freedom Rider John Lewis (*above, left*) were beaten by a mob in Montgomery, Alabama.

On May 26, 1961, two days after her arrest as a Freedom Rider, Lucretia Collins (*right*) speaks to the press while waiting at the Jackson, Mississippi, airport for a plane back to college.

ing reporters and smashing cameras. The female protestors escaped in taxis, but the men could not. Three were beaten so badly they had to be taken to local hospitals, as was James Seigenthaler, an aide to the U.S. Attorney General who had been sent to Alabama to help handle the crisis.

Two nights later, as the demonstrators were honored at a mass meeting of about 1,500 people at Montgomery's First Baptist Church, federal marshals could barely restrain the angry whites gathered outside. A stone shattered a church window, and tear-gas canisters thrown at the mob by marshals were hurled back toward the meeting. Despite the suffocating gas that filled the church, the Reverend S. S. Seay, a local civil rights leader, led the crowd in prayer, and Martin Luther King, Jr., also spoke.

A few days later, the Freedom Riders got back on the bus. But in Jackson, Mississippi, the next stop, city police arrested the protestors as they sat in the white waiting room and charged them with disturbing the peace and trespassing. Several served their 60-day sentences, but Lucretia Collins asked to be bailed out so

that she could attend Tennessee State's graduation. Collins later discovered that administrators had decided not to confer her degree because of her absence on the ride. "I also learned that our classmates had planned to walk out if they did not let me graduate," she added. "Perhaps because of this, I got my degree."

The First Baptist Church rocks with applause (*above*) as a speaker announces the presence of the Freedom Riders on May 21, 1961. When tear gas drifted into the church, the crowd covered their noses with handkerchiefs against the suffocating vapors (*left*).

MISSISSIPPI MARTYRDOM

In 1946, Medgar Evers returned home to Mississippi from World War II. He, his brother Charlie, and four other young black men registered to vote—something only about five percent of black Mississippians did at that time, even though African Americans made up about 45 percent of the state's population. But when the six went to cast their ballots on election day, they were blocked by about 200 armed whites. "After the Germans and the Japanese hadn't killed us," Evers later re-

called, "it looked as though the white Mississippians would." He and the others went home.

As the incident suggests, Mississippi was far from a land of opportunity for African Americans. In 1954, two years after graduating from Alcorn Agricultural and Mechanical College, Evers applied to the University of Mississippi Law School but was rejected because he refused to supply recommendations from whites. Despite these and other setbacks, however, Evers never

lost faith that change was possible in his home state. Later in 1954, he became the NAACP's first field secretary in Mississippi, responsible for recruiting new members, encouraging black voter registration, and investigating racial harassment and lynchings (including that of Emmett Till in 1955). These duties made him a natural target for white supremacists. According to his wife, Myrlie, his family received frequent telephone death threats. She and Medgar kept a gun in every room

In a blurry photograph taken at her husband's funeral in Jackson, Myrlie Evers comforts her nine-year-old son Darrell Kenyatta. The couple's other two children, aged eight and three, also attended the ceremony, after which an estimated 3,000 black men and women marched behind the hearse bearing Medgar Evers's body. He was buried in Arlington National Cemetery, just outside Washington, D.C., four days later.

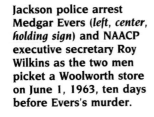

Jackson police arrest Medgar Evers (*left, center, holding sign*) and NAACP executive secretary Roy Wilkins as the two men picket a Woolworth store on June 1, 1963, ten days before Evers's murder.

of the house and taught their three children to lie on the floor if shooting broke out.

In spring 1963, Evers and other NAACP leaders held a mass meeting in Jackson, the state capital, calling for an end to all forms of segregation in the city. When the mayor rebuffed their demands, the NAACP launched sit-ins at a Woolworth store on May 28. That night someone threw a Molotov cocktail at Evers's home. Some days later, police clubbed and arrested hundreds of black high-school students marching in support of the NAACP.

Evers wanted to organize fur-

ther protests, and when NAACP headquarters in New York would not approve the additional bail money, he began to raise money on his own, arranging for a benefit concert by Lena Horne. "Freedom has never been free," Evers told the concert crowd. "I love my children and I love my wife with all my heart. And I would die, and die gladly, if that would make a better life for them."

Four days later, on the morning of June 11, he left home as usual to attend meetings and other functions connected to the protests. "During that day, he called two or three times," Myrlie Evers later remembered, "which was a little unusual with all of the activity that was going on." Medgar Evers worked late that night, but the family was still up when he pulled into the driveway just after midnight. "We heard him get out of the car and the car door slam," Myrlie recalled, "and in that same instant, we heard the loud gun-

fire." When she rushed to the front door, she found her husband had been shot in the back. Evers, 37, died within an hour—the first prominent civil rights leader of the 1960s to become a martyr for the movement.

Byron de la Beckwith, a local fertilizer salesman and ardent segregationist, was charged with the murder. His fingerprints were found on a rifle and scope discovered near the murder scene, and several witnesses recalled seeing him in Jackson on the night in question. But at two trials in 1964, all-white juries failed to reach a verdict. In 1992, citing new evidence, prosecutors called for a third trial. Some questioned whether a judgment could be reached on so old a crime. For those in the civil rights community, however, holding the trial symbolized part of the movement's unfinished business—the countless racial murders that remain unsolved or unprosecuted.

A QUARTER OF A MILLION STRONG

"Woke up this morning with my mind set on freedom, hallelu, hallelu, hallelujah!" chorused hundreds of travelers as they poured out of their train at Washington, D.C.'s, Union Station. The morning was Wednesday, August 28, 1963, and their destination was the Lincoln Memorial. There, at the marble feet of the president who had signed the Emancipation Proclamation 100 years earlier, they would gather with some 250,000 other Americans, including 60,000 white supporters, for the largest demonstration of its time—the March on Washington for Jobs and Freedom.

A century after the Civil War, most black families still had to struggle to make ends meet, earning an average of only $3,500 a year compared with a white family's $6,500. And that was when they could find work at all, for black unemployment hovered around 11 percent; meanwhile just five percent of the white work force went jobless. Civil rights activists A. Philip Randolph and Bayard Rustin—the organizers of the march—first planned the event as a protest against discrimination in employment. Soon, though, their goals expanded to include demands for other civil rights—decent housing, education, and the right to vote.

Some 2,000 chartered buses and more than 30 trains con-

The official button of the march, which sold for 25 cents, showed black and white hands clasped in a symbol of unity.

Members of the congregation of Cincinnati's Carmel Presbyterian Church donate money to the March on Washington. Funds were needed for such essentials as toilets and a sound system.

On August 11, 1963, Congress of Racial Equality (CORE) volunteers visit a Cincinnati-area home, spreading word of the march and selling buttons. Such efforts helped carry the message to so many people that more than twice the number expected took part.

CORE members swing to rock, jazz, and twist tunes in Cincinnati's Club Ramon at a benefit titled "Jam for Freedom." The civil rights group hoped to raise enough funds to send its members to the march, only two weeks away.

221

Like countless civil rights workers in other organizations across the country, a young NAACP volunteer in Cincinnati distributes fliers announcing the March on Washington for Jobs and Freedom.

Fired by leaflets like this one, listing endorsements by well-known activists and the basic demands of black Americans, an unprecedented crowd descended on Washington, where they surrounded the Lincoln Memorial to listen to speeches and songs (*background*).

Sitting beside a stack of protest signs near the base of the Washington Monument, march participant Roosevelt Nesmith of Camden, New Jersey, introduces his three-year-old son to the civil rights movement.

verged on the nation's capital that day, carrying schoolteachers and students, church groups, labor leaders and union workers, clerks, cooks, and priests, as well as thousands of poor and unemployed black Americans—all having learned of the event through local churches and civil rights organizations. One of several chartered airplanes brought celebrities from Hollywood. An African American youth roller-skated in from Chicago, wearing a red sash proclaiming "Freedom," and other demonstrators—including an 82-year-old man—arrived by bicycle from as far away as South Dakota. "Black people voted that day with their feet," said Bayard Rustin. "They came from every state, they came in jalopies, on trains, buses, anything they could get—some walked."

They also came from Savannah, Georgia—where police had sprayed tear gas at crowds of demonstrators on June 19—and from Danville, Virginia, where on June 10, the notorious "Bloody

Monday," police officers had kicked down the door of an African American church and injured 65 civil rights workers with clubs and fire hoses. In the midst of a year racked by violence, many expected the march to erupt into an angry mob scene, and the government put thousands of local police, National Guardsmen, and U.S. troops on the alert.

But such fears proved groundless. The swell of marchers peacefully carried signs calling for "Voting Rights Now" and "Jobs for All Now" up Independence and Constitution avenues to the Lincoln Memorial; and in a celebration of racial harmony, black and white singers such as Marian Anderson and Bob Dylan, Mahalia Jackson and Joan Baez, inspired the crowd with renditions of "Oh Freedom" and "He's Got the Whole World in His Hands." Afterward, Randolph kicked off the program of speakers, which included prominent figures in civil rights, labor, and the church. "Let the nation and the world know the meaning of our numbers," he proclaimed. "We are not a mob. We are the advance guard of a massive moral revolution for jobs and freedom."

Late in the afternoon, Randolph called the last speaker, Dr. Martin Luther King, Jr., to the microphone. As television networks ABC, CBS, and NBC turned their cameras on him, King began the litany of dreams that would pull cheering thousands to their tired feet and move the hearts of an entire nation. At the end of it, he marked the historic day with a prayer that "all God's children, black men and white men, Jews and gentiles, Protestants and Catholics, will be able to join hands and sing in the words of the old Negro spiritual: 'Free at last! Free at last! Thank God Almighty, we are free at last!'"

TRAINING FOR A BRUTAL SUMMER

"The reality of Mississippi gets closer every day," wrote SNCC civil rights volunteer Margaret Aley in June 1964, partway through a training session in Ohio. "We know the blood is going to flow this summer and it's going to be our blood. And I'm scared. I'm very scared."

As part of the Mississippi Summer Project, more popularly known as Freedom Summer, hundreds of volunteers like Aley swept into the state in the summer of 1964 to register black voters, organize informal schools, and establish health clinics. As Aley's words suggest, the violence and harassment the volunteers encountered along the way was utterly predictable. It was also a key part of the paradox of nonviolence, which makes the greatest impact when set against brutality. In the case of Mississippi, especially, many in SNCC believed that only unprovoked segrega-tionist assaults on young volunteers would stir the federal government to action. And yet, of course, no one wanted the volunteers to be hurt or killed. In two separate week-long training sessions, SNCC veterans tried to give the northern, predominantly white, newcomers some rudimentary survival skills. If nothing else, they tried to convey just what life in Mississippi as a civil rights worker would be like.

"We didn't concentrate on how to protect yourself," SNCC executive secretary James Forman, who helped run the training, later explained. Instead, by rehearsing the kinds of ugly insults volunteers might encounter, or the physical attacks that could happen, the trainers would "get people acclimated," he said, so that, whatever occurred, "they would have already done it, so it wouldn't be as deadly."

As an introduction to the sum-

Andrew Goodman (*below, left*) and two other workshop participants hurl insults at fellow trainees as part of a training exercise. The following week, 20-year-old Goodman would become one of three civil rights workers to die in a single incident.

SNCC volunteers practice how to react to an attack by lying close together and protecting their heads, with one participant keeping a lookout.

mer, these dry runs of possible tragedy had a powerful effect on the participants. One volunteer wrote about seeing a group of stunned trainees in a role-playing exercise "riveted to the frozen tableau of a violence that till that moment had existed for them only in grade-B movies and tabloid spreads." For others, simply meeting the veteran activists who served as trainers was sobering. "I'd venture to say that every member of the Mississippi staff has been beaten at least once and he who has not been shot at is rare," wrote one participant.

Early in their training week, the second group of volunteers were further shaken by news of the disappearance of two experienced civil rights workers and fellow trainee Andrew Goodman, who had been in the first workshop group (*page* 196). (All three who vanished were later found dead.) And the horror was just begin-

ning. By the end of the summer, the official tally stood at four civil rights workers dead, four others critically wounded, and 80 beaten. Thirty-seven churches and 30 black homes and businesses were either bombed or burned.

In the midst of the violence, the young people accomplished much of the grass-roots work they had set out to do. But the August defeat of the SNCC-inspired Mississippi Freedom Democratic party (*pages* 226-229), combined with the weeks of brutality, contributed to a sense of overall failure. For many SNCC regulars, including James Forman, nonviolence had lost its appeal. "The Mississippi Summer Project," Forman wrote in 1972, "confirmed the absolute necessity for self-defense."

Struggling trainees pile on top of workshop director James Forman, SNCC's executive secretary, in a rehearsal of a mob beating.

As she leaves for Mississippi on a chartered SNCC bus, volunteer Penny Patch says good-bye to an unidentified fellow participant.

MISSISSIPPI'S FIGHT FOR FREEDOM

"Nineteen sixty-four could really be the year for Mississippi," predicted John Lewis, the national chairman of the Student Non-Violent Coordinating Committee, early in that presidential election year. With all but six percent of the state's black citizens barred from voting by Jim Crow laws and terrorism, SNCC had targeted Mississippi for major change. "Before the Negro people get the right to vote, there will have to be a massive confrontation," Lewis stated. "We are going to Mississippi in force."

And they did. Perhaps as many as a thousand volunteers began flooding into the Magnolia State in June 1964 as part of the SNCC project called Freedom Summer. Not only would they register African American voters, they would also sign the voters up in a new political party: the Mississippi Freedom Democrats (MFDP). SNCC had organized the MFDP in April to challenge Mississippi's whites-only regular Democratic party. Open to everyone, regardless of race, the Freedom Democrats planned to unseat the regular party at the Democratic national convention, scheduled for the end of August in Atlantic City, New Jersey.

Emerging as a natural leader in the new party was Fannie Lou Hamer, a poor black woman from

Testifying before the Credentials Committee of the Democratic national convention on August 22, 1964, Fannie Lou Hamer urges the committee members to repudiate the racist Mississippi Democratic party and instead seat the "only honest" party—the Freedom Democrats.

the town of Ruleville whose now-famous words "I'm sick and tired of being sick and tired" would become a motto in the civil rights movement. The 20th child of a sharecropping family, Hamer had experienced some of the worst of her state's racial hatred. When she was a child, neighbors had poisoned the family's live-stock, destroying their chance to run their own farm. At age six Hamer began picking cotton and by 13 was forced to abandon school altogether to work in the fields. She married and twice gave birth to stillborns. In 1961, at age 43, a white doctor steri-lized her without her knowledge, much less her consent.

But the course of Hamer's life was destined to change the fol-lowing year, when she attended a rally where SNCC's executive director, James Forman, urged black Mississippians to dare to vote. "When they asked for those to raise their hands who'd go down to the courthouse the next day, I raised mine. Had it up high as I could get," Hamer said. "The only thing they could do to me was kill me, and it seemed like they'd been trying to do that a little bit at a time ever since I could remember."

Hamer traveled to the court-house with the group as planned but then failed a literacy test and could not register. Merely for

making the attempt, though, she lost her job and her home. Un-daunted, she tried to register again in December and finally succeeded in January 1963. Soon afterward, Hamer began teaching others how to pass the voting test and in 1964 turned to civil rights work full-time in the Mis-sissippi Freedom Democratic party, where her dedication and eloquence earned her the posi-tion of vice-chairman. In August of that year, 2,500 members elected her to help lead the MFDP delegation in Atlantic City.

On the first day of the conven-tion, the Freedom Democrats took their case to represent Mis-sissippi before the Credentials

Mississippi Freedom Democrats and their sup-porters gather for an all-night vigil on August 24. Rita Schwerner, widow of one of three civil rights workers murdered in June in Mississippi, stands at near center.

We Shall Overcome

Committee, whose members would decide which of the competing delegations to seat. In a nationally televised hearing that would prove to be the convention's most dramatic event, Hamer described horrors committed against black Americans in her home state: the arrest of a busload of people trying to register to vote in Indianola, her own job loss and eviction for trying to register, and the violent beating she suffered in the Winona jailhouse during June 1963 on her return from a civil rights meeting. "If the Freedom Democratic party is not seated now, I question America," she concluded. "Is this America, the land of the free and the home of the brave, where we have to sleep with our telephones off of the hook because our lives be threatened daily, because we want to live as decent human beings in America?"

President Lyndon Johnson, who backed the standard Mississippi Democratic party and wanted a peaceful convention, watched Hamer begin her stirring testimony on television and tried to preempt her by ordering an immediate press conference. But viewers had seen enough: The committee was soon overwhelmed with calls and telegrams from outraged Americans supporting Hamer's delegation.

Ironically, the standard Mississippi party did not support Johnson's nomination—while the Freedom party did—yet Johnson pressured members of the Credentials Committee to stick with the status quo. He also put Hubert Humphrey to work on a compromise proposal, intimating that he would choose the Minnesota senator as his running mate only if the Freedom Democrats were silenced. Learning of the aspiring candidate's dilemma, Hamer recalled that she asked him directly, "Mr. Humphrey, do you mean to tell me that your position is more important to you than four hundred thousand black people's lives?"

On August 27, after their disappointing defeat, members of the Mississippi Freedom Democratic party join hands in prayer at the convention hall.

The compromise eventually offered to the MFDP called for seating the standard delegation and giving two of the Freedom delegates a pair of at-large seats on the convention floor. Hamer's response was characteristically fiery: "We didn't come all this way for no two seats when all of us is tired." The rest of the party agreed and rejected the compromise. "We would have been betraying those very many people back there in Mississippi," delegate Victoria Gray explained.

In the face of rejection by both the president they supported and the Democratic party, the MFDP marched onto the convention floor with borrowed passes, singing songs of freedom in their determination to be heard. When a reporter asked Hamer whether she wanted to be equal with white men, her reply was both scathing and inspiring. "What would I look like fighting for equality with the white man?" she demanded. "I don't want to go down that low. I want the true democracy that'll raise that white man up—raise America up." Fannie Lou Hamer and the Mississippi Freedom Democrats went down fighting, thereby pushing the nation's politics closer to the goal of raising America up. Never again would a major party convention seat a discriminatory delegation.

Television newscaster John Chancellor watches New Jersey police bar Fannie Lou Hamer, MFDP chairman Aaron Henry (*near right*), and other members of the party who are trying to enter the convention hall. The delegates managed to get in using passes borrowed from supporters.

"OUR OWN BLACK SHINING PRINCE"

On March 8, 1964, Malcolm X announced his break with the Nation of Islam, the religious group that had raised him out of despair in prison (*pages* 197-198). After 17 years, the rift between them had grown too wide. In the months that followed, he would go through enough political and philosophical transformation to fill most people's lifetimes.

Malcolm X immediately formed his own Islamic community, the Muslim Mosque, Inc. He also began making political statements more openly than he had been permitted to do as a spokesman for the Nation. He repeatedly called for "the ballot before the bullet" in speeches that positioned him as a black militant willing to try conventional politics. "Well, if you and I don't use the ballot," he would say, "we're going to be forced to use the bullet." He went on: "So let us try the ballot. And if the ballot doesn't work, we'll try something else. But let us try the ballot."

Malcolm also began exploring new religious territory after his break with the Nation. In April 1964, he changed his name to Malik El-Shabazz and went on hajj, or a pilgrimage, to Mecca. There he encountered Muslims of many colors meeting together as equals. He had had similar experiences on a 1959 trip to Saudi Arabia, but had said little at the time. Now, in a spate of postcards and letters, he marveled at eating, living, and praying "with fellow Muslims whose eyes were the bluest of blue, whose hair was the blondest of blond, and whose skin was the whitest of white." Although his anger at white American racism still burned, he moved away from the religious black separatism of his Nation of Islam days.

For a month after the hajj, Malcolm X (as he was usually still called) traveled throughout the Middle East and Africa as a guest of state. Then he returned home to found the Organization of Afro-American Unity (OAAU). Malcolm determined that the group would accept no contributions from whites, on the grounds that "a man who tosses worms in the river isn't necessarily a friend of the fish." Anticipating the themes of the later Black Power movement, the OAAU charter stressed self-defense as well as education, economic empowerment, community outreach, and reclaiming African culture. The OAAU was also meant to draw African nations into the race struggle within the United States. In July, Malcolm circulated a document at an international conference of African nations in Cairo, urging the delegates to petition the United Nations on behalf of black Americans; the paper argued that the physical and economic oppression of African Americans violated UN conventions on both human rights and genocide. But no African nation leaped to join his cause for fear of losing American financial aid.

During his many travels, which accounted for a total of six months in 1964 alone, Malcolm met with Arab leaders, debated at Oxford University, and addressed the Council of African Organizations in London. He attempted to speak to African students in Paris, but was turned away at Orly Airport by French authorities who feared racial strife.

Expanding horizons abroad did nothing to change the fact that trouble was brewing at home, where a constant stream of letters and telephone calls threatened his life. The Nation tried for months to evict Malcolm X from a house the group owned in Queens. Early on February 14, the house was firebombed. No one was injured, but Malcolm X, his pregnant wife, Betty, and their four daughters moved out four days later. Although Malcolm believed he was a marked man, he refused police protection, convinced that no one could guard him effectively enough.

On February 21, 1965, Malcolm X was scheduled to speak at an OAAU rally at the Audubon Ballroom in upper Manhattan. He was nervous on his arrival. "I feel that I should not be here," he said to an aide when none of the expected platform guests appeared. "Something is wrong." Yet he refused to cancel the meeting. As he uttered the Muslim greeting As *salaamu alaikum* ("Peace be unto you") to the crowd of several hundred, a shouting match erupted in the front row and a smoke bomb exploded. Suddenly, a man fired a shotgun twice at Malcolm's chest; two other gunmen blasted his body where it fell. The eloquent voice of Malcolm X had been silenced at the age of 39. Three men were later convicted of his murder.

At the funeral on February 27, African American actor Ossie Davis captured what the fallen hero had meant to many. Referring to Harlem, where the service was held, he said: "It is not in the memory of man that this beleaguered, unfortunate but nonetheless proud community has found a braver, more gallant champion than this Afro-American who lies before us—unconquered still." He went on to eulogize him as "our manhood, our living black manhood," and "our own black shining prince." In death, as in life, Malcolm X became a symbol of racial pride and uncompromising moral principle. He remains for many the voice of the black underclass, his legacy embedded forever in the defiant hope of his words and life.

POWER TO THE PEOPLE

The scene was extraordinary: Twenty-four black men and six black women—many wearing black leather jackets and berets, some carrying .45s and .357 magnums—walked toward the California state capitol in Sacramento on May 2, 1967. The demonstration was meant to protest a bill then before the California state legislature that would forbid civilians to carry loaded firearms in public. On the capitol steps, the group's leader, Bobby Seale, read a statement calling on African Americans to arm themselves; then the 30 protestors entered the building. They had intended to make their way to the spectators' gallery, but, surrounded by reporters, the gun-toting activists were carried straight onto the assembly floor. They were immediately asked to leave and did so, only to be arrested outside. Images of armed blacks in the state legislature made news nationwide.

Thus were many Americans first introduced to the Black Panthers. Unlike most nationally known black political groups of the 1960s, which arose in the South or the Northeast, the Black Panther Party for Self-Defense was born in the American West,

Clad in black jackets and caps, armed Black Panthers (*left*) protest on the steps of the California legislature on May 2, 1967, against a bill—directed against the Panthers—banning the carrying of loaded firearms. Bobby Seale, cofounder of the group, is at far right.

in Oakland, California. Founded in October 1966 by two Oakland residents, 24-year-old Huey P. Newton and 29-year-old Bobby Seale, the party took its name from the black panther symbol of the Lowndes County Freedom Organization, a political party formed in Alabama in 1965. Newton and Seale had met while working at the North Oakland Neighborhood Anti-Poverty Center, where they came into frequent contact with victims of police brutality—an issue that

would be a key Panther concern.

The organization had visions far beyond municipal matters, however. Influenced by Malcolm X, Mao Zedong, Karl Marx, and revolutionary political theorist Frantz Fanon, among others, Newton and Seale conceived a "10-point program" (*below*) calling for "land, bread, housing, education, clothing, justice and peace."

The Panthers began putting some of those ideals into practice in December 1966, when Seale, Newton, and others start-

BLACK PANTHER 10-POINT PROGRAM

1. WE WANT FREEDOM. WE WANT POWER TO DETERMINE THE DESTINY OF OUR BLACK COMMUNITY.

2. WE WANT FULL EMPLOYMENT FOR OUR PEOPLE.

3. WE WANT AN END TO ROBBERY BY THE CAPITALIST OF OUR BLACK COMMUNITY.

4. WE WANT DECENT HOUSING, FIT FOR SHELTER OF HUMAN BEINGS.

5. WE WANT EDUCATION FOR OUR PEOPLE THAT EXPOSES THE TRUE NATURE OF THIS DECADENT AMERICAN SOCIETY. WE WANT EDUCATION THAT TEACHES US OUR TRUE HISTORY AND OUR ROLE IN THE PRESENT-DAY SOCIETY.

6. WE WANT ALL BLACK MEN TO BE EXEMPT FROM MILITARY SERVICE.

7. WE WANT AN IMMEDIATE END TO POLICE BRUTALITY AND MURDER OF BLACK PEOPLE.

8. WE WANT FREEDOM FOR ALL BLACK MEN HELD IN FEDERAL, STATE, COUNTY AND CITY PRISONS AND JAILS.

9. WE WANT ALL BLACK PEOPLE WHEN BROUGHT TO TRIAL TO BE TRIED IN A COURT BY A JURY OF THEIR PEER GROUP OR PEOPLE FROM THEIR BLACK COMMUNITIES, AS DEFINED BY THE CONSTITUTION OF THE UNITED STATES.

10. WE WANT LAND, BREAD, HOUSING, EDUCATION, CLOTHING, JUSTICE AND PEACE. AND AS OUR MAJOR POLITICAL OBJECTIVE, A UNITED NATIONS-SUPERVISED PLEBISCITE TO BE HELD THROUGHOUT THE BLACK COLONY IN WHICH ONLY BLACK COLONIAL SUBJECTS WILL BE ALLOWED TO PARTICIPATE, FOR THE PURPOSE OF DETERMINING THE WILL OF BLACK PEOPLE AS TO THEIR NATIONAL DESTINY.

Armed with a shotgun and ammunition-packed bandoleer, Panthers cofounder Huey Newton personifies revolutionary change in this August 1969 portrait. Frequently at odds with the law, by 1974 he was in voluntary exile in Cuba.

ed following police in black neighborhoods, carrying guns—and law books. Their purpose was to show young blacks that they had a right to expect ordinary courtesy and due process from the police. One result of this action, however, was the legislature's law against civilians carrying loaded firearms.

In early 1967, Seale and Newton welcomed a new ally in Eldridge Cleaver. Recently released from Soledad Prison on parole from a rape conviction, Cleaver was a former member of the Nation of Islam and a senior editor at *Ramparts* magazine. In a letter written the following year, he

described his first glimpse of the Panthers as "the most beautiful sight I had ever seen: four black men wearing black berets, powder-blue shirts, black leather jackets, black trousers, shiny black shoes—and each with a gun." Cleaver helped Seale and Newton plan the state legislature gun-law protest, supervised the publication of the Black Panther newspaper, and wrote articles for white publications.

Less welcome publicity came on October 28, 1967, when Huey Newton was arrested for fatally shooting an Oakland police officer. The matter became a cause célèbre with the rallying cry of

Bill Whitfield, a Kansas City Black Panther, serves local children breakfast on April 16, 1969, as part of the Panther free breakfast program. Party members arrived at 6:00 a.m. to feed the children at 7:00 or 7:30 in local churches or community centers.

"Free Huey." Newton was convicted twice on charges related to the incident; ultimately both verdicts were overturned.

By late the next year, the Panthers had spread from Oakland to 25 cities, including New York, Los Angeles, Des Moines, and Denver. Meanwhile, the Federal Bureau of Investigation had expanded its antiradical counterin-

A dramatic sign (*above*) marks the Panthers' international headquarters in Algeria, established by Eldridge Cleaver in 1969 after he fled to that country to avoid prosecution in connection with a shootout with police in Oakland.

telligence program, COINTELPRO, to include the Panthers. In memos obtained and published by the *New York Times*, FBI Director J. Edgar Hoover asked field offices to develop "imaginative and hard-hitting counterintelligence measures aimed at crippling the BPP."

Despite harassment and growing infiltration by informers, the party continued to expand in 1969, establishing free breakfast programs—funded by black businessmen—in several cities. Some chapters also organized free health clinics. By the end of the year, membership stood at several hundred.

Not all was well, however. According to press reports, an estimated four police officers and 28 Panthers were slain in clashes between the Panthers and law-enforcement agencies. In one incident, Fred Hampton, a charismatic Panther who had helped establish the Illinois

chapter, was killed with fellow Panther Mark Clark in a predawn raid by Chicago police. The police said their knock was met with shotgun fire, which they returned. The Panthers claimed their comrades had been murdered in bed. A series of investigations failed to resolve the issue, although it is now known that there were several FBI informers in the Chicago group.

As the 1970s began, the Panthers, staggered by the killings, were being torn apart. Newton was still in jail, and Seale was also incarcerated, one of eight people charged in the murder of an allegedly disloyal party member. Cleaver had fled to Algeria after being charged with a parole violation involving a shootout. Other Panthers were under arrest on a variety of charges. A split also developed between those favoring a paramilitary emphasis and those wanting to focus on community programs.

Yet the Panthers persisted—and even broke new ground. In 1974, longtime Panther Elaine Brown became the group's first female leader. In her three years at the helm, Brown returned the focus to Oakland, augmenting the free breakfast program and devising an award-winning learning center for poor children. Brown ran, unsuccessfully, for the Oakland City Council. She also organized a drive that registered nearly 100,000 new voters, who in 1977 helped elect Lionel Wilson the first black mayor of Oakland.

A technician looks on as Panthers cofounder Bobby Seale examines a microscope slide (*left*) at the Panthers' clinic in Oakland in 1972. Clinics were also set up in San Francisco, Los Angeles, and Chicago.

A CIVIL RIGHTS LEGEND ON THE COURT

On June 13, 1967, President Lyndon Johnson called his solicitor general, Thurgood Marshall, to the White House and asked him to accept nomination to the United States Supreme Court. The offer was not entirely unexpected, but Marshall telephoned his wife, Cissy, from the Oval Office so Johnson could tell her himself. "Take a deep breath and sit down slowly," Marshall cautioned in mock seriousness before putting the president on the line. Four months later, after winning a tough confirmation fight led by conservative southern senators, Marshall was sworn in, becoming at age 59 the first black justice on the highest court in the land.

Marshall's decades of work as an NAACP lawyer—capped by his success in 1954 in the landmark school desegregation case, *Brown v. the Board of Education of Topeka, Kansas* (pages 191-192)— had made him a legend in the African American community, where he was often called the little man's lawyer. He had also served notably in the federal government. In 1961, President Kennedy had appointed Marshall a federal appeals court judge. He went on to serve with distinction, writing 98 majority

The son of a yacht-club steward and the great-grandson of a Maryland slave, civil rights crusader Thurgood Marshall wears his judge's robes on October 2, 1967, the day he was sworn in as a justice of the United States Supreme Court.

opinions, none of which were overturned by the Supreme Court on appeal. President Johnson made Marshall solicitor general in 1965, and in that position he had again excelled, successfully representing the United States in 14 of 19 appearances before the Supreme Court.

In his third and final government role, Supreme Court Justice Marshall at first found a comfortable intellectual home. Led by Chief Justice Earl Warren, the majority of justices held an expansive, liberal view of the Constitution that fit well with Marshall's devotion to the rights of the oppressed. But as Warren and some of those who had voted with him began to leave the Court and were replaced by more conservative jurists, the winds of change began to blow.

By 1972, just five years after his appointment, Marshall could eke out only a five-to-four majority in *Furman v. Georgia*, a case in which the Court overturned the sentencing procedures used by states to impose the death penalty and pronounced a moratorium on executions. Many consider Marshall's opinion in the case—a 60-page, exhaustively researched masterwork—to be his finest. Capital punishment, he declared, is meted out unequally, violating the constitutional provision against cruel and unusual punishment. It is "usually the poor," he wrote, "the illiterate, the underprivileged, the member of the minority group—the man who, because he is without means and is defended by a court-appointed attorney—who becomes society's sacrificial lamb." Marshall also challenged the very notion of capital punishment. "Death is irrevocable. Life imprisonment is not," he wrote. "Death, of course, makes rehabil-

itation impossible. Life imprisonment does not."

Four years later, in 1976, the increasingly conservative Court reinstated capital punishment. That night, Marshall had a mild heart attack that permanently affected his health. Undaunted, he persisted. For 15 more years, often outvoted on the cases he cared about most, he argued for the principles he had always championed: the rights of the individual, the end of the death penalty, the legitimacy of remedies such as affirmative action.

Refusing to compromise, Marshall became one of the Court's great dissenters, writing minority opinions that spoke to the ages even if they could not sway his colleagues on the Court. In 1978, when the majority assumed a poor woman had enough money to post a bond, he wrote, in a stinging dissent: "I cannot remain silent as the Court demonstrates, not for the first time, an attitude of callous indifference to the realities of life for the poor." When the other justices overturned a Richmond city ordinance setting aside funds for minority contractors, Marshall wrote that the Court was "constitutionalizing its wishful thinking" by assuming that racial discrimination no longer existed. In the late 1980s and early 1990s, the Court several times approved law-enforcement tactics in the "war on drugs" that Marshall viewed as unconstitutional. "Precisely because the need for action against the drug scourge is manifest, the need for vigilance against unconstitutional excess is great," he wrote, dissenting from a 1991 decision that upheld the testing of railroad employees for drug use. "The majority's acceptance of dragnet blood and urine testing ensures that the first, and

worst, casualty of the war on drugs will be the precious liberties of our citizens."

In addition to his written dissents, Marshall used a mixture of humor and personal anecdotes to bring to life issues of poverty, racism, and inequity for the other justices. Sandra Day O'Connor, a conservative jurist and the nation's first female justice, wrote that Marshall "imparted not only his legal acumen, but also his life experiences, constantly pushing and prodding us to respond not only to the persuasiveness of legal argument, but also to the power of moral truth."

Despite his declining health during the 1980s, Marshall scoffed at any notion of retirement. "I have a lifetime appointment and I intend to serve it," he often told reporters. It was thus a shock to Court watchers when in 1991 he decided to retire, after all. Marshall died on January 24, 1993, four days after the inauguration of President Bill Clinton; he had been too ill to administer the vice-presidential oath to Albert Gore, as had been planned.

The memorial service honoring Marshall filled Washington's National Cathedral beyond capacity, and he was lauded by the famous and the powerful. But Marshall might have appreciated most the tribute paid to him a few days earlier by an estimated 20,000 ordinary citizens, black and white, who lined up quietly in the cold to wait hours for a chance to pass his coffin as it lay in state in the Supreme Court's Great Hall. The working men and women, parents with children, and elderly people who paid their respects honored Thurgood Marshall for a lifetime of service—as protector of the defenseless, champion of the underdog, and hero of the little man.

ACKNOWLEDGMENTS

Voices of Triumph has been made possible by the generous support of Time Warner Inc.

The editors wish to thank the following individuals and institutions for their valuable assistance in the preparation of this volume:
Don Anderson, Senior Adviser to the Chairman and CEO, Time Warner Inc., New York City; Dr. Samuel Barnes, Washington, D.C.; Dr. Thomas Battle, Director, Karen Jefferson, Curator of Manuscripts, Moorland Spingarn Research Center, Washington, D.C.; Christine Smith Benjamin, Consulting Director, Retail Marketing and Sales, River Forest, Illinois; Charles L. Blockson, Temple University Afro-American Collection, Philadelphia, Pennsylvania; Carroll Ann Bowers, Historic Charleston Foundation, Charleston, South Carolina; Herb Boyd, New York City; Reginald K. Brack, Jr., Chairman and CEO, Time Inc., New York City; Marie Brown, Marie Brown Associates, New York City; Wesley Brown, Washington, D.C.; Randall K. Burquett, Director, W. E. B. Du Bois Research Center, Harvard University, Cambridge, Massachusetts; Gen. Sherian G. Cadoria, U.S. Army (Retired), Pineville, Louisiana; Vicki Chiro, New Haven Colony Historical Society, New Haven, Connecticut; Jamie W. and Marcia W. Constance, Chicora Wood Plantation, Georgetown, South Carolina; Chester Cowan, Oklahoma Historical Society, Oklahoma City; Timothy Cronen, National Air and Space Museum, Washington, D.C.; Jean P. Dillard, Hampton, Virginia; Mr. and Mrs. Patrick J. Doyle, Georgetown, South Carolina; Kenny Drayton, Debbie Dugan, Mark Johnson, Jay Lance, Plantersville Turf Farm, Georgetown, South Carolina; Dr. James Dunn, Corps of Engineers, Fort Belvoir, Virginia; Toni Fay, Vice President, Community Relations, Time Warner Inc., New York City;

James A. Fitch, Director, Pat Balthis, Rice Museum, Georgetown, South Carolina; Therez Fleetwood, Phe-Zulu Collection, New York City; James Forman, Washington, D.C.; Christraud M. Geary, Amy J. Staples, Dr. Rosalyn Walker, National Museum of African Art, Smithsonian Institution, Washington, D.C.; Jason Gwardiak, Georgetown, South Carolina; Maxine Hernandez, The Jekyll Island Authority, Jekyll Island, Georgia; Amy Hilliard-Jones, Senior Vice President, Esther Terrell, Vice President, Burrell Communications, Chicago, Illinois; Myrtle Holloman, Saltspring Island, British Columbia; Bill Hora, Dickenson, Texas; Juanita James, Senior Vice President, Book-of-the-Month Club, New York City; Jesse J. Johnson, Hampton, Virginia; Gerald Levin, Chairman and CEO, Time Warner Inc., New York City; Byron Lewis, Chairman and CEO, Rosalie Roman, Manager of Special Events and Promotions, Lynne Scott, Director of Public Relations, Uniworld Group, New York City; Rev. Harold Lewis, Belin Methodist Church, Georgetown, South Carolina; Dolores Littles, Falls Church, Virginia; Don Logan, President and COO, Time Inc., New York City; John Lovett, University of Oklahoma Library, Western History Collection, Norman; Judy Lund, New Bedford Whaling Museum, New Bedford, Massachusetts; Dr. Dolly A. McPherson, Wake Forest University, Winston-Salem, North Carolina; Deborah J. Maples, Army Medical Department, Fort Sam Houston, Texas; Liliana Meazza, Mondadori, Milan, Italy; E. Ethelbert Miller, Director, African American Resource Center, Howard University, Washington, D.C.; Roy Moore, Jr., Petersburg, Virginia; Jones Morgan, Petersburg, Virginia; Giovanna Moro, Rome, Italy; Gloria Morton-Finney, Joan Morton-Finney, Indianapolis, Indiana; Colleen Murphy, Director of Corporate Communi-

cations, Time Inc. Books, New York City; Princess Asie Ocansey and Dayo B. Babalola, ABC International, New York City; Donald Packard, Houston, Texas; Jacquelyn Paschal, Navy Recruiting Command, Arlington, Virginia; Genevieve Chandler Peterkin, Murrells Inlet, South Carolina; Lucille Quattlebaum, Arundel Plantation, Georgetown, South Carolina; Nancy E. Reagor, Department of the Army, U.S. Military Academy, West Point, New York; Victoria E. Reese, Executive Director, Metropolitan Lynchburg Chapter, American Red Cross, Lynchburg, Virginia; C. E. Graham Reeves, Annandale Plantation, Georgetown, South Carolina; Teresa Roane, The Valentine Museum, Richmond, Virginia; Maj. Ken Roberts, Deputy Director, Joint Task Force, Somalia, U.S. Army, Mogadishu, Somalia; Richard Sanders, Ashland, Virginia; Lamen Sbita, Howard University, Washington, D.C.; Gidget Smith, *Stars and Stripes*, Darmstadt, Germany; Michelle Spellman, Graphic Design Director, Spellman, Bostic and Williams, Silver Spring, Maryland; Geraldine R. Stepp, Paul Stewart, Black American West Museum and Heritage Center, Denver, Colorado; Paul Stillwell, Director, History Division, U.S. Naval Institute, Annapolis, Maryland; Doug Stover, National Capital Parks East, Washington, D.C.; Kathy Swan, Denver Public Library, Denver, Colorado; Eugene Thompson, Alexandria Black History Museum, Alexandria, Virginia; Leanne Walker, Marketing Research Manager, Time Life Inc., Alexandria, Virginia; Ernest E. Washington, Jr., Mattapan, Massachusetts; John D. Weaver, Durham, North Carolina; John Wiley, Georgetown, South Carolina; Deborah Willis-Braithwaite, Collections Coordinator, National African Museum Project, Smithsonian Institution, Washington, D.C.; Lossie Winters, Richmond, Virginia.

PICTURE CREDITS

Artwork by Floyd Cooper. **26, 27:** National Archives #111-BA-1103. **28, 29:** Moorland Spingarn Research Center, Howard University, Washington, D.C., #2345; © Maggie Steber 1992/JB Pictures, New York. **30, 31:** National Archives #111-BA-4687. **32:** Valentine Museum, Richmond, Va. **33, 34:** Jackson Hill, courtesy Louisiana State Museum, New Orleans, La. **35:** Charleston Museum, Charleston, S.C. **37:** Photos by Larry Sherer, courtesy Moorland Spingarn Research Center, Howard University, Washington, D.C. **38:** Jackson Hill, courtesy Louisiana State Museum, New Orleans, La. **39:** Library of Congress #39380. **40:** Schomburg Center for Research in Black Culture, New York Public Library, New York #SC-CN-93-0571. **41:** National Archives #111-B-75. **42, 43:** Background, Robin Smith/Tony Stone Images, Chicago, Ill. Map by Mike Reagan; Granger Collection, New York. **44, 45:** Background, Robin Smith/Tony Stone Images, Chicago, Ill. Dr. Gerald J. Rizzo, MD (2); photograph by Eliot Elisofon, 1970, National Museum of African Art, Washington, D.C.—photograph by Christraud M. Geary, 1990, National Museum of African Art, Washington, D.C.; © John Elk III, 1979/Bruce Coleman, Inc., New York. **46, 47:** Background, Robin Smith/Tony Stone Images, Chicago, Ill. Library of the Society of Friends, London; Wilberforce House, Hull City Museums and Art Galleries, Humberside, England; Jean-Loup Charmet, Paris (2)—Wilberforce House, Hull City Museums and Art Galleries, Humberside, England. **48, 49:** Background, Frank and Marie-Therese Wood Print Collection, Alexandria, Va. Craig Moran, courtesy Rice Museum, Georgetown, S.C. (2). **50, 51:** Background, from *Down by the Riverside: A South Carolina Slave Community* by Charles Joyner, University of Illinois Press, Urbana, Ill., 1984. From *Slavery and Rice Culture in Low Country Georgia 1750-1860* by Julia Floyd Smith, University of Tennessee Press, Knoxville, Tenn., 1985; Craig Moran, courtesy Rice Museum, Georgetown, S.C. (2); from *Down by the Riverside: A South Carolina Slave Community* by Charles Joyner, University of Illinois Press, Urbana, Ill., 1984; Craig Moran, courtesy Rice Museum, Georgetown, S.C. (1)—Craig Moran, courtesy Jamie Constance, Georgetown, S.C. (2). **52, 53:** Background, from *Slavery and Rice Culture*

in Low Country Georgia: 1750-1860 by Julia Floyd Smith, University of Tennessee Press, Knoxville, Tenn., 1985. Craig Moran, courtesy Mrs. Lucille Quattlebaum; Library of Congress #307015—Craig Moran, courtesy Jamie Constance, Georgetown, S.C. (2)—Craig Moran, courtesy Mr. and Mrs. Patrick J. Doyle; Paul Hester, courtesy Bill Hora, Dickenson, Tex.; Craig Moran, courtesy Jamie Constance, Georgetown, S.C. **55:** Culver Pictures, Inc., New York—Library of Congress #40597; Library of Congress #33451. **56:** New Haven Colony Historical Society, gift of Dr. Charles B. Purvis, 1898, New Haven, Conn.—New Haven Colony Historical Society, New Haven, Conn. **57:** New Haven Colony Historical Society, gift of Simeon E. Baldwin, 1919, New Haven, Conn. **58, 59:** Artwork by Yvette Watson; Library of the Society of Friends, London—Hulton Deutsch Collection, London; Massachusetts Historical Society, Boston, Mass. **60:** Copied by J. R. Eyerman for LIFE. **61:** Moorland Spingarn Research Center, Howard University, Washington, D.C., #401—photos by Larry Sherer, courtesy Moorland Spingarn Research Center, Howard University, Washington, D.C. (2). **62-67:** Artwork by Yvette Watson. **68:** Henry E. Huntington Library and Art Gallery, San Marino, Calif.—photo by Larry Sherer, courtesy Temple University Afro-American Collection, Philadelphia, Pa. **69:** Map by Time-Life Books, based on research by Charles Blockson—© 1992 Louis Psihoyos/Contact Press Images, New York (2). **70, 71:** Massachusetts Historical Society, Boston, Mass.; Grey Villet for LIFE. **72, 73:** Painting by Warren Sheppard, courtesy Jekyll Island Museum, Jekyll Island, Ga., photographed by Daryl J. Bunn, insets, reproduced by permission of the American Anthropological Association from *American Anthropologist* 10:4, Oct.-Dec. 1908. Not for sale or further reproduction (4). **74, 75:** Background, National Park Service, Harpers Ferry National Historical Park, Harpers Ferry, W.Va. Granger Collection, New York; Library of Congress #627821; Granger Collection, New York—Library of Congress #61748; Bettmann Archive, New York; Larry Sherer, courtesy National Park Service, Harpers Ferry National Historical Park, Harpers Ferry, W.Va.—Library of Congress #38900. **76, 77:** Hulton Deutsch Collection, London. **78:** Courtesy the William Gladstone

Collection, Westport, Conn. **79:** South Carolina Historical Society, Charleston, S.C. **80:** Courtesy the Historic New Orleans Collection Museum/Research Center, accession number 1979.183, New Orleans, La. **81:** Frank and Marie-Therese Wood Print Collection, Alexandria, Va. **82:** Library of Congress #99507. **83:** Herb Peck, Jr. **84, 85:** Solomon D. Butcher Collection, Nebraska State Historical Society, Lincoln, Nebr. **86:** Photo Ben Wittick, courtesy School of American Research Collections in the Museum of New Mexico, neg. no. 15889, Santa Fe, N.Mex. **89:** Courtesy the Montana Historical Society, gift of the artist, Helena, Mont. **90:** Minnesota Historical Society, Saint Paul, Minn. **92:** Map by Time-Life Books. **93:** Robbie McClaran, courtesy Oregon State Archives, Provisional and Territorial Documents, Salem, Ore.—Oregon Historical Society, ORHI #11917-A, Portland, Ore. **94:** Denver Public Library, Western History Department, Denver, Colo. **96:** From *Pony Tracks* by Frederic Remington, University of Oklahoma Press, Norman, Okla., 1961. **97:** Black American West Museum and Heritage Center, Paul W. Stewart Collection, Denver, Colo. **98:** Kansas State Historical Society, Topeka, Kans. **100, 101:** Chicago Historical Society, Chicago, Ill. (2); Du Sable Museum of African American History, Inc., Chicago, Ill. **102:** Nevada Historical Society, Reno, Nev. **103:** Map by Time-Life Books; from *Jim Beckwourth* by Elinor Wilson, University of Oklahoma Press, Norman, Okla., 1972—Colorado Historical Society, Denver, Colo.; Universal City Studios, Inc., courtesy MCA Publishing Rights, a Division of MCA Inc. **104:** Betty Peters, courtesy Myrtle Holloman. **105:** Map by Time-Life Books—Betty Peters, courtesy Myrtle Holloman (2). **106:** Denver Public Library, Denver, Colo.; Guthrie Public Library Collection in the Western History Collections, University of Oklahoma Library, Norman, Okla.—Archives and Manuscripts Division of the Oklahoma Historical Society, Oklahoma City, Okla. **107:** Denver Public Library, Denver, Colo.; Security Pacific National Bank Photograph Collection/Los Angeles Public Library; Montana Historical Society, Helena, Mont.—Arizona Historical Society, Tucson, Ariz. **108:** Archives of the Big Bend Sul Ross State University, Alpine, Tex. **109:** Western History Collections, University of Oklahoma, Norman, Okla.; Phillips Collection in the Western History Collections, University of Oklahoma Library, Norman, Okla. **110:** Bennett Collection, Archives and Manuscripts Division of the Oklahoma Historical Society, Oklahoma City, Okla.—Archives and Manuscripts Division of the Oklahoma Historical Society, Oklahoma City, Okla. **111:** Courtesy Colorado Historical Society, Denver, Colo.; Denver Public Library, Western History Department, Denver, Colo. **112, 113:** Noah H. Rose Collection in the Western History Collections, University of Oklahoma Library, Norman, Okla.; Walter Ferguson Collection in the Western History Collections, University of Oklahoma Library, Norman, Okla.—Denver Public Library, Denver, Colo.; Eagan/Denver Public Library, Western History Department, Denver, Colo. **114, 115:** General Personalities Collection in the Western History Collections, University of Oklahoma, Norman, Okla.; Denver Public Library, Western History Department, Denver, Colo.—Mrs. Ottie Lee Collection in the Western History Collections, University of Oklahoma, Norman, Okla.; Black American West Museum and Heritage Center, Paul W. Stewart Collection, Denver, Colo. (2). **116, 117:** National African American Museum Project, Smithsonian Institution, Washington, D.C.; Cincinnati Historical Society, Cincinnati, Ohio— Montana Historical Society, Helena, Mont. (3). **118, 119:** Kansas State Historical Society, Topeka, Kans. (2); © William K. Geiger Photography, Washington, D.C.—map by Time-Life Books; Archives and Manuscripts Division of the Oklahoma Historical Society, Oklahoma City, Okla. (3). **120:** Denver Public Library, Western History Department, Denver, Colo. (2); Black American West Museum and Heritage Center, Paul W. Stewart Collection, Denver, Colo. **121:** Allensworth State Historic Park, Earlimart, Calif. (2); California State Library, California Section, Sacramento, Calif. (2). **122:** National Cowboy Hall of Fame, Oklahoma City, Okla.—Phillips Collection in the Western History Collections, University of Oklahoma Library, Norman, Okla.; Oklahoma Collection in the Western History Collections, University of Oklahoma, Norman, Okla. **123:** Fred Nyulassy—Black American West Museum and Heritage Center, Paul W. Stewart Collection, Denver, Colo.—Fred Nyulassy.

124, 125: Joel Grimes, courtesy Black American West Museum and Heritage Center, Denver, Colo. **126, 127:** U.S. Army Military History Institute, Carlisle Barracks, Pa. **128:** Larry Sherer, courtesy National Archives #NP-89P-2. **130:** Massachusetts Historical Society, Boston, Mass. **131:** U.S. Senate Collection, Washington, D.C. **132:** Smithsonian Institution, Washington, D.C.—Moorland Spingarn Research Center, Howard University, Washington, D.C., #630. **133:** Library of Congress, courtesy Preston E. Amos. **134:** Moorland Spingarn Research Center, Howard University, Washington, D.C., courtesy Jerry Anderson—Historical Pictures/Stock Montage, Inc., Chicago, Ill. **136, 137:** Renée Comet, courtesy Elizabeth Gibbs Moore—courtesy Elizabeth Gibbs Moore—Culver Pictures, Inc., New York. **138, 139:** U.S. Army photographs #196151; #198659. **140:** U.S. Marine Corps, Washington, D.C. **141:** Naval Photographic Center, Washington, D.C. **142:** Ernest E. Washington, Jr. **144:** Shelby L. Stanton Collection, Bethesda, Md. **145:** U.S. Department of Defense, Washington, D.C. **146, 147:** Background, artwork by Yvette Watson. Hunter Clarkson, courtesy South Carolina Department of Archives and History, Columbia, S.C.; Virginia Historical Society, Richmond, Va. **148:** From *History of the Fifty-fourth Regiment of Massachusetts Volunteer Infantry, 1863-1865* by Luis Fenollosa Emilio, Boston Book Company, Boston, Mass., 1894—private collection, photographed by Nick Whitman (2). **149:** Sculpture by Augustus Saint-Gaudens, City of Boston Art Commission, photographed by Jack Leonard. **150, 151:** Eli Reichman, courtesy Frontier Army Museum, Fort Levenworth, Kans.—Larry Sherer, courtesy National Archives #81433. **152:** National Archives #SC-97120-A, copied by Larry Sherer— Eli Reichman, courtesy Frontier Army Museum, Fort Levenworth, Kans. **153:** Joel Grimes, courtesy Black American West Museum and Heritage Center, Denver, Colo.; courtesy Butler University, Indianapolis, Ind.—Welton Doby III. **154, 155:** From *The Brownsville Raid* by John D. Weaver, W. W. Norton & Co., New York, 1970 (2); courtesy John D. Weaver. **156, 157:** Background, UPI/Bettmann, New York. Bettmann Archive, New York—UPI/ Bettmann, New York; Eli Reichman, courtesy Liberty Memorial Museum, Kansas City, Kans.; Bettmann Archive, New

York—UPI/Bettmann Newsphotos, New York. **158, 159:** National Air and Space Museum, Washington, D.C. **160, 161:** U.S. Army Corps of Engineers, Office of History. **162:** Courtesy Navy Recruiting Command, Arlington, Va. **163:** Photo by Vories Fisher, courtesy Dr. Samuel E. Barnes—courtesy Navy Recruiting Command, Arlington, Va. **164:** Moorland Spingarn Research Center, Howard University, Washington, D.C. #3924—from *History of the American Negro in the Great World War* by W. Allison Sweeney, Negro Universities Press, New York, 1969. **165:** LTC Jesse Johnson—National Archives #SC337 995-1, copied by Larry Sherer. **166:** Brig. Gen. Marcelite J. Harris— National Archives #297439, copied by Larry Sherer. **167:** LTC Jesse Johnson—© Donna Ferrato/Black Star, New York. **168, 169:** United States Military Academy, West Point, N.Y. (2)—from *History of the American Negro in the Great World War* by W. Allison Sweeney, Negro Universities Press, New York, 1969. **170, 171:** Courtesy J. Alfred Phelps (2)—courtesy J. Alfred Phelps, DOD/Still Media Research Center. **172, 173:** Courtesy Brig. Gen. Sherian G. Cadoria. **174:** Evan Sheppard, courtesy John W. Listman, Jr., National Museum of Health and Medicine, Washington, D.C. **175:** Courtesy the Joel family. **176, 177:** Courtesy Office of the Chairman, Joint Chiefs of Staff, Washington, D.C. **178, 179:** Background, © Greg English/Sygma, New York. © Chris Rainier/JB Pictures, New York; © Peter Turnley Newsweek/Black Star, New York; © Klaus Reisinger/Black Star, New York—© Greg English/Sygma, New York—© Les Stone/Sygma, New York. **180:** © Burt Glinn/Magnum Photos, New York. **182:** UPI/Bettmann, New York. **183:** From *A Pictorial History of the Negro in America* by Langston Hughes and Milton Meltzer, Crown Publishing, Inc., New York, 1968. **184:** Gilman Paper Company Collection, New York. **187:** Library of Congress #33793. **188, 189:** Library of Congress #33790. **190, 191:** Culver Pictures, Inc., New York. **192, 193:** Library of Congress #99293—Library of Congress #35344. **194:** Don Cravens for LIFE. **195:** AP/Wide World Photos, New York. **196, 197:** Paul Schutzer for LIFE. **198, 199:** © Charles Moore/Black Star, New York. **200:** Library of Congress #105252. **201:** John Dominis. **202:** © 1986 by James Van Der Zee, all rights

BIBLIOGRAPHY

A MIGHTY NATION ON THE NIGER

BOOKS

Ajayi, J. F. A., and Michael Crowder (eds.). H*istory of West Africa* (Vol. 1). New York: Columbia University Press, 1972.

Chu, Daniel, and Elliott Skinner. A *Glorious Age in Africa.* Trenton, N.J.: Africa World Press, 1990.

Davidson, Basil, F. K. Buah, and J. F. A. Ajayi. *The Growth of African Civilisation: A History of West Africa 1000-1800.* New York: Longmans, 1965.

Diop, Cheikh Anta. *Precolonial Black Africa.* Translated by Harold Salemson. Westport, Conn.: Lawrence Hill, 1987.

The Horizon History of Africa. New York: American Heritage, 1971.

Leo, Africanus. *The History and Description of Africa and of the Notable Things Therein Contained* (Vol. 3). Edited by Robert Brown. New York: Burt Franklin, 1896.

Levtzion, Nehemia. *Ancient Ghana and Mali.* New York: Africana, 1980.

Murphy, E. Jefferson. H*istory of African Civilization.* New York: Dell, 1972.

Naylor, Kim. M*ali.* New York: Chelsea House, 1987.

The New Encyclopædia Britannica (Vols. 12 and 19). Chicago: Encyclopædia Britannica, 1984.

Opoku, Kofi Asare. *West African Traditional Religion.* Accra, Ghana: FEP International Private Limited, 1978.

Saad, Elias N. *Social History of Timbuktu: The Role of Muslim Scholars and Notables 1400-1900.* Cambridge: Cambridge University Press, 1983.

Woodson, Carter G. *African Heroes and Heroines* (3d ed.). Washington, D.C.: Associated Publishers, 1969.

PERIODICALS

Imperato, Pascal James. "The Dance of the Tyi Wara." *African Arts,* 1970, Vol. 4, no. 1.

1
FREEDOM DENIED, FREEDOM WON

BOOKS

Adams, Russell L. *Great Negroes: Past and Present* (3d ed.). Chicago: Afro-Am Publishing, 1991.

The African American Experience: A History. Englewood Cliffs, N.J.: Globe Book Company, 1992.

Anderson, Osborne P. A *Voice from Harper's Ferry.* New York: World View Publishers, 1974.

Aptheker, Herbert. *American Negro Slave Revolts.* New York: International Publishers, 1974.

Aptheker, Herbert (ed.). A *Documentary History of the Negro People in the United States* (Vol. 1). New York: Citadel Press, 1951.

Asante, Molefi K., and Mark T. Mattson. *The Historical and Cultural Atlas of African Americans.* New York: Macmillan, 1991.

Barber, John W. (comp.). A H*istory of the Amistad Captives.* New Haven, Conn.: E. L. & J. W. Barber, 1840.

Bennett, Lerone, Jr. *Before the Mayflower: A History of Black America* (5th ed.). New York: Penguin Books, 1984.

Bibb, Henry. *Narrative of the Life and Adventures of Henry Bibb, an American Slave.* Miami, Fla.: Mnemosyne, 1969 (reprint of 1859 edition).

Blassingame, John W. *The Slave Community: Plantation Life in the Antebellum South* (rev. ed.). New York: Oxford University Press, 1979.

Bracey, John H., Jr., August Meier, and Elliott Rudwick (eds.). *Blacks in the Abolitionist Movement.* Belmont, Calif.: Wadsworth, 1971.

Bradford, Sarah H. *Harriet: The Moses of Her People.* New York: George R. Lockwood & Son, 1886.

Campbell, Edward D. C., Jr., and Kym S. Rice (eds.). *Before Freedom Came: African-American Life in the Antebellum South.* Charlottesville: University Press of Virginia, 1991.

Catterall, Helen Tunnicliff, and James J. Hayden (eds.). *Judicial Cases Concerning*

American Slavery and the Negro (Vol. 4). New York: Octagon Books, 1968.

Craft, William. *Running a Thousand Miles for Freedom; or, The Escape of William and Ellen Craft from Slavery.* Miami, Fla.: Mnemosyne, 1969 (reprint of 1860 edition).

Davidson, Basil. *The African Slave Trade.* Boston: Little, Brown, 1980.

Douglass, Frederick. *Narrative of the Life of Frederick Douglass, an American Slave.* New York: Penguin Books, 1986 (reprint of 1845 edition).

Du Bois, W. E. B. *Black Reconstruction in America.* New York: Atheneum, 1992 (reprint of 1935 edition).

Fehrenbacher, Don. *Slavery, Law, and Politics: The Dred Scott Case in Historical Perspective.* New York: Oxford University Press, 1981.

Fifty Years in Chains; or, The Life of an American Slave. Miami, Fla.: Mnemosyne, 1969 (reprint of 1858 edition).

Foner, Eric, and John A. Garraty (eds.). *The Reader's Companion to American History.* Boston: Houghton Mifflin, 1991.

Franklin, John Hope. *Reconstruction: After the Civil War.* Chicago: University of Chicago Press, 1961.

Franklin, John Hope, and Alfred A. Moss, Jr. *From Slavery to Freedom: A History of Negro Americans* (6th ed.). New York: McGraw-Hill, 1988.

Freedman, Florence B. *Two Tickets to Freedom: The True Story of Ellen and William Craft, Fugitive Slaves.* New York: Peter Bedrick Books, 1971.

Gara, Larry. *The Liberty Line: The Legend of the Underground Railroad.* Lexington: University of Kentucky Press, 1961.

Gates, Henry Louis, Jr. (ed.). *The Classic Slave Narratives.* New York: New American Library (Mentor), 1987.

Genovese, Eugene D.: *From Rebellion to Revolution.* Baton Rouge: Louisiana State University Press, 1979.

Roll, Jordan, Roll: The World the Slaves Made. New York: Vintage Books, 1976.

Gorée: Island of Memories. Paris: Unesco, 1985.

Graham, Leroy. *Baltimore: The Nineteenth Century Black Capital.* Washington, D.C.: University Press of America, 1982.

Graham, Lorenz. *John Brown's Raid: A Picture History of the Attack on Harpers Ferry, Virginia.* New York: Scholastic Book Services, 1972.

Gratus, Jack. *The Great White Lie: Slavery, Emancipation, and Changing Racial Attitudes.* New York: Monthly Review Press, 1973.

Greene, Lorenzo Johnston. *The Negro in Colonial New England.* New York: Atheneum, 1968.

Herskovits, Melville J. *The Myth of the Negro Past.* Boston: Beacon Press, 1958.

Higginbotham, A. Leon, Jr. *In the Matter of Color.* Oxford: Oxford University Press, 1978.

Hogg, Peter. *Slavery: The Afro-American Experience.* London: British Library, 1979.

Hornsby, Alton, Jr. *Chronology of African-American History.* Detroit: Gale Research, 1991.

Hughes, Langston, Milton Meltzer, and C. Eric Lincoln. *A Pictorial History of Blackamericans* (5th ed.). New York: Crown Publishers, 1983.

Hughes, Louis. *Thirty Years a Slave: From Bondage to Freedom.* Milwaukee: South Side Printing, 1897.

Hurmence, Belinda (ed.). *Before Freedom, When I Just Can Remember.* Winston-Salem, N.C.: John F. Blair, 1989.

Jacobs, Harriet A. *Incidents in the Life of a Slave Girl.* Edited by L. Maria Child and Jean Fagan Yellin. Cambridge, Mass.: Harvard University Press, 1987.

Jones, Howard. *Mutiny on the Amistad: The Saga of a Slave Revolt and Its Impact on American Abolition, Law, and Diplomacy.* New York: Oxford University Press, 1987.

Joyner, Charles. *Down by the Riverside: A South Carolina Slave Community.* Urbana: University of Illinois Press, 1984.

Katz, William Loren (ed.). *The Negro in Virginia.* New York: Hastings House, 1969.

Koger, Larry. *Black Slaveowners: Free Black Slave Masters in South Carolina, 1790-1860.* Jefferson, N.C.: McFarland & Company, 1985.

Libby, Jean. *Black Voices from Harpers Ferry: Osborne Anderson and the John Brown Raid.* Palo Alto, Calif.: Jean Libby, 1979.

Litwack, Leon F. *Been in the Storm So Long: The Aftermath of Slavery.* New York: Alfred A. Knopf, 1979.

Litwack, Leon F., and August Meier (eds.). *Black Leaders of the Nineteenth Century.* Urbana: University of Illinois Press, 1988.

Logan, Rayford W., and Michael R. Winston (eds.). *Dictionary of American Negro Biography.* New York: W. W. Norton, 1982.

Low, W. Augustus, and Virgil A. Clift (eds.). *Encyclopedia of Black America.* New York: Da Capo Press, 1981.

McClard, Megan. *Harriet Tubman: Slavery and the Underground Railroad.* Englewood Cliffs, N.J.: Silver Burdett Press, 1991.

McFeely, William S. *Frederick Douglass.* New York: Simon & Schuster, 1991.

McPherson, James M. *The Negro's Civil War.* New York: Ballantine Books, 1991.

Meltzer, Milton (ed.). *The Black Americans: A History in Their Own Words, 1619-1983.* New York: Thomas Y. Crowell, 1984.

Nichols, Charles H. *Many Thousand Gone: The Ex-slaves' Account of Their Bondage and Freedom.* Leiden, Netherlands: E. J. Brill, 1963.

Osofsky, Gilbert (ed.). *Puttin' On Ole Massa.* New York: Harper & Row, 1969.

Phillips, William D., Jr. *Slavery from Roman Times to the Early Transatlantic Trade.* Minneapolis: University of Minnesota Press, 1985.

Price, Richard (ed.). *Maroon Societies: Rebel Slave Communities in the Americas* (2d ed.). Baltimore: Johns Hopkins University Press, 1979.

Quarles, Benjamin: *Allies for Freedom: Blacks and John Brown.* New York: Oxford University Press, 1974.

Black Abolitionists. New York: Oxford University Press, 1969.

The Negro in the Making of America (3d ed.). New York: Collier Books, 1987.

Rémy, Mylène. *Senegal Today.* Paris: Editions Jeune Afrique, 1974.

Renaudeau, Michel. *Gorée.* Périgueux, France: Société Africaine d'Edition, 1978.

Rice, C. Duncan. *The Rise and Fall of Black Slavery.* New York: Harper & Row, 1975.

Scott, John Anthony. *Hard Trials on My Way.* New York: New American Library (Mentor), 1974.

Smith, Jessie Carney (ed.). *Notable Black American Women.* Detroit: Gale Research, 1992.

Smith, Julia Floyd. *Slavery and Rice Culture in Low Country Georgia 1750-1860.* Knoxville: University of Tennessee Press, 1985.

Stampp, Kenneth M. *The Peculiar Institution: Slavery in the Antebellum South.* New York: Vintage Books, 1956.

Sterling, Dorothy. *Captain of the Planter: The Story of Robert Smalls.* Garden City, N.Y.: Doubleday, 1958.

Sterling, Dorothy (ed.). *We Are Your Sisters: Black Women in the Nineteenth Century.* New York: W. W. Norton, 1984.

Still, William. *The Underground Railroad.* Chicago: Johnson Publishing, 1970 (reprint of 1871 edition).

Taylor, Joe Gray. *Negro Slavery in Louisiana.* Baton Rouge: Louisiana Historical Association, 1963.

Tunnell, Ted. *Crucible of Reconstruction.* Baton Rouge: Louisiana State University Press, 1984.

Wiggins, William H., Jr. *O Freedom! Afro-American Emancipation Celebrations.* Knoxville: University of Tennessee Press, 1987.

Wood, Peter. *Black Majority: Negroes in Colonial South Carolina.* New York: Random House, 1974.

Yee, Shirley J. *Black Women Abolitionists: A Study in Activism, 1828-1860.* Knoxville: University of Tennessee Press, 1992.

PERIODICALS

Berlin, Ira. "How the Slaves Freed Themselves." *Washington Post*, December 27, 1992.

Blockson, Charles L. "Escape from Slavery: The Underground Railroad." *National Geographic*, July 1984.

"A Crime to Remember." *New York Times*, February 14, 1993.

Jackson, Edmund. "The Virginia Maroons." *Philadelphia Freeman*, January 1, 1852.

Johnson, Clifton. "The Amistad Case and Its Consequences in U.S. History." *Journal of the New Haven Colony Historical Society*, Spring 1990.

Montgomery, Charles J. "Survivors from the Cargo of the Negro Slave Yacht Wanderer." *American Anthropologist*, 1908, Vol. 10.

Morganthau, Tom. "Slavery: How It Built the New World." *Newsweek: Columbus Special Issue*, Fall/Winter, 1991.

Motley, Constance Baker. "The Legal Aspects of the Amistad Case." *Journal of the New Haven Colony Historical Society*, Spring 1990.

Palmer, Colin. "African Slave Trade: The Cruelest Commerce." *National Geographic*, September 1992.

Thompson, Winfield M. "Historic American Yachts." *Rudder* (New York), February 1904.

OTHER SOURCES

McCain, Diana R. "Free Men: The Amistad Revolt and the American Anti-Slavery Movement." Brochure from an exhibit at the New Haven Colony Historical Society, September 22, 1989-January 19, 1990.

2
THE SURGE WESTWARD
BOOKS

Asante, Molefi K., and Mark T. Mattson. *The Historical and Cultural Atlas of African Americans.* New York: Macmillan, 1991.

Bancroft, Hubert Howe. *The Works of Hubert Howe Bancroft, Volume XX: History of California: Vol. III, 1825-1840.* New York: McGraw-Hill, 1992 (reprint of 1886 edition).

Bean, Walton. *California: An Interpretive History.* New York: McGraw-Hill, 1988.

Bennett, Lerone, Jr. *Before the Mayflower: A History of Black America* (5th ed.). New York: Penguin Books, 1984.

Berry, Mary Frances. *Black Resistance, White Law.* New York: Meredith, 1971.

Berwanger, Eugene H. *The Frontier against Slavery.* Urbana: University of Illinois Press, 1971.

Bontemps, Arna, and Jack Conroy. *Anyplace but Here* (American Century series). New York: Hill & Wang, 1966.

Burton, Arthur T. *Black, Red and Deadly: Black and Indian Gunfighters of the Indian Territory, 1870-1907.* Austin, Tex.: Eakin Press, 1991.

Carroll, John M. *The Black Military Experience in the American West.* New York: Liveright, 1971.

Carruth, Gorton. *The Encyclopedia of American Facts & Dates* (8th ed.). New York: Harper & Row, 1987.

Clyman, James. *Journal of a Mountain Man.* Edited by Linda M. Hasselstrom. Missoula, Mont.: Mountain Press, 1984.

Cortesi, Lawrence. *Jean duSable: Father of Chicago.* Philadelphia: Chilton Book Company, 1972.

Crockett, Norman L. *The Black Towns.* Lawrence: Regents Press of Kansas, 1979.

Cromwell, Arthur, Jr. (ed.). *The Black Frontier.* Omaha: University of Nebraska Television, 1970.

Durham, Philip, and Everett L. Jones. *The Negro Cowboys.* New York: Dodd, Mead, 1965.

Ebony Pictorial History of Black America (Vol. 1). Nashville: Southwestern Company, 1971.

Forbes, Jack D. *Black Africans and Native Americans.* Oxford: Basil Blackwell, 1988.

Franklin, John Hope, and Alfred A. Moss, Jr. *From Slavery to Freedom: A History of Negro Americans* (6th ed.). New York: McGraw-Hill, 1988.

Gibbs, C. R. *Black Explorers.* Silver Spring, Md.: Three Dimensional Publishing, 1992.

Gilber, Paul, and Charles Lee Bryan. *Chicago and Its Makers.* Chicago: F. Mendelsohn, 1929.

Goode, Kenneth G. *California's Black Pioneers: A Brief Historical Survey.* Santa Barbara, Calif.: McNally & Loftin, 1974.

Hamilton, Kenneth Marvin. *Black Towns and Profit: Promotion and Development in the Trans-Appalachian West, 1877-1915.* Urbana: University of Illinois Press, 1991.

Hanes, Bailey C. *Bill Pickett, Bulldogger: The Biography of a Black Cowboy.* Norman: University of Oklahoma Press, 1989.

Harris, Richard E. *The First Hundred Years: A History of Arizona Blacks.* Apache Junction, Ariz.: Relmo Publishers, 1983.

Heard, J. Norman. *The Black Frontiersmen: Adventures of Negroes among American Indians, 1528-1918.* New York: John Day, 1969.

Huggins, Nathan I., Martin Kilson, and Daniel M. Fox (eds.). *Key Issues in the Afro-American Experience* (Vol. 1). New York: Harcourt Brace Jovanovich, 1971.

Katz, William Loren: *Black Indians: A Hidden Heritage.* New York: Atheneum, 1986.
Black People Who Made the Old West. New York: Thomas Y. Crowell, 1977.
The Black West (3d ed.). Seattle: Open Hand Publishing, 1987.

Kilian, Crawford. *Go Do Some Great Thing: The Black Pioneers of British Columbia.* Vancouver: Douglas & McIntyre, 1978.

Kranz, Rachel C. *The Biographical Dictionary of Black Americans.* New York: Facts On File, 1992.

Lapp, Rudolph M. *Blacks in Gold Rush California.* New Haven, Conn.: Yale University Press, 1977.

Levenson, Dorothy. *Women of the West.* New York: Franklin Watts, 1973.

Logan, Rayford W., and Michael R. Winston (eds.). *Dictionary of American Negro Biography.* New York: W. W. Norton, 1982.

McLagan, Elizabeth. *A Peculiar Paradise:*

A *History of Blacks in Oregon, 1788-1940*. Portland: Georgian Press (Oregon Black History Project), 1980.

Miller, Robert H. *Reflections of a Black Cowboy*. Englewood Cliffs, N.J.: Silver Burdett Press, 1991.

Painter, Nell Irvin. *Exodusters: Black Migration to Kansas after Reconstruction*. Lawrence: University of Kansas Press, 1986.

Porter, Kenneth Wiggins. *The Negro on the American Frontier*. New York: Arno Press, 1971.

Riley, Glenda: A *Place To Grow: Women in the American West*. Arlington Heights, Ill.: Harlan Davidson, 1992.

"Western Territories." In *Black Women in American History from Colonial Times through the Nineteenth Century*, edited by Darlene Clark Hine. Brooklyn, N.Y.: Carlson, 1990.

Savage, W. Sherman. *Blacks in the West*. Westport, Conn.: Greenwood Press, 1976.

Scott, Victoria, and Ernest Jones. *Sylvia Stark: A Pioneer*. Seattle: Open Hand Publishing, 1991.

Smith, Jessie Carney (ed.). *Notable Black American Women*. Detroit: Gale Research, 1992.

Snyder, Gerald S. *In the Footsteps of Lewis and Clark*. Washington, D.C.: National Geographic Society, 1970.

Stewart, Paul W., and Wallace Yvonne Ponce. *Black Cowboys*. Broomfield, Colo.: Phillips Publishing, 1986.

Terrell, John Upton. *Estevanico the Black*. Los Angeles: Westernlore Press, 1968.

Twombly, Robert C. *Blacks in White America since 1865*. New York: David McKay, 1971.

Wheeler, B. Gordon. *Black California: The History of African-Americans in the Golden State*. New York: Hippocrene Books, 1993.

White, Richard. "*It's Your Misfortune and None of My Own*": A History of the American West. Norman: University of Oklahoma Press, 1991.

Wilson, Elinor. *Jim Beckwourth: Black Mountain Man and War Chief of the Crows*. Norman: University of Oklahoma Press, 1972.

PERIODICALS

Andrews, Thomas F. "Freedmen in Indian Territory: A Post-Civil War Dilemma." *Journal of the West*, July 1965.

Bentz, Donald N. "William and Anna Neal of Oracle." *Oracle Historian* (Oracle, Ariz.), Summer 1982.

Brinan, William D. "Jesse Stahl." *Western Horseman*, June 1975.

de Graaf, Lawrence B. "Race, Sex, and Region: Black Women in the American West, 1850-1920." *Pacific Historical Review*, May 1980.

Dillard-Rosen, Sandra. "Forgotten Cowboys: Blacks of Old West Remembered in Museum." *Denver Post*, March 25, 1989.

Hewitt, Mary Jane. "The Long Black Line." *California History*, Spring 1981.

"The Inter-Ocean." *Rocky Mountain News*, October 22, 1973.

Lang, William L. "The Nearly Forgotten Blacks on Last Chance Gulch, 1900-1912." *Pacific Northwest Quarterly*, April 1979.

Lapp, Rudolph. "The Negro in Gold Rush California." *Journal of Negro History*, April 1964.

McDermott, Burton. "The Incredible Saga of the Black Marshal Who Tamed Colorado." *Frontier West*, April 1974.

"Oracle and the Colorful Sting of the Mountain View Hotel." *Tucson Magazine*, November 1948.

Porter, Kenneth W. "Negroes and Indians on the Texas Frontier, 1834-1874." *Southwestern Historical Quarterly*, October 1949.

Ringolsby, Tracy. "Hitching onto a Career: Young Roper Finds Success on Pro-Circuit." *Dallas Morning News*, January 30, 1991.

Taylor, Quintard. "Slaves and Free Men: Blacks in the Oregon Country, 1840-1860." *Oregon Historical Quarterly*, Summer 1982.

Taylor, Ronald B. "Cowboy Charles Sampson Rides Off with World Championship." *Los Angeles Times*, January 5, 1983.

Wasmund, Laurie Marr. "Inter-Ocean Statesman Barney Ford." *True West*, April 1992.

West, Hollie I. "Once a Town of Hope, Now a Fading Dream." *Washington Post*, February 9, 1975.

White, Evelyn C. "How Paul Stewart Mines Lost 'Gold' with a Tape Recorder." *Smithsonian*, August 1989.

OTHER SOURCES

Coar, Valencia Hollins. "A Century of Black Photographers: 1840-1960." Exhibition catalog. Providence: Museum of Art, Rhode Island School of Design, 1983.

Spangenberg, Kristin L. (ed.). "Photographic Treasures from the Cincinnati Art Museum." Catalog. Cincinnati: Cincinnati Art Museum, 1989.

Stark, Maria Albertina (daughter of Sylvia Stark). Notes from the recollections of her mother, located in the archives of the Victoria Provincial Museum, Victoria, British Columbia, no date.

U.S. National Park Service. "Seminole-Negro Indian Scouts." Pamphlet (Fort Davis, National Historic Site). Washington, D.C.: U.S. Department of the Interior, no date.

3
SOLDIERS IN THE SHADOWS

BOOKS

Above and Beyond: A History of the Medal of Honor from the Civil War to Vietnam. Boston: Boston Publishing, 1985.

Adams, Russell L. *Great Negroes: Past and Present* (3d ed.). Chicago: Afro-Am Publishing, 1991.

Adams, Virginia Matzke (ed.). *On the Altar of Freedom: A Black Soldier's Civil War Letter from the Front*. Amherst: University of Massachusetts Press, 1991.

Andersen, Richard. *The Reluctant Hero and the Massachusetts 54th Colored Regiment*. Nashville: Winston-Derek, 1991.

Binkin, Martin, et al. *Blacks and the Military*. Washington, D.C.: Brookings Institution, 1982.

Brawly, Benjamin. *Negro Builders and Heroes*. Chapel Hill: University of North Carolina Press, 1937.

Carroll, John M. *The Black Military Experience in the American West*. New York: Liveright, 1971.

Cornish, Dudley Taylor. *The Sable Arm: Black Troops in the Union Army, 1861-1865*. Lawrence: University Press of Kansas, 1987.

Davis, Benjamin O., Jr. *Benjamin O. Davis, Jr., American: An Autobiography*. New York: Plume, 1991.

Davis, Burke. *Black Heroes of the American Revolution*. New York: Harcourt Brace Jovanovich, 1976.

Downey, Fairfax. *The Buffalo Soldiers in the Indian Wars*. New York: McGraw-Hill, 1969.

Early, Charity Adams. *One Woman's Army: A Black Officer Remembers the WAC*.

College Station: Texas A&M University Press, 1989.

Emilio, Louis. *A Brave Black Regiment: History of the 54th Regiment of the Massachusetts Volunteer Infantry 1863-1865.* New York: Arno Press, 1969.

Foner, Jack D. *Blacks and the Military in American History: A New Perspective.* New York: Praeger Publishers, 1974.

Francis, Charles E. *The Tuskegee Airmen.* Boston: Branden, 1988.

Franklin, John Hope, and the Editors of Time-Life Books. *An Illustrated History of Black Americans.* New York: Time-Life Books, 1970.

Glatthaar, Joseph T. *Forged in Battle: The Civil War Alliance of Black Soldiers and White Officers.* New York: New American Library, 1991.

Greene, Robert Ewell: *Black Defenders of America, 1775-1973.* Chicago: Johnson Publishing, 1974.

Black Defenders of the Persian Gulf War: Desert Shield-Desert Storm. Fort Washington, Md.: R. E. Greene, 1991.

Hardesty, Von, and Dominick Pisano. *Black Wings: The American Black in Aviation.* Washington, D.C.: Smithsonian Institution National Air and Space Museum, 1984.

Hargrove, Hondon B.: *Buffalo Soldiers in Italy: Black Americans in World War II.* Jefferson, N.C.: McFarland, 1985.

Black Union Soldiers in the Civil War. Jefferson, N.C.: McFarland, 1988.

Johnson, Jesse J. (ed.). *A Pictorial History of Black Soldiers (1619-1969) in Peace and War.* Hampton, Va.: Hampton Institute, 1970.

Kaplan, Sidney, and Emma Nogrady Kaplan. *The Black Presence in the Era of the American Revolution.* Amherst: University of Massachusetts Press, 1989.

Lanker, Brian. *I Dream a World.* New York: Stewart, Tabori & Chang, 1989.

Leckie, William H. *The Buffalo Soldiers: A Narrative of the Negro Cavalry in the West.* Norman: University of Oklahoma Press, 1967.

Low, W. Augustus, and Virgil A. Clift (eds.). *Encyclopedia of Black America.* New York: Da Capo Press, 1981.

McGovern, James R. *Black Eagle: General Daniel "Chappie" James, Jr.* Tuscaloosa: University of Alabama Press, 1985.

Marszalek, John F., Jr. *Court-Martial: A Black Man in America.* New York: Charles Scribner's Sons, 1972.

Motley, Mary Penick (ed.). *The Invisible Soldier: The Experience of the Black Soldier, World War II.* Detroit: Wayne State University Press, 1975.

Nalty, Bernard C. *Strength for the Fight: A History of Black Americans in the Military.* New York: Free Press, 1986.

Nalty, Bernard C., and Morris J. MacGregor (eds.). *Blacks in the Military: Essential Documents.* Wilmington, Del.: Scholarly Resources, 1981.

Nell, William C. *The Colored Patriots of the American Revolution.* New York: Arno Press, 1968.

Nelson, Dennis D. *The Integration of the Negro into the U.S. Navy.* New York: Farrar, Straus and Young, 1951.

Ploski, Harry A., and James Williams (eds.). *The Negro Almanac: A Reference Work on the African American* (5th ed.). Detroit: Gale Research, 1989.

Potter, Lou, William Miles, and Nina Rosenblum. *Liberators: Fighting on Two Fronts in World War II.* New York: Harcourt Brace Jovanovich, 1992.

Quarles, Benjamin: *The Negro in the American Revolution.* New York: W. W. Norton, 1961.

The Negro in the Civil War. New York: Da Capo Press, 1953.

Sandler, Stanley. *Segregated Skies: All-Black Combat Squadrons WW II.* Washington, D.C.: Smithsonian Institution, 1992.

Scott, Emmett J. *Scott's Official History of the American Negro in the World War.* Emmett J. Scott, 1919.

Stanton, Shelby. *U.S. Army Uniforms of the Vietnam War.* Harrisburg, Pa.: Stackpole Books, 1989.

Stillwell, Paul (ed.). *The Golden Thirteen: Recollections of the First Black Naval Officers.* Annapolis, Md.: Naval Institute Press, 1992.

Sweeney, W. Allison. *History of the American Negro in the Great World War.* New York: Negro Universities Press, 1969.

Terry, Wallace. *Bloods: An Oral History of the Vietnam War by Black Veterans.* New York: Ballantine Books, 1984.

Todd, Frederick P. *American Military Equipage, 1851-1872.* New York: Charles Scribner's Sons, 1978.

Twitchell, Heath. *Northwest Epic.* New York: St. Martin's Press, 1992.

U.S. Department of Defense. *Black Americans in Defense of Our Nation.* Washington, D.C.: U.S. Government Printing Office, 1984.

Weaver, John D. *The Brownsville Raid.* College Station: Texas A&M University Press, 1992.

Weigley, Russell F. *History of the United States Army.* New York: Macmillan, 1967.

The Wild West. Alexandria, Va.: Time-Life Books, 1993.

PERIODICALS

Bartholet, Jeffrey, and Marcus Mabry. "U.S. Troops: Black like Me." *Newsweek,* December 21, 1992.

"Buffalo Soldiers: Forgotten Black Heroes of the Old West." *Washington Post,* January 20, 1991.

Charles, N. S. "Black Soldiers in Somalia: Mixed Emotions, Vanishing Euphoria." *Emerge,* May 1993.

"Colonel Charles Young: Pointman." *Crisis,* May 1977.

"A Different Centennial: Henry O. Flipper, USMA 1877, First Black Graduate." *Assembly,* June 1977.

Dwiggins, Don. "Coliseum Named for Medal of Honor Recipient." *Winston-Salem Journal,* August 22, 1989.

East, Bill. "He Never Did Feel Comfortable as a Celebrity." *Winston-Salem Journal,* February 6, 1984.

Farrell, Christopher. "The Military Is Pretty Good at Fighting Racism, Too." *Business Week,* March 11, 1991.

"The Fairness Doctrine." *Economist,* January 12, 1991.

"First Negro Ensigns." *Life,* April 24, 1944.

Gilmore, Jane. "Diversity of Harris' Career Prompted Renaming Award." *Journal Record,* October 22, 1992.

"The Golden Thirteen." *Proceedings/Naval Review,* 1987.

Harvey, Betty Jane. "Peggy Howard Named Corporate Woman of the Year: Marcelite Harris Presented Woman of Enterprise Award." *Journal Record,* October 22, 1992.

Healy, John. "Joel Is Given a New Honor." *Winston-Salem Journal,* February 26, 1991.

Hilbert, Mary A. "Aileen Cole Stewart: First Black Nurse." *Eagle and Swan,* 1975.

"It's Such a Pleasure to Learn." *Parade,* March 18, 1990.

Kolb, Richard K. "The Vietnam Army—Second to None." *Wall Street Journal,* January 25, 1991.

Krakauer, Jon. "Ice, Mosquitoes, and Muskeg-Building the Road to Alaska." *Smithsonian,* July 1992.

Lacayo, Richard. "Why No Blue Blood

Will Flow." *Time*, November 26, 1990.

Mackay, Mike. "Veterans Recall Joel's Heroism." *Winston-Salem Journal*, August 29, 1989.

Massaquoi, Hans J. "Trying to Put the Past Behind." *Ebony*, September 1989.

Means, Howard. "From Mean Streets to Four Stars." *Washingtonian*, October 1992.

Morgan, Lael. "Miles and Miles." *Daily News-Miner* (Fairbanks), February 9, 1992.

Moskos, Charles C. "Success Story: Blacks in the Army." *Atlantic Monthly*, May 1986.

"Nourished by a Hunger for Learning." *Boston Globe*, April 26, 1990.

"100-Year-Old Son of Slave Feted for Love of Learning." *Boston Herald*, April 26, 1990.

Powell, Colin. "U.S. Forces: Challenges Ahead." *Foreign Affairs*, Winter 1992/93.

Robinson, Randall. "The Story behind Somalia." *Essence Magazine*, March 1993.

Santoli, Al. "Work Hard and Win the Future." *Parade*, June 30, 1991.

Schatzman, Dennis. "The Proud and Patriotic Legacy of Lawrence Joel." *Phoenix*, February 1988.

"West Point and the First Negro Cadet." *Military Affairs*, October 1971.

"Where Troop Cuts Will Be Cruelest." *Business Week*, June 8, 1992.

OTHER SOURCES

Barnacle, Mike. "A Private Peace." Videotape, CityLine. Boston: WCVP, November 11, 1985.

"Remember Doris Miller." Videotape, Better with Age (Evelyn Hoffman, host and producer). Waco, Tex.: 1986.

Terry, Wallace. "The Bloods of Nam." Videotape, Frontline. Boston: PBS, 1985.

4

ADVOCATES FOR CHANGE

BOOKS

Asante, Molefi K., and Mark T. Mattson. *The Historical and Cultural Atlas of African Americans*. New York: Macmillan, 1991.

Ayers, Edward L. *The Promise of the New South: Life after Reconstruction*. New York: Oxford University Press, 1992.

Bailey, R. W., and M. Furst (eds.). *Let Us March On! Civil Rights Photographs of Ernest C. Withers 1955-1968*. Boston: Massachusetts College of Art and the Department of African-American Studies, Northeastern University, 1992.

Berry, Mary Frances, and John W. Blassingame. *Long Memory: The Black Experience in America*. New York: Oxford University Press, 1982.

Branch, Taylor. *Parting the Waters: America in the King Years, 1954-1963*. New York: Touchstone, 1988.

Carmichael, Stokely, and Charles V. Hamilton. *Black Power: The Politics of Liberation in America*. New York: Vintage Books, 1967.

Carson, Clayborne: *In Struggle: SNCC and the Black Awakening of the 1960s.* Cambridge, Mass.: Harvard University Press, 1981.

Malcolm X: The FBI File. New York: Carroll & Graf, 1991.

Carter, Dan T. *Scottsboro: A Tragedy of the American South.* New York: Oxford University Press, 1969.

Cartwright, Joseph H. *The Triumph of Jim Crow: Tennessee Race Relations in the 1880s.* Knoxville: University of Tennessee Press, 1976.

Clarke, John Henrik (ed.). *Malcolm X: The Man and His Times.* Trenton, N.J.: Africa World Press, 1990.

Clark, John Henrik, and Amy Jacques Garvey (eds.). *Marcus Garvey and the Vision of Africa.* New York: Vintage Books, 1974.

Cleaver, Eldridge. *Soul on Fire.* New York: Dell, 1992.

Cronon, E. David. *Black Moses: The Story of Marcus Garvey and the Universal Negro Improvement Association.* Madison: University of Wisconsin Press, 1969.

Davis, Michael D., and Hunter R. Clark. *Thurgood Marshall: Warrior at the Bar, Rebel on the Bench.* New York: Birch Lane Press, 1992.

Davis, Thulani. *Malcolm X: The Great Photographs.* New York: Stewart, Tabori & Chang, 1993.

Du Bois, W. E. Burghardt (ed.). *The Negro American Family.* Cambridge, Mass.: MIT Press, 1970 (reprint of 1909 edition).

Durham, Michael S. *Powerful Days: The Civil Rights Photography of Charles Moore.* New York: Stewart, Tabori & Chang, 1991.

Farmer, James. *Lay Bare the Heart: An Autobiography of the Civil Rights Movement.* New York: Arbor House, 1985.

Fellman, David. *The Defendant's Rights Today.* Madison: University of Wisconsin Press, 1976.

Forman, James. *The Making of Black Revolutionaries.* Seattle: Open Hand Publishing, 1990.

Franklin, John Hope, and Alfred A. Moss, Jr. *From Slavery to Freedom: A History of Negro Americans* (6th ed.). New York: McGraw-Hill, 1988.

Franklin, John Hope, and August Meier (eds.). *Black Leaders of the Twentieth Century.* Urbana: University of Illinois Press, 1982.

Gallen, David. *Malcolm X as They Knew Him.* New York: Carroll & Graf, 1992.

Garrow, David J.: *Bearing the Cross: Martin Luther King, Jr., and the Southern Christian Leadership Conference.* New York: William Morrow, 1986.

Protest at Selma: Martin Luther King, Jr., and the Voting Rights Act of 1965. New Haven, Conn.: Yale University Press, 1978.

Garvey, Amy Jacques (comp.). *The Philosophy and Opinions of Marcus Garvey; or Africa for the Africans* (Vols. I and II). Dover, Mass.: Majority Press, 1986.

Gentile, Thomas. *March on Washington: August 28, 1963.* Washington, D.C.: New Day Publications, 1983.

Goldman, Roger, and David Gallen. *Thurgood Marshall: Justice for All.* New York: Garroll & Graf, 1992.

Grant, Joanne (ed.). *Black Protest: History, Documents, and Analyses, 1619 to the Present* (2d ed.). New York: Fawcett, 1986.

Grofman, Bernard, and Chandler Davidson (eds.). *Controversies in Minority Voting: The Voting Rights Act in Perspective.* Washington, D.C.: Brookings Institution, 1992.

Hambourg, Maria Morris, et al. *The Waking Dream: Photography's First Century.* New York: Metropolitan Museum of Art, 1993.

Hampton, Henry, and Steve Fayer, with Sarah Flynn. *Voices of Freedom: An Oral History of the Civil Rights Movement from the 1950s through the 1980s.* New York: Bantam Books, 1990.

Hine, Darlene Clark (ed.). *Black Women in America: An Historical Encyclopedia* (Vol. 1). Brooklyn, N.Y.: Carlson, 1993.

Hornsby, Alton, Jr.: *Chronology of African-American History.* Detroit: Gale Research, 1991.

Milestones in 20th-Century African-American History. Detroit: Visible Ink Press, 1993.

Hughes, Langston, Milton Meltzer, and C. Eric Lincoln. *A Pictorial History of Blackamericans* (5th ed.). New York: Crown Publishers, 1983.

Hunter-Gault, Charlayne. *In My Place.* New York: Farrar Straus Giroux, 1992.

Jaynes, Gerald David, and Robin M. Williams, Jr. (eds.). *A Common Destiny:*

Blacks and American Society. Washington, D.C.: National Academy Press, 1989.

Kellogg, Charles Flint. NAACP: A *History of the National Association for the Advancement of Colored People* (Vol. 1). Baltimore: Johns Hopkins University Press, 1967.

Kluger, Richard. *Simple Justice: The History of Brown v. Board of Education and Black America's Struggle for Equality.* New York: Vintage Books, 1975.

Kousser, J. Morgan. *The Shaping of Southern Politics: Suffrage Restriction and the Establishment of the One-Party South, 1880-1910.* New Haven, Conn.: Yale University Press, 1974.

Lawler, Mary. *Marcus Garvey.* New York: Chelsea House Publishers, 1988.

Lewis, David L. *King: A Biography.* Urbana: University of Illinois Press, 1978.

Litwack, Leon F., and August Meier (eds.). *Black Leaders of the Nineteenth Century.* Urbana: University of Illinois Press, 1988.

Lofgren, Charles A. *The Plessy Case: A Legal-Historical Interpretation.* New York: Oxford University Press, 1987.

McAdam, Doug. *Freedom Summer.* New York: Oxford University Press, 1988.

Malcolm X: *The Autobiography of Malcolm X.* New York: Ballantine Books, 1965.

Malcolm X Talks to Young People: Speeches in the U.S., Britain, and Africa. New York: Pathfinder, 1991.

Margo, Robert A. *Race and Schooling in the South, 1880-1950: An Economic History.* Chicago: University of Chicago Press, 1990.

Martin, Tony. *Race First: The Ideological and Organizational Struggles of Marcus Garvey and the Universal Negro Improvement Association.* Dover, Mass.: Majority Press, 1976.

Meier, August, and Elliott Rudwick. CORE: *A Study in the Civil Rights Movement, 1942-1968.* Urbana: University of Illinois Press, 1975.

Mills, Kay. *This Little Light of Mine: The Life of Fannie Lou Hamer.* New York: New American Library, 1993.

Mills, Nicolaus. *Like a Holy Crusade: Mississippi 1964—The Turning of the Civil Rights Movement in America.* Chicago: Ivan R. Dee, 1992.

Moody, Anne. *Coming of Age in Mississippi.* New York: Laurel, 1968.

Moore, Gilbert. *A Special Rage.* New York: Harper & Row, 1971.

Nalty, Bernard C. *Strength for the Fight: A History of Black Americans in the Military.* New York: Free Press, 1986.

Norris, Clarence, and Sybil D. Washington. *The Last of the Scottsboro Boys: An Autobiography.* New York: G. P. Putnam's Sons, 1979.

Oates, Stephen B. *Let the Trumpet Sound: The Life of Martin Luther King, Jr.* New York: New American Library (Mentor), 1985.

Olsen, Otto H. (ed.): *The Negro Question: From Slavery to Caste, 1863-1910.* New York: Pitman Publishing, 1971.

The Thin Disguise: Turning Point in Negro History—Plessy v. Ferguson: A Documentary Presentation, 1864-1896. New York: Humanities Press, 1967.

Ploski, Harry A., and James Williams (eds.). *The Negro Almanac: A Reference Work on the African American* (5th ed.). Detroit: Gale Research, 1989.

Powledge, Fred. *Free at Last? The Civil Rights Movement and the People Who Made It.* Boston: Little, Brown, 1991.

Raines, Howell. *My Soul Is Rested: The Story of the Civil Rights Movement in the Deep South.* New York: Penguin Books, 1984.

Report of the National Advisory Commission on Civil Disorders. New York: Bantam Books, 1968.

Robinson, Jo Ann Gibson. *The Montgomery Bus Boycott and the Women Who Started It.* Edited by David J. Garrow. Knoxville: University of Tennessee Press, 1987.

Rout, Kathleen. *Eldridge Cleaver.* Boston: Twayne Publishers, 1991.

Rowan, Carl T.: *Breaking Barriers: A Memoir.* New York: HarperPerennial, 1991.

Dream Makers, Dream Breakers: The World of Justice Thurgood Marshall. Boston: Little, Brown, 1993.

Rubel, David. *Fannie Lou Hamer: From Sharecropping to Politics.* Englewood Cliffs, N.J.: Silver Burdett Press, 1990.

Salzman, Jack, with Adina Back and Gretchen Sullivan Sorin (eds.). *Bridges and Boundaries: African Americans and American Jews.* New York: George Braziller, 1992.

Saunders, Doris E. (ed.). *The Day They Marched.* Chicago: Johnson Publishing Company, 1963.

Seale, Bobby. *Seize the Time: The Story of the Black Panther Party and Huey P. Newton.* Baltimore: Black Classic Press, 1991 (reprint of 1970 edition).

Sitkoff, Harvard. *The Struggle for Black Equality, 1954-1980* (American Century series). New York: Hill & Wang, 1981.

Smith, Jessie Carney (ed.). *Notable Black American Women.* Detroit: Gale Research, 1992.

Tushnet, Mark V. *The NAACP's Legal Strategy against Segregated Education, 1925-1950.* Chapel Hill: University of North Carolina Press, 1987.

Weisbrot, Robert. *Freedom Bound: A History of America's Civil Rights Movement.* New York: Plume, 1991.

Whitfield, Stephen J. *A Death in the Delta: The Story of Emmett Till.* Baltimore: Johns Hopkins University Press, 1988.

Williams, Juan. *Eyes on the Prize: America's Civil Rights Years, 1954-1965.* New York: Penguin Books, 1987.

Wright, Sarah E. *A. Philip Randolph: Integration in the Workplace.* Englewood Cliffs, N.J.: Silver Burdett Press, 1990.

Zangrando, Robert L. *The NAACP Crusade against Lynching, 1909-1950.* Philadelphia: Temple University Press, 1980.

PERIODICALS

Applebome, Peter. "Court Allows 3d Trial in '63 Medgar Evers Slaying." *New York Times,* December 17, 1992.

Booth, William. "Third Trial Ordered for Supremacist Beckwith." *Washington Post,* December 17, 1992.

Boyd, Herb. "All Power to the People." *Emerge,* February 1993.

Bray, Rosemary L. "A Black Panther's Long Journey." *New York Times Magazine,* January 31, 1993.

"Complicated Hospitality." *Time,* February 22, 1960.

Frady, Marshall. "The Children of Malcolm." *New Yorker,* October 12, 1992.

Mayfield, Mark. " 'Forgive and Forget?' Not If It's Murder." *USA Today,* September 25, 1992.

Minor, W. F. "The Suspect: A Man with a Mission." *New York Post,* June 24, 1963.

"New Evers Autopsy Replaces Original, Reported as Missing." *New York Times,* June 7, 1991.

"The Panthers and the Police." *New Yorker,* February 13, 1971.

"The Panthers: Cutting Edge of Black Revolt." *Life,* February 6, 1970.

"Second Look at Murder." *Time,* December 25, 1989.

Schanche, Don A. "Panthers against the Wall: Liberty, Fraternity, Insanity." *Atlantic,* May 1970.

Steele, Shelby. "Malcolm Little." *New Republic,* December 21, 1992.

"Youth Will Be Served." *Time,* March 21, 1960.

INDEX

Numerals in boldface indicate an illustration of the subject mentioned.

in, 197; founding, 88-89, 101; restaurant sit-in, 212; riots, 197, 200

Chicasaw: 91, 108

Chicora Wood plantation: 53

Choctaw: 108, **110**

Cilucängy: **73**

Cincinnati: Carmel Presbyterian Church members, **220;** preparations for March on Washington, **220-224**

Cinque: **56,** 57

Civilian Pilot Training Act: 158

Civil Rights Act of 1964: 195

Civil Rights Bill of 1866: 78

Civil rights legislation: 78, 82

Civil rights movement, 20th century: 181, 182, 185-199, **206-229;** and Malcolm X, 198; and polarization, 200-201; precursor of, 185; and Vietnam War, 143-144

Civil War: 128, 129, 132-134, 148-149; black casualties, 134; and black POWs, 133-134, 148; Bureau of Colored Troops, 133; and slaves, 40-41, 132-133; and women, 164

Clark, Jim: 196

Clark, Kenneth: 191

Clark, Mark: 235

Cleaver, Eldridge: 234, 235

Cleveland: riots, 200

Clinton, Bill: 237

Cloud, Kitty: and family, **111**

Cochise: 151

Cody, Buffalo Bill: 107

Coffee, Alvin: 93

Coffin, Levi: 68

COINTELPRO: 235

Collar, slave: **38**

Collingwood, Luke: 46

Collins, Lucretia: **216,** 217

Colonial militias: 129-130

Colonization: 62; opponents of, 62, 63; supporters of, 62

Colorado: antiblack laws, 94; civil rights act, 95; saloon, **97**

Colored Patriots of the American Revolution, The (Nell): 65

Color quebrados: 87

Comanche: 110, 111, 151

Communist party: 200; and Scottsboro Boys, 207

Compromise of 1850: 93, 90

Compromise of 1877: 83

Conductors, Underground Railroad: 68-69

Congressional Medal of Honor:

111, 132, 134, 135, 141, 142, **148,** 174

Congressmen, black: 60, 80, 82

Congress of Racial Equality (CORE): 194, 199, 212; and March on Washington, **221**

Conley, Elvira: 107

Connecticut: black regiments, 133

Conner, Bull: 176

Constitution, United States: Fifteenth Amendment, 83; Fourteenth Amendment, 78, 83, 183, 191; and slavery, 31, 131; Thirteenth Amendment, 76, 183

Constitutions, state: 79-80; convention delegates, **80**

Continental Army: 130-131

Cook, George: 37

Cook, John F.: 37

Cook, Mary: 37

Coolidge, Calvin: 205

Cooper, George C.: 162, **163**

Copeland, John: **74,** 75

Cornwallis, Lord: 146

Corry, William: 72

Cotton: and development of cotton gin, 31

Cowboys: **96, 97, 122-123;** on trail and in town, 97

Covey, Edward: 60

Covey, James: 57

Cowles, Robert: 94

Craft, Ellen: **58, 59**

Craft, William: **58, 59**

Creeks: 129; and slavery, 91, 108, 110

Croix de Guerre: 138, **156**

Cromwell, Oliver: 130

Crops: slave-intensive, 31

Crow: 102

Crozer Theological Seminary: 214

Cuba: and *Amistad,* 56, 57; San Juan Hill, 135, 152

Cuffe, Paul: 62

Custer, George A.: 108

D

Dart, Isom (Ned Huddleston): **113**

Davis, Angela: **200**

Davis, Benjamin O., Sr.: 139, 168-169

Davis, Jefferson: 80

Davis, John W.: 191

Davis, Nelson: 71

Davis, Ossie: 231

Dearfield (Colorado): **120**

Declaration of Rights of the Negro Peoples of the World: 204

Defense industry: desegregation of, 189

Democratic party: and Mississippi Democratic party, 227-229

Dennis, David: **196-197**

Detroit: riots, 200

Dexter Avenue Baptist Church: 214

Diggs, Charles C., Jr.: 182

Djenné: 14

Dockum Drugs: **212**

Dorman, Isaiah: 108

Douglas, James: 104

Douglass, Frederick: **60-61,** 62, 74, 133; and colonization, 63; and Harpers Ferry, 75; and violence, 67

Douglass, Sarah Mapps: 64, 67

Dow, George Francis: 46

Du Bois, William Edward Burghardt (W. E. B.): 5, 136, 138, 139, 185, 186, 191, 201, 204

Du Sable, Jean Baptiste Pointe: 88, 101; property, **100-101**

Dunmore: 130

Dunn, Oscar J.: **80**

Dylan, Bob: 223

E

Ebenezer Baptist Church: 214, 215

Echeandía, José María: 88

Eckford, Elizabeth: **209**

Economic development: and Garvey, 203; v. social equality, 185, 195

Economic disparities: 201

Education: campaign against segregation, 187, 188, 190-192, 194, **208-211;** disparities, 201; universal public, 80. *See also* Schools

Eisenhower, Dwight D.: 194

Emancipation: **41**

Emancipation Proclamation: 40-41, **76,** 132

Enforcement Act: 81

Equiano, Olaudah (Gustavus Vassa): 27-28, 32, 46

E. S. *Newman:* 135

Estes, Sylvia: *See* Stark, Sylvia

Estevanico: 87

Etheridge, Richard: 135

Europe, James Reese: **156**

Evans, Bob C.: **171**

Evers, Charlie: 218

Evers, Darrell Kenyatta: **219**

Evers, Medgar: **218-219**

Evers, Myrlie: 218, **219**

Executive Order 9981: 190

Exodusters: 98

F

Fabanna: **57**

Factories: slaves in, 35

Families, slave: 32-33, 37

Fanon, Frantz: 233

Faubus, Orval: 194, 208

Federal Bureau of Investigation (FBI): and Black Panthers, 234-235; and A. Davis, 200; and M. L. King, 214-215

Federal Writers' Project: 29

Fellowship of Reconciliation: 194

Ferrer, Ramón: **56**

Fields, Mary: **107**

Fisher, Ada Lois Sipuel: **208**

Fisk University: 78

Fleetwood, Christian A.: **132**

Fletcher, Diane: **109**

Flipper, Henry Ossian: 151-152, 168

Florida: government, 80; runaway slaves in, 91

Food: plantation rations, 34; on rice plantations: 52

Foraker, Joseph Benson: **155**

Ford, Barney: **94,** 95

Forest, Nathan Benedict: 134

Forman, James: 224, **225,** 227

Fort Brown: **154-155**

Fort Wagner: battle of, 148, 149

Forten, Charlotte: 67

Forten, James: **62,** 64, 65, 67

Forten, Margaretta: 67

Fortune, Robert L.: **115**

Fortune, T. Thomas: 185

France: and black WWI troops, 138, 156

Franklin, John Hope: 5

Free blacks: 36-37; and military, 128, 129, 131; papers, **37**

Freedmen's Bureau: 67. *See also* Bureau of Freedmen, Refugees, and Abandoned Lands

Freedom paper: **37**

Freedom Rides: 194-195, 199, **216-217**

Freedom suits: 38-39

Freedom Summer: 196-197, **224-225,** 226